Public
Integrity

Public Integrity

J. Patrick Dobel

The Johns Hopkins University Press

BALTIMORE AND LONDON

The Johns Hopkins University Press
2715 North Charles Street
Baltimore, Maryland 21218-4363
www.press.jhu.edu

Library of Congress Cataloging-in-Publication Data

Dobel, J. Patrick.
Public integrity / J. Patrick Dobel.
    p.   cm.
Includes bibliographical references and index.

1. Public administration—Moral and ethical aspects. 2. Politics, Practical—
Moral and ethical aspects. 3. Political ethics. 4. Integrity. I. Title.
JF1525.E8 D63 1999
172—dc21   99-21569
                                                                CIP

A catalog record for this book is available from the British Library.

FOR HILARY AND MATTHEW

Contents

Preface

> The most interesting thing about responsibility is that we carry it with us everywhere. That means responsibility is ours, that we must accept and grasp it *here, now,* in this place in time and space where the Lord has set us down, and that we cannot lie our way out of it.
>
> Václav Havel, *Living in Truth*

POLITICS is a world of moral attrition. Ideals and integrity corrode under the acid of power, opposition, frustration, imperfection, and constraint. In a haunting paradox, moral commitments imposed with zealous power can produce more harm than good. Greed, violence, betrayal, and the stubborn limits of human nature can lead individuals to bitterness, revenge, violence, or the lust for power for its own Faustian sake. The imperatives of great causes and responsibilities can challenge the most basic moral commitments, as President Franklin Roosevelt admitted when he acknowledged that he would have lied or cheated to win World War II.

Václav Havel has seen both sides of political power. As a writer and playwright, he suffered persecution and imprisonment under Communist regimes and later rose to become president of Czechoslovakia and of the Czech Republic. He points out that public officials live in a world of half-truth, which saps the soul and integrity of any person. Based on his experiences, Havel insists that only responsible individuals of integrity risking the moral dangers of politics and persisting in their quest for a better public life can make a difference in the world. This book grows out of that belief and the tradition of Machiavelli, Weber, and Acton, all of whom insist that politics proceeds from the actions of individuals. Great ideas, great theories, and great nightmares gain their reality from the judgments and decisions of individuals.

This book is written as variations upon the theme of how people exercise their integrity in office. Personal integrity is crucial to keeping promises and judging well. Integrity glues the social world of organizations together. Personal and public integrity join through the medium of promises and judgment. Individuals link their integrity to office through promises they make to obey the law, live up to the obligations of office, and frame their discretion around the dictates of office and the values of a liberal and democratic regime. Yet the moral structure of office and the institutional structure of public power generate inherent tensions and dangers for integrity. These tensions and ironies suffuse this study and challenge individuals to engage and surmount them. The book explores these encounters by first laying out a conception of public integrity, then discussing the major threats to integrity in office, and finally examining critical situations in which individuals must live out their integrity in office. The thematically related essays are true to integrity's nature because integrity means attending to the relevant promises and obligations in each setting. Each setting poses a different but related set of issues and potential balancing among obligations. No one theoretical model of integrity can capture this moral complexity.

In his writings, Havel warns about the dangers of "anonymous" and "innocent" power, in which individuals escape responsibility for their actions by surrendering their moral humanity to the imperatives of a cause, an order, or a superior. They can also escape by defining their identity solely by one aspect of themselves—such as ethnicity, gender, or religion—and subsuming their own splendid moral complexity under one definition of self. Within these structures of ideology, power, or identity, individuals can act without taking responsibility for the consequences of their actions. As Adolf Eichmann demonstrated at Auschwitz, people will surrender their judgment to the dictates of a cause, an identity, or an institution that transcends and absolves them. When individuals lose their capacity to act with moral discernment or courage, they lose their conscience.

This book explores the moral life of public agency, of individuals who act in public life. It focuses upon individuals as responsible political actors and pays special attention to people who possess explicit power and responsibility: people who hold office. "Office" conjures up visions of presidents, governors, senators, or cabinet members —even police chiefs. Although the responsibilities of the democratic citizen lie outside the scope of this book, Aristotle reminded us that office pervades public life; the good citizen and the good person are not one and the same. All citizens hold an office and co-responsibility for their public life. The human polity does not occur spontaneously. Amid the magnificent indifference of nature, humans create, sustain, and change their political institutions and culture. These efforts can generate great good or terrifying harm, but the moral center remains human beings acting with other human beings amid conflict and cooperation, friendship and hostility. Within this world, any political action, whether as a democratic citizen or as a head of a public agency, links a person to a web of connectedness, of enabling and disabling, of vulnerability and reliance, of obligations and consequences.

I believe the moral structure of holding office—whether legislative or executive, whether elected, appointed, or career—is the same. All involve people in a promise to live up to obligations of office in a web of reliance and to frame their judgments by standards embedded in the office's responsibilities. For citizens participating in an election, using these standards may mean asking which candidates or policies serve the public interest rather than personal self-interest. For public officials it means subordinating and informing judgment by the standards linked to the office. Yet each decision involves a complex interaction among the obligations of office, personal moral commitments and capacities, and political prudence. The obligations and tensions remain the same in each office, although the weightings and range of discretion will vary widely. This book studies a wide range of public officials in elected, appointed, and career positions to illustrate the range of issues across offices. By focusing on individuals, it seeks to do justice to the complexity of the actual lives of public officials, rather than dictate to them from external moral or philosophical principles. Many of the examples derive from high-level offices because of the availability of memoirs, cases, and biographies, but most of the moral insights apply across all levels of office because the moral structure remains the same. I believe the insights and guidelines the book presents can help a wide range of officials, especially those in senior management and leadership positions, in making better judgments.

Obviously, institutional design and accountability matter profoundly to the moral quality of politics. My arguments do not deny this reality or the importance of studying them. In fact, I believe institutions could be made more effective by placing public integrity at the core of their strategies. This book's arguments insist that integrity and judgment form the bedrock of public morality. Integrity involves the capacity of people to make sense of their life and link belief and practice. It enables them to make and keep promises—to take responsibility and hold together in one person the complex domains of obligations to office, personal commitments and capacity, and political prudence. Judgment involves a person's capacity to scan a situation, discover the significant aspects of a case, make sense of them, and decide on the proper course of action. It ends with the capacity to provide honest public justifications in terms fellow citizens can understand. Integrity helps to ensure clarity of reflection and to resist temptation to self-deception. It provides the moral coherence and discipline to implement decisions. The book concludes that the design and leadership of institutions should focus on the quality of integrity and judgment that they produce.

The book's focus remains resolutely upon the individual as a complex moral being and studies the moral difficulty of public action. My arguments reject any attempt to reduce individuals to simple products of an identity or role. My conclusions do not state clear theoretical prescriptions or rules for action. In general, such approaches seldom help real individuals in public life and can do more harm than good, as Machiavelli liked to point out. I want to work through issues from the internal moral view of public officials seeking to maintain integrity in complex and pressured environments. The real world of individuals is more complex and paradoxical than that posed by principled theories of public morality or by a focus on legal mandates of office. To accommodate the complexity of public action, the book is militantly interdisciplinary. It uses classical and modern moral and political theory and draws upon the resources of history, social psychology, and organizational theory. In an effort to stay with a person-focused view, it makes extensive use of biography, memoirs, interviews, and case studies. These texts help us to understand the political actor's world from the inside, as experienced, not as prescribed. Throughout the book and especially in Chapters 3 and 4, I use drama and fiction, because good art provides some of the richest and most nuanced insights into the conflict between moral integrity and the demands of public office. I use some long cases to work through complex issues mapping the moral dimensions, and at other times I use briefer examples to illustrate the issues I discuss.

My approach focuses on individuals trying to act with integrity in a complex world, which constantly presents not only ethical challenges but also challenges to a person's integrity and soul. With its emphasis upon cases, I try to do justice to the wisdom of practitioners while teasing out analytic and moral insight and generalizations. By this strategy, I hope to expand the range of moral resources available to leaders. My conclusions strive to present insights into the dilemmas and tensions that public officials need to acknowledge and engage. I seek to articulate guidelines for which individuals should be accountable and to identify morally significant issues to which individuals have an obligation to attend. In the end, I hope to increase the self-awareness of political actors and provide insights that support public integrity and good judgment. I believe this book can be especially helpful to students preparing for public service and to reflective practitioners who possess or aspire to positions of leadership in public life.

Politics remains one of the most difficult of human activities. The dense world of interests, beliefs, alliances, opposition, friendship, hatred, cooperation, conflict, passion, calculation, organized power, and institutional pathologies makes achievement difficult, costly, and precarious. Individuals face resistance and challenges when they seek to accomplish good in public life. Over time, the interactions can wear people down and change them for good or ill. Each day an individual's integrity and judgment are exercised and challenged. I hope to generate some moral resources to help actors navigating the treacherous currents of public action.

Chapter 1 lays the foundation for the book by examining the moral obligations of individuals who take on public responsibilities. People in public life face legal, constitutional, and institutional demands that demarcate the bounds of their discretion while personal commitments and capacities support and influence judgment. The political environment exerts a never-ending pressure to exercise prudence to engage the power of other people and to achieve durable results. I argue that a conception of public integrity provides the most solid moral vessel for navigating the moral shoals of this political sea. In particular, integrity sustains the promises that bind people as moral agents to the responsibilities of office. It involves an ability to balance judgments among the domains of obligations of office, personal commitments and capacities, and prudence. Chapter 2 examines how the exercise of public power enmeshes individuals in a number of psychological and social traps that can undermine their integrity. It reaffirms and deepens the classical observations that substantial power tempts personal integrity and can subvert public commitment over time.

Chapters 3 and 4 use fiction and drama to examine the moral dilemmas and paradoxes that subvert integrity in politics. In Chapter 3 relations with other people, the undertow of conflicting loyalties, and the irony of rectitude all haunt participation in public life. Each dilemma generates considerable confusion within people seeking to keep their integrity intact and achieve some good in the world. The chapter develops a moral stance towards public life that accounts for these complexities. Chapter 4 examines a fundamental problem in public life: provocations to and the erosion of integrity in public officials who serve in positions in which they are asked to perform actions that violate basic moral norms. The use of evil means for good ends exacts a steady and deep cost to anyone who must participate in such actions.

Continuing a theme of Chapter 4, the next four chapters study how individuals maintain their integrity when facing critical junctures or challenges where their integrity is on the line. Chapter 5 examines the hazards individuals face when they participate in the making of a policy with which they morally disagree. This is a defining moment of integrity when people are caught between the need to maintain credibility and access by participation in policy making and their duty to dissent and change the policy if they find it morally wrong. This chapter maps out the dilemmas and advantages of trying to stay in office yet changing the policies with which one disagrees.

Chapter 6 examines the other side of staying in. It argues that resigning from office remains one of the basic moral resources of public integrity. The possibility of resigning ensures the responsibility of actors, supports increased accountability, and provides an essential way to maintain integrity. The chapter argues that if the conditions of the promise an official makes when taking office become eroded, he or she should resign.

Chapter 7 examines the pervasive hazards of political sleaze—the use of public office to serve personal ends. Sleaze has three major variations: the raw pursuit of self-interest in office, the corruption of idealism in office, and the subversion of office by moral absolutists or zealots who impose their personal values on official action. The chapter concludes with a defense of an updated conception of public honor as an alternative way to think about the relation between private interests and commitments and between the requirements of office and accountability.

Chapter 8 explores one of the most vexing questions of political life: how to square public integrity with the demands of human differences. On the one hand, differences generate creativity and innovation; they support freedom and the development of human identity. Yet, on the other hand, differences can also be the source of mistrust, exclusion, injustice, and conflict. As an organizing principle of government policy, claims of difference can hide political accountability, encourage fractional politics, or be used to constrict the identity of individuals. In this light, I argue that the ideal of public integrity should be expanded to include the responsibility to build peace within political order, construct and sustain an inclusive political community, and engender social trust and common bonds of interest, affiliation, and solidarity across differences.

The two concluding chapters return to the domains of public integrity. Chapter 9 explores the importance of private life and privacy in maintaining balance and integrity in public office. It discusses how the privacy of public officials has been ruptured in modern politics by the dynamics of media coverage and political conflict. More paradoxically, the chapter explores how private lives do intrude into public office and can become a reasonable object of scrutiny. It concludes that even a commitment to the privacy of public officials generates no hard and fast guidelines for limiting the scrutiny of private lives. Consequently a set of standards is offered for assessing the private lives of public officials after they have been publicly revealed.

Chapter 10 examines the third domain of public integrity: political prudence. It argues that political prudence should be a fundamental moral resource of public leaders. Political prudence can be understood as the virtue whose requirements arise from the demands of excellence in political achievement. Individuals risk moral negligence as leaders if they do not attend to the framework of political prudence, which includes critical aspects of judgment such as disciplined reason, openness to knowledge, timing and momentum, acquiring power, and minimizing coercion.

Behind my arguments lies Havel's insistence that individuals in politics never abandon responsibility for their actions, even if acknowledging it requires betrayal, pain, and sacrifice. These arguments explore not only the dangers and anguish of public action but also the joy of companionship, the satisfaction of making people's lives better, and the dignity of living up to obligations. I suggest some preliminary guidance and weightings to help frame judgment and support integrity in public life. There are no guarantees, however, of coherence or success in politics. Nor do I deny the fact that, in very rare moments, public integrity may require a person to decide and rely upon the mercy of God or the judgment of history. But these moments are rare. For most of us integrity plays out in the cumulative pilgrimage of daily interactions and judgments. In this journey, integrity remains the means and the end.

Acknowledgments

I COULD NOT have written this book without the help of my students. For the last fifteen years students at the University of Michigan–Dearborn and in the Evans School of Public Affairs at the University of Washington have challenged me to teach ethics in a way that is relevant to their lives. In classes and seminars they have taught me about the limits of modern moral philosophy and political theory for individuals trying to make good decisions in complex and constrained situations. They have pushed me to find terms, ideas, and approaches that could help them live better lives as public officials. The ideas in this book emerged from my continuing dialogue with my students, and I am forever grateful to them for teaching me.

I have also benefited from the advice and discussion of many colleagues over the years. Bayard Catron, Kathryn Denhardt, John Rohr, Terry Cooper, Dennis Thompson, Carol Lewis, Gene Bardach, Chris DiStefano, Jamie Mayerfeld, Howard McCurdy, and Erwin Hargrove all read various chapters and helped with their comments. Jim Doig has been a constant source of guidance and help on these ideas since graduate school. My colleagues Walter Williams, Dick Zerbe, Bill Zumeta, Paul Hill, Jon Brock, and Hubert Locke helped with their reading and by their wonderful hallway conversation. Dean Margo Gordon created the environment that sustained my work. Dick Thompson and Nancy Campbell exemplify the ideal of "reflective practitioner" and immensely benefited my thinking with their honest conversation. I owe a special thanks to Henry Tom, of the Johns Hopkins University Press, for believing in the book; his candor and advice helped me immensely. The editing of Alice Copp Smith contributed greatly to the clarity of my thought and writing.

ACKNOWLEDGMENTS

Portions of this book have appeared in the *Public Administration Review*, *Administration and Society*, *American Review of Public Administration*, and *Public Personnel Management*.

While I was writing *Public Integrity*, my father died. He was the man who first taught me the meaning of loving integrity, and he handed on a passion and commitment to public service. I hope he would be proud of the book. My children, Hilary and Matt, acted as growing children do during the writing of the book. They kept me human. They also reminded me of the stakes involved in having excellent public service led by individuals of integrity. Finally, I thank my wife and best friend, Lea Vaughn, scholar and teacher in her own right. She grounds my integrity.

Public Integrity

1

Integrity in Office

A reaffirmed human responsibility is the most natural barrier to all irresponsibility.

Václav Havel, *Living in Truth*

Every subject's duty is the King's, but every subject's soul is his own.

Henry V 4.1.176

LIBERAL AND DEMOCRATIC SOCIETIES have always distrusted public officials. For liberals, official discretion invites abuse, vests too much power in the officeholder rather than in the law, and undermines the political liberties of citizens. For democrats, official discretion usurps sovereignty and undermines the accountability and participation so central to democratic life. Yet every elected, appointed, and career official must exercise judgment and discretion in carrying out the duties and responsibilities of office. Society depends upon their conscientious judgment and skill to provide the foundations of public order. A theory of public integrity can guide these public officials in exercising judgment and discretion.

By *public official* I mean any individual who holds any position at any level of government or public authority. Obviously the range of effective discretion, obligation, and responsibility associated with public office varies immensely. As a general rule the level of discretion increases directly with an office's position in the hierarchy of authority, although street-level bureaucrats can also possess immense discretion. Discretion, along with the directness of accountability, also expands tremendously if an official is elected. Yet the moral structure of discretion remains essentially the same for all officials because they are all charged to obey and implement the law and respect legal process in exercising their power and judgment. All such public officials have to weigh their personal moral commitments in making the decisions they face, and all must strike a balance among the institutional, prudential, and personal dimensions of public judgment.[1]

Three models have traditionally been offered to resolve the conflicts between public discretion and liberal, democratic life. The *legal-institutional model* emphasizes the public official's subordination to legal and institutional authority, which has been refined by popular participation.[2] The *personal-responsibility model* argues that personal responsibility should be incorporated in judgments of public officials.[3] The *effectiveness* or *implementation model* highlights the inescapable discretion and political dimension of all judgments made by public officials, even those in the middle ranks and at the street level; this model posits the need to use power, to be flexible, and to act effectively.[4] In general, each model accentuates one set of standards at the expense of others.

The question of public discretion and judgment can be thought of as an inquiry into what standards and considerations individuals in office should use to frame their judgments. Each model identifies one crucial domain of reasoning vital to good public judgment. I believe, however, that none of the models covers the entire range of moral resources that public officials need. Additionally, each domain by itself can generate abuses inherent in its logic, and these abuses can be avoided only by ensuring that each domain reinforces and checks the other two.

A theory that will frame the exercise of official discretion and judgment must meet several standards. It should be compatible with the moral and constitutional foundations of liberal and democratic government and should do justice to the legal and political warrants of office. It should plausibly connect personal integrity and public discretion in a way that supports official authority without losing the initiative, dynamism, and "checking" value personal integrity offers.[5] Last, it should be true to the demands of effectiveness and prudence without reducing to political expediency. Because none of the above models alone meets all three standards, I believe we should think about public discretion and integrity in office as an iterative process in which public officials move within a triangle of judgment. They move back and forth among the domains—obligations of office, personal capacity and commitments, and prudence and effectiveness—holding them in balanced tension when framing judgments.

The key to developing such a theory of official judgment and discretion lies with personal integrity. As a moral goal, integrity represents a cognitive and psychological state that anchors personal responsibility and judgment. As its root meaning suggests, integrity flows from the capacity to integrate different parts of oneself into a whole or completeness. Individuals achieve integrity when they make sense of their multiple obligations or roles in a manner that creates coherence or wholeness across the different aspects of their life. People of integrity possess the capacity to hold the triangle of judgment and its three domains in a productive tension and to resist obstacles in living up to their obligations. They also have the capacity to change their commitments and actions after reflective judgment. In this chapter I present an account of public integrity that can ground the discretion and judgment of public officials in a liberal and democratic order.

Personal Integrity

No matter how strictly written the mandates or how clearly prescribed the hierarchy, at some point commitments will come into conflict. High officials regularly feel cross-cutting tensions amid the requirements of protecting an institution, building support for a policy, and accounting to superiors. But even an inspector who vigilantly fills out a priority checklist must make the choice between sending it to an overworked agency that may be slow in acting on it and trying to negotiate immediate compliance. An official drawing up a budget proposal not only must decide what his or her division needs to fulfill its goals but also assess the nature of competing budgetary claims and the politics of the budgetary process. In any public office, goals and values will compete and collide. No one should assume that clear judgment will come out of any of these situations.[6]

The ideal of personal integrity is a state in which people hold multiple domains of judgment in tension while keeping some coherence in their actions and lives. In this sense, personal integrity is a normative ideal for which people should and almost always do strive. The notion of moral responsibility depends upon the assumption that individuals can achieve integrity in their actions. Integrity provides a vital framework in which to discuss how individuals can simultaneously hold several commitments and achieve a morally defensible balance among them. In a complex world, integrity is the essential virtue for a moral life.

Personal integrity has several aspects. First, it demands consistency between inner beliefs and public actions. Integrity depends upon people

3

possessing the self-discipline and moral courage to act on a commitment even if doing so requires sacrifice and effort. Second, integrity presupposes that people have the reflective capacity to make a commitment, recognize what the commitment entails, and act on it. Integrity cannot be reduced to rigidity about received beliefs; it presumes that people reflect upon and understand their beliefs in order to make them their own. Third, integrity assumes a oneness or unity in the moral life of individuals. People can create coherence across their roles and commitments by linking and adjusting their public roles to their central web of values and commitments.[7]

Personal integrity builds upon the unity of people's lives. The reality of one's body automatically imposes a continuity between past and future and gives human life a unity in terms of consequences of actions and promises. It forces individuals to consider themselves as a moral unity over time and establishes a causal continuity both across actions over time and within the person. Personal integrity, then, arises from people's ability to build a moral coherence by shaping their activities and roles to values and commitments that they view as centering their selfhood.[8]

Personal integrity resembles a network of roles and promises all held together by a central web of values and commitments. Integrity is not a rigid hierarchical structure with foundation values to which all other actions, roles, and commitments can be reduced. Such a notion is too static to account for the growth and change in central values and commitments. Basic personal capacities of character, temperament, and physicality support commitments; they include physical buttresses such as levels of energy, strength, health, and endurance, and aspects of character and temperament such as optimism, courage, caution, empathy, imagination, conscientiousness, and self-discipline—as well as their opposites. Self-conscious reflection depends upon the capacities of character and body along with central commitments.[9] Individuals can reflect across roles and actions and judge their compatibility with each other as well as with the central web of commitments. This enables people to create a plausible connectedness or wholeness to a life and among roles and actions. Such reflection may lead individuals to revise roles and actions to achieve coherence and make them more compatible with each other and with the individuals' central values and commitments. This sense of selfhood also extends historically across the roles people held in the past.[10] Individuals who assess performance of office should judge not only professed beliefs but also people's physical and moral capacity to act upon commitments.

Personal commitments at the center of the web form the moral, intellectual, and emotional links that individuals use to connect other clusters of commitments embedded in roles. These central values have been acquired independently of, and usually prior to, office. The central values can be revised in light of experience, and such values are often reinforced by intersecting threads of family, religious, or professional commitments. These values provide the capacity for critical reflection and judgment, which enables individuals to stand back from, hold together, and reshape roles. The moral philosopher John Rawls has called this process *reflective equilibrium*, a state in which individuals seek a balance and coherence across actions, roles, and commitments.[11] For a public official, these central values would include respect for self and others, commitment to truthfulness and public good, care, fairness, and honor. In maintaining integrity across their lives, individuals use reflection, will, and character to assess their various roles and commitments. Each role can be lived with different amounts of empathy, conscientiousness, courage, optimism, or respect. Individuals personalize roles and change the shape of each job they do by integrating their own personal values and character through the office.

This model of personal integrity as a moral ideal does not envision integrity as a hard, implacable nugget but as something dynamic. The experience of some roles can lead people to modify their central commitments in light of the demands of the roles. They might learn to expand or deepen their definition of respect or of professionalism. Given the unity of people's lives, most values and commitments crisscross, intersect, and often reinforce one another. Individuals have difficulty when commitments or roles pull at the centering values. Within a role, actions that violate central values disturb all other aspects of people's lives and raise most of the serious issues of personal integrity in office. In these situations, the strains and pressures on the web of values can be so great as to destroy health or energy.

In response to such tensions, people sometimes disentangle themselves from commitments that can no longer be sustained, and they resign from office. At other times, they may dissent in office or modify or resist actions to make them compatible with personal integrity. Sometimes the demands of a role so strain the central web of values that connections snap, leaving certain roles intact but loosely dangling from the rest of oneself. People go to work but perform their jobs as if sleepwalking, with the job having no relation to the rest of their life. People can fall into selfdeception and not acknowledge their role as part of their identity. When individuals' lives disintegrate like this, personal integrity and responsibility fragment. People in office lose commitment, burn out, deny responsibility; their performance and their personal lives suffer. In another variant of undermined integrity, the personal infiltrates the official, and people can confuse personal desires with office. On the other hand, integrity can also be undermined when the requirements of the role so dominate self-consciousness that the central web of values unravels. It no longer functions as a center of balance; the job takes over one's life. In such cases, people lose not only perspective on their actions in office but also the capacity to integrate and change roles through reflection and will.

The central commitments and capacities anchor the moral and cognitive personality of a self and provide the matrix by which people can judge and ground their actions and role commitments. When central commitments or character capacities are undermined, individuals themselves change in a moral sense. When basic attributes of self can no longer be relied upon or when they change, then the centering identity that held the roles and commitments of life together no longer holds. This violation or unraveling of integrity calls into question all the commitments and promises made on the basis of the older self and can undermine people's ability to commit and keep promises in the future.

Individuals of integrity can give accurate and plausible accounts of how the domains of their lives fit together with each other and how roles and commitments link to central values and commitments.[12] Ironically, although the capacity and desire to make life plausible and whole is crucial, it is not sufficient to guarantee that people face their lives honestly. In fact, self-deception gains much of its attractiveness from the desire to keep one's sense of "integrity" intact. True personal integrity requires selfreflective honesty as well as friends and colleagues with whom people can check personal assessments. This reflective honesty should play out in the capacity of individuals to change their lives to align their various roles with each other and with their central commitments. All commitments are ultimately personal because, whatever the requirements of a role or office, individuals commit to them; individuals still do the judging and acting. People's abilities to live up to legal, official, or professional expectations reside in their own personal capacity for integrity. Their commitments remain *their* commitments as personally reflected upon and affirmed. A public role can provide morally acceptable special excuses and dispensations for actions not normally permitted in personal life. These exceptions are grounded in moral conditions set by the people who can grant the dispensations. No roles, however, can exonerate individuals from some responsibility.[13]

Roles or offices that individuals freely accept presume personal integrity on the individual's part. From the view of personal integrity, all such offices and roles can be conceived of as promises by people to discipline judgment and action by the standards and procedures of the office. Morally speaking, office commits individuals of integrity to hold themselves responsible and accountable to such standards and procedures as a public trust.[14] A personal oath or promise connects personal commitments with the moral horizons and commitments of office. The promise conditions the performance of official duties upon one's integrity. It does not excuse people from moral responsibility to their basic commitments but becomes a "warrant for continuous scrutiny of one's own conduct in relation to the changing conditions of office to ensure that the conditions still hold."[15]

Integrity and the Conditions of Delegation

Public office relies upon individuals to frame their judgments by authorized standards and procedures and to exercise power in an accountable manner. Even given the wide discretion of elective legislative and executive positions, it makes no sense for citizens to delegate authority unless they believe that elected officials will also discipline their desires, prejudices, and self-interests and will focus their judgments within circumscribed ranges.[16]

In a liberal democracy, the powers of office come with several crucial conditions that detail the democratic responsibility of public officials:

1. Public officials should act in accord with the basic principles or regime values that legitimize the authority of the constitutional government. Officeholders are expected to see all citizens as possessing dignity, basic rights, and equality under the law.

2. They agree to subordinate their personal judgments to the outcomes of legitimate processes and to frame judgments by the legal and professional directives in their areas of authority.

3. They agree to remain accountable for their actions to relevant authorities and the public and to try to be honest and accurate in accounting for their actions.

4. They agree to act competently and effectively to achieve the purposes within the above constraints.

5. They agree to avoid favoritism, striving to be independent and objective while responding to relevant and appropriate reasons in making official decisions.

6. They agree to use public funds with care and efficiency for authorized public purposes, not for their own gain or the private gain of others.

7. They agree to protect the trustworthiness and legitimacy of their institutions.

Obligations of Office: The Legal-Institutional Model

In light of these conditions, the legal-institutional model legitimizes public service by limiting discretion in public office. Public officials should serve the will of the people as it is articulated and refined through authoritative executive, legislative, and judicial processes.[17] Officials are bound by the same limits although they possess wider discretion. General decisions on moral-political matters of policy should rest ultimately with elected officials and their appointees, acting lawfully, and all decisions by public officials should be traceable to either defined mandates or clear lines of authority.

The legal-institutional model jealously guards popular prerogatives and fears the abuse of power inherent in discretion. In this model, government institutions would be designed to minimize discretion and to maximize oversight of career and appointed officials by elected executives, courts, and legislatures. Even elected officials, especially executives, would be expected to limit their discretion by law and accountability. Laws and regulations should be as clear and unambiguous as possible; only the implementation of details would be delegated, and even such limited discretion would be closely monitored. Public career officials would be expected, in Emerson's phrase, to "speak truth to power" and to provide information and aid when necessary to their elected counterparts who craft legislation and rules. Career officials could also legitimately point out inconsistencies and problems that they recognize on the basis of their skills or experience. They would be expected to possess "neutral competence" and to serve different elected and appointed officials with skill and conscientiousness. All nonelected officials would act to implement law but would not actively create law and policy. Their major discretionary judgments would reside in ensuring that procedures were followed and that information was accurate and available to maintain accountability. When issues of vagueness, conflict of directives, or failure arise in implementation, appointed and career officials would dutifully return to their executive and legislative superiors, possibly with informed recommendations, to have the positions refined, or they might rely on determinations by courts.[18] These processes make professional government consistent with democratic governance.

In this domain, the integrity of nonelected public officials resides in several basic commitments. First, they commit to master the expertise their jobs require and to perform conscientiously in their office. Second, they commit to implement the laws and policies articulated by the formal processes of constitutional government even when they personally disagree with them. Max Weber argues that a true public servant should obey orders "exactly as if the order agreed with his own convictions. This holds even if the order appears wrong to him, and if, despite the civil servant's remonstrance, the authority insists on the order. Without this moral discipline and self-denial, in the highest sense, the whole apparatus would fall apart."[19] Third, public officials commit to act impartially and overcome their own personal prejudices and preferences and provide conscientious service to all citizens. Judgment based on any other commitments constitutes an arbitrary exercise of tyrannical power.

From the perspective of public integrity, the legal-institutional model has several profound limits, even linked to democratic responsibility. Insistence upon strict, hierarchical accountability produces timid, reactive, and rule-bound public officials. This model often severs the connection between personal capacity and values and public integrity. It encourages individuals to think of office mainly in terms of self-interest or reputation. At the same time, paradoxically, it presumes that they will continue to act on the basis of their conscientiousness, self-discipline, and other character attributes. For many individuals, this discontinuity between one's role and one's personal center will lead to either a self-interested and reputation-based pursuit of the job or a leaden and uninspired performance in the office.[20] Disconnecting most commitments of personal integrity from the office can undermine personal initiative and stifle dissent within government. Individuals lose the sense of responsibility for institutional judgments. The legal-institutional model disconnects the role from the central web of commitments and encourages what Stanley Milgram called an "agentic shift," in which individuals surrender their judgments and responsibilities to superiors. This shift effectively eliminates them as checks upon government abuse or as sources of initiative and new ideas.[21]

This model invites an excessively legalistic narrowing of concern. Except for reasons of reputation or self-interest, individuals feel little motivation to identify and correct wrong or harm within the system, and they are discouraged from feeling responsibility towards precedents that they set or procedures that they follow. The model strips them of the moral resources they need either to initiate positive actions or to resist immoral or illegal actions within their institutions.

Also, the legal-institutional model ignores the inescapable fact that public officials must always exercise discretion.[22] Public processes inevitably produce laws and policies that are vague, contradictory, and underdetermined. Yet elected, appointed, and career public officials not only must implement these policies but must do so in uncertain political environments, against opposition. Even clearly written laws and orders often require interpretation and negotiation in context.[23]

Finally, although the model relies heavily upon a formal notion of democratic accountability, it takes little account of the reality of democratic life. Democratic politics is often dominated by wealthy or well-organized constituencies and interest groups. The most vulnerable members of society—the poor, the unorganized, children, and future generations—are not well represented. The legal-institutional model gives public officials no moral resources to address such limitations; they are not permitted to inject fiduciary judgments on behalf of those not represented or to encourage nonparticipants to make themselves heard. Additionally, it profoundly misunderstands the nature of accountability by restricting all interpretive power to a superior. In the United States, at least, the legislature and courts legitimately share in oversight of institutions and in the interpretation of laws. All laws and actions in a liberal constitutional order are subject to assessment in light of the underlying regime values of the constitution.[24] Public officials' institutional responsibility can be robustly interpreted to include answering to authority vested in these branches of government as well as to the constitutional values.

For public integrity the domain of obligations of office keeps the traditional premises but incorporates the above criticisms. It lays out several essential dimensions of public integrity that become moral resources needed to exercise discretion. First, the proximate and presumptive standards to guide judgment reside with the laws, policies, court decisions, and procedures that bound the office.[25] Second, accountability and accurate reporting lie at the very center of the delegation and exercise of power. Accountability can be legitimately limited to certain officials or publics to whom one reports, but this limitation does not undermine the obligations of honesty and accuracy. Third, public officials are trustees of the law and of constitutionally sanctioned process but also of the basic constitutional and regime values. Superiors have no right to violate the standards of law, procedure, legislature, and courts. Public officials can legitimately refer to these other authorities to defend the integrity of law and process as well as promote fair participation. Fourth, competence, conscientiousness, and efficiency belong at the center of public obligation. Last, all actions performed under a constitutional warrant depend upon respect for the basic rights and dignity of all citizens. Constitutional and regime values remain as background moral conditions, and individuals can refer to them as values for limiting abuses and guiding actions.[26]

Personal Capacity and Commitment: The Personal-Responsibility Model

For public officials a focus on personal responsibility can compensate for some of the limits of the legal-institutional model. The commitments, capacities, and character that individuals have prior to taking office form the heart of integrity. They hold together the various roles individuals play and are usually entwined with religious, familial, professional, and civic commitments. Personal commitments and capacity become even more important when public officials take on leadership responsibilities. Here the range of responsibility and discretion increases, and the roles of vision, exemplary action, personal judgment, and initiative become crucial.

At a minimum, maintaining personal integrity and responsibility in public office means that individuals cannot deny responsibility for their actions. They cannot place blame on institutional structures or on others. Under the rubric of public integrity, all commitments are personal commitments. No rules or strict orders totally exonerate people from responsibility for outcomes to which they contribute and that they judge immoral, illegal, or wasteful. Public officials should be subject to praise and blame, guilt or shame or satisfaction for such actions.

In public life, laws, rules, and orders can provide strong and good reasons to justify and even excuse, but individuals may not disavow their own obligations to judge. An office can set some limits on levels of responsibility, but these limits exist as excuses or dispensations because individuals in office are committed to respect authority, process, and law. The obligations of office remain personal commitments subject to scrutiny and connected to central commitments.

However, if individuals are assigned responsibility for their actions in office, they can claim the right to introduce personal valuations. For responsibility requires integrity, which poses the obligation to keep coherence and connections between personal commitments and public office. To assign personal responsibility and yet deny officials the right to inject personal valuations contradicts the premise of the assignment. This assignment of responsibility means that integrity-based values can sometimes intrude into public judgments. In a liberal democracy, no one can legitimately claim "They made me do it." Public servants may be obliged on the basis of personal moral judgments to initiate actions for good, to dissent, to resign, or to work to change a policy that causes wrong or harm. When they take on leadership positions, they are obliged to provide direction and energy that draw upon personal commitments.

The arguments for bringing personal responsibility into public discretion flow from several claims. The first is that public officials, even those at relatively low levels, possess a degree of unavoidable responsibility in the classic sense because their actions contribute to results.[27] Personal responsibility is strengthened because officials create precedents or procedures that implicate them as responsible for results that follow because of their precedents or procedures.[28] Each action also builds or undermines the legitimacy of the public institution. Additionally the warrants of law and procedure are always being modified through negotiation, and in the "organized anarchy" of public life, officials often participate in these negotiations and influence outcomes.[29]

Furthermore successful public officials draw upon personal capacities and commitments. Stephen Bailey argued correctly that the attributes of optimism, courage, empathy, honesty, and conscientiousness, as well as an understanding of the paradoxes of procedure and moral ambiguity, are central to good public judgment.[30] The capacities to keep promises, to discipline judgments, or to limit self-interest and prejudice permeate personality, and they do not necessarily divide at the line between personal and official. Additionally, many offices call upon prior professional competencies, connections, or style.[31]

Assigning personal responsibility also fits the reality of power more accurately than the legal-institutional model. It links effective responsibility to real power, not simply formal position. In institutions, real power is often independent of formal position, held instead by those with special skills, expertise, or long service. It can also accrue through informal networks built up across other divisions. Too often individuals who possess such power deny it when convenient by pointing to the official hierarchy. Formal responsibility serves as the minimum condition of responsibility; but integrity ties officials to effective responsibility based upon real power. A focus on personal responsibility and integrity insists that officials see themselves in light of the reality of their actual power, unofficial as it may be, and act in accord with it.

The reality of the political process offers scope for immense discretion and often contains an element of serendipity. This is especially true of budget and implementation efforts in which elected, career, and appointed officials all interact. All law reflects multiple intents that provide little definitive guidance, and when standards do exist they may be multiple and conflicting. Within such situations, in which implementation can be uncertain and complex, individuals can rely upon personal commitments and capacities.[32]

A focus on personal responsibility can lead to better decisions and serve as a check on governmental abuse. Personal, professional, or associational insights and assessments can enrich deliberation as well as increase the scope of options and the honesty of evaluations. New directions can be suggested, unanticipated normative aspects can be discovered, and imaginative ways of proceeding can be proposed. Additionally, strength of character and judgment buttressed by personal commitments and capacity can produce the energy to oppose not only illegal actions but also immoral or mistaken ones.

Leadership builds upon personal attributes. The ability to provide direction, address obstacles, motivate others, and provide a guiding vision draw deeply upon an individual's personal moral commitments. These abilities become doubly important when public officials must provide new directions for an institution or respond to the demands of a changing political environment.[33]

Paradoxically, the commitments to respect public processes and legitimate values of governance now become personal commitments enmeshed in integrity. The central values of personal integrity entwine with the commitments to public service, giving them coherence and resiliency. The promises become a source of honor to the individual and the institution. The boundary between personal integrity and public commitments blurs more than the legal-institutional model allows.

But personal moral commitments and capacities are not the grounds upon which the fiduciary trust and discretionary power of government institutions are granted. Just as one could imagine the nightmare of an office in which every individual acted only on the basis of rules and orders with no personal style or commitment, so one can imagine an office in which every individual acted only on personal moral values in making each decision. Neither situation is morally or politically acceptable. Many alternatives have been offered to define what moral standards individuals should use when exercising public discretion. These standards range from social equity, to maximizing participation, to maximizing social wealth creation, to using the personal values that one believes are linked to a particular issue.[34] All of these attempts to define the correct personal moral standards to inform discretion ignore the conditions of the grant of power. Personal judgments, even personal interpretations of democracy, do not lie on a pure continuum with public judgments. The exercise of power in office is justified by the integrity-based promise to abide by provisions of the grant of power. These official duties carry presumptive weight as commitments of integrity.

Most recent attempts to integrate personal moral integrity with public service correctly urge public officials to map out all their obligations in making a judgment. Too often, however, these obligations flow from external standards of right and are not linked to the obligations of the office in question.[35] The Iran-Contra affair demonstrates what can happen when individuals, acting upon their zealous moral commitment against Communism, bypass procedure, law, policy, and accountability. What Benjamin Cardozo said of a judge's discretion could well be said of a public official: "He is not to innovate at pleasure. He is not a knight-errant roaming at will in pursuit of his own ideal of beauty or governance."[36]

Personal commitments and capacities can integrate personal integrity with the obligations of office. The conditions of the delegation of power deserve primary loyalty. Individuals should judge first on the basis of law and rules, then on the basis of the constitutional and regime values behind the authorizing laws. This leaves the central group of personal commitments as background conditions of critical evaluation or initiative, not as foreground directives for action. They should be viewed as benchmarks for judging actions that violate central moral commitments or as sources to direct action where initiative is justified.

Initiating action on the basis of personal commitments requires further caution. Because obligations to prevent wrong or harm are stronger than positive obligations, personally grounded initiatives are most defensible when an official is acting to rectify illegal results or abuse of office. These understandings should be based on the effective, not just formal, power and history of one's responsibility and power. This includes policies and precedents to which one has contributed. Some interventions may legitimately occur even beyond the effective range of responsibility if the wrong is great enough. Debra Stewart has proposed what she calls the "Kew Gardens Principle" to guide actions from personal principle in office. These conditions include the following:

- Need—there is a clear need for aid to prevent or rectify compelling wrong;
- Proximity—the agent is "close" to the situation, that is, he or she is physically close, accessible, and knowledgeable;
- Capability—the agent has some means to aid the one in need without undue risk to herself or himself;
- Indispensability—no one else is likely to know about or act on the situation.[37]

These conditions provide a warrant to inject personal judgments.

On the other hand, many personal commitments have no place in public office. The basic grant of public power in a liberal democracy protects citizens against public officials who might act with prejudice on the basis of morally illegitimate considerations such as sex, race, or religion. Additionally, family, ethnic, or religious loyalties should be set aside in the exercise of official judgment or the allocating of benefits. Personal gain or private gain of one group should not influence an official's decisions, nor should official decisions or promises to one interest group dominate policy.[38] Even claims of friendship need to be limited. Friendship and loyalty are central to political life and success, but the limits of friendship are exceeded when public officials use their office to benefit their friends or when, as often happens, loyalty blinds them to their friends' incompetence or impropriety.[39]

Many individuals bring strong professional commitments into office, and these are often required by the position, as in attorneys general's offices or public health agencies. There are many times, however, when such professional norms may be misplaced in a particular office. The military norms claimed by Vice Admiral Poindexter during Iran-Contra in trying to protect his commander in chief, President Reagan, subverted more basic norms of accountability and oversight and undermined the accuracy of information going to major decision makers. In a similar way, during the Watergate affair lawyers such as John Dean III and John Mitchell misidentified the person of Richard Nixon as their client rather than seeing themselves as trustees of public office and law. Five senators, known as "the Keating five," misconceived of themselves as legal advocates for Charles Keating when they tried to secretly influence federal regulators who were investigating Keating's illegal activities. In doing this, they undermined their more fundamental senatorial obligations of due process, fairness to colleagues, and independent judgment.[40]

However, because the legal and constitutional warrants for action are notoriously underdetermined, public officials must constantly initiate actions, not just react to abuses. In the day-to-day battles over interpretation, public life often resembles a "republic of politics, not laws."[41] In this light, three other limitations based on obligations of office are needed to constrain the judgments that flow from personal commitments and capacities.

First, these judgments, especially as initiatives to reinterpret or change policy, should be made in an accountable and truthful manner. This does not imply that they need to be open to the entire world, but that relevant authorities and publics should be aware of the actions and have the opportunity to respond. This makes the moral initiatives consistent with the tenets of the obligations of office and recognizes that individuals can legitimately defer to democratic procedures to decide some moral outcomes.[42] Normal procedures for refining and authorizing decisions should be respected, and these should be designed where possible to accommodate exceptional circumstances.[43] Being accountable and using procedures mitigate the claims that such judgments are tyrannical and arbitrary impositions because decision makers create a public record. Insistence on accountability and deliberation reinforces public integrity by forcing individuals to articulate their positions and to persuade others. Deliberation refines their position and helps them avoid self-deception or ideological rigidity. It can also minimize the dangers of "groupthink," in which decisions are reinforced by like-minded individuals and are never subjected to searching criticisms.

Second, public officials should avoid freelance endeavors. Outcomes should be implemented by professionals and should have institutional support with regular oversight. As both Watergate and Iran-Contra demonstrated, groups such as the extralegal "plumbers" or the Contra-aid networks invite abuse, are of limited competence, and violate basic tenets of democratic accountability. Actions that end as ad hoc or personalized initiatives are presumptively illegitimate in democratic life.

Finally, official initiatives cannot be justified exclusively by personal beliefs. Public officials should use the public language and justifications of constitutional or regime values in one of two ways. Either individuals can work to change the terms of justification surrounding an issue, or they can adapt their own moral concerns to the existing rhetoric. In the first case, individuals might use their positions as "bully pulpits" and work to change the rhetoric and understanding of a problem or policy. In the second, individuals refine and translate their own personal beliefs, whatever their sources, into a more broadly based language of public discourse. As long as a socially and legally legitimated group of reasons cluster around a policy, public officials should try to link with or transform them. This forces individuals to engage the mores of a society and to enter into the deliberative process; it also means that such initiatives based on personal commitment and capacities must earn legitimacy and broader public acceptance.[44]

Prudence and Effectiveness: The Effectiveness or Implementation Model

Focusing upon moral commitments or the obligations of office can sound pompous and even dangerous to experienced political actors. Machiavelli explains why: "There's such a difference between the way we really live and the way we ought to live that the man who neglects the real to study the ideal will learn how to accomplish his ruin, not his salvation."[45] As the third referent of the triangle of judgment of public integrity, prudence adds the dimension of power and effectiveness to the obligations of office and personal commitments and capacity. Prudence encompasses the considerations needed to achieve an excellent political outcome. I build this account around prudence, a traditional virtue, to place effectiveness concerns in a strong moral context and avoid reducing prudent action to political expediency.

Machiavelli reminds public officials that strong individuals and institutions of power and conviction often oppose them. He also reminds them that their own self-interest will affect their judgments, and that a world of limited resources and moral ambiguity confines them. In such a world, prudence dictates that public officials should work to get the best knowledge possible about the situation and to acquire the power and resources to achieve their goals.

The relation of prudence to public integrity flows from the "effectiveness imperative."[46] This stipulates that if an individual has goals derived from morally defensible commitments, the moral significance of these goals obliges people to work to acquire the means necessary to overcome the obstacles and achieve the goals. Public office never comes with enough knowledge or authority to achieve mandated goals. At a minimum, officials of integrity are obligated to seek the knowledge and the authoritative power to meet the obligations of office. Lack of power is not an excuse but a charge. Officials who passively accept their lack of power are negligent.

Prudential obligations reinforce the link between responsibility and the capacity to do something about goals or wrongs. Any decision to initiate or oppose actions should involve judgments about the action's importance given a person's obligations. But individuals must also ask whether they possess enough authoritative power to succeed. If they can acquire enough power, they need to know whether the actions they contemplate will affect their ability to accomplish other goals or undermine their office. They might also need to judge the proper timing for the best chance of success and to consider whether the balance between the resources expended and the goal sought is proportionate.

The virtue of prudence takes its normative importance from the nature of a politically successful outcome. This ideal of success is linked to political success and carries prescriptive weight within the practice of democratic politics. Each reference point of success then provides good prudential reasons to justify action. A truly successful political outcome includes the obligations of office but in addition charges officials to pursue the actions needed to achieve the power required to gain success. The ideal of democratic political success that informs political prudence begins with the claim that official actions should not unleash great harm or backlash. A successful outcome should endure; it should possess institutional stability as well as consistent political and budgetary support. A good durable policy should not require great coercion and manipulation to carry it out but should generate acceptance. Good effective policy either connects to or transforms the beliefs of the organizational culture or the broader political culture. It either changes or fits with the perceived interests of the relevant political actors. Such a connection with these perceived self-interests maintains long-term support and avoids the backlashes that undermine policy and legitimacy. Finally, a successful public outcome should build political community and legitimacy.[47]

Prudent judgment matters because politics is not a frictionless plane. The political reality is that passing laws and making policy is a complex and difficult process of building coalitions. Most laws and policies embody multiple goals that reflect these coalitions. The laws then carry a symbolic import. They are a pledge of effort for broad purposes that are contingent on resources and leadership. In most cases, resources are insufficient and goals are multiple or unclear, so public officials must exercise leadership to adjust the resources to the possibilities while addressing opposition and unanticipated consequences. Prudence also highlights the public official's responsibility to sustain the institutional foundations necessary for political achievement. Without adequate budgets and staffing, goals will not be achieved. Building institutional capacity and credibility makes achievement possible over time and creates power and competence for the future. This institutionalization also supports accountability.

Prudence, with its focus on effectiveness, also has its own limits. It invites individuals to focus their energies on immediate tasks of their office. This has the salutary effect of connecting them to official goals and energizing them, but it can lead to a narrowed spectrum of concern as officials fight to protect funds and support. This narrowed commitment can ignore broader political purposes. Officials can become so beholden to supporting groups that they give them privileged access and control, thus skewing the democratic process of participation. The push to achieve results can clash with a democratic focus on continuing accountability and respect for rights through procedure. The time and frustration of implementation can drive many effective public officials to seek to bypass accountability and procedures to achieve goals. It can also motivate officials to focus on short-term achievement rather than long-term institution building. Under these pressures, goal displacement can occur too easily. If individuals connect their personal commitments to the office, even if only in a purely self-interested way, they can fix too narrowly on personal or institutional status, power, or budget. If everyone acts this way, politics becomes a "game," and the gaming aspects can usurp the real goals. Reasonable efforts to protect budgets, expand effectiveness, or preserve credibility can easily slide into budget mongering, bureaucratic predation, or institutional shirking.[48] Individuals, as Machiavelli knew, can grow to enjoy the exercise of power at the expense of their obligations.

Prudence pervades every aspect of public life and is necessary to give shape to the obligations of office and personal commitments. Good prudential reasons can change easily into vices, and such justifications need to be constrained by the same concerns that limit personal judgments. Public officials should integrate prudence into the triangle of judgment to balance and interact with the obligations of office and personal commitments and capacities. Only all three domains held together by people of integrity will enable prudence to flourish within its limits.

The Commitments of Public Integrity

Responsible judgment by public officials requires a wide range of moral resources. I believe that public integrity should be seen as an iterative process among three mutually supporting domains of judgment—obligations of office, personal commitment and capacity, and prudence. We can think of public integrity as involving individuals moving within a triangle of judgment, with each point one of the domains. Individuals need integrity to hold these multiple commitments in a productive tension. Each domain provides references for judgment, and from these a range of contingently acceptable possibilities emerge. Each domain can be viewed as a ray of light illuminating a range of outcomes. Individuals should seek areas where the beams reinforce one another to illuminate the clearest and strongest outcomes. Each domain might also be thought of as a lens through which the goals and terrain are clarified and made more textured and dimensional. By using each domain to view a situation, individuals can come to clearer and more realistic assessments of the goals they seek and strategies they should follow.

Although this approach violates a desire for clean and neat solutions, it does cover all the relevant aspects of public judgment. It does not ask for spurious precision or emphasize one domain to the exclusion of other legitimate considerations. It also understands that each domain by itself is prone to its own vices and limits. The focus on individual integrity highlights the fact that individuals should deliberate within the triangle of judgment and remain responsible. All decisions are made by individual human beings and remain personal although bound by norms to which people hold themselves accountable. The three domains overlap and reinforce each other in crucial areas. These overlaps support seven standards that I propose as focal commitments for public integrity.

1. Be truthfully accountable to relevant authorities and publics. The honest and accurate monitoring and reporting of actions and results are central to all three domains. Without accountability and truthfulness, public deliberation is undermined, policy cannot improve, and the number of abuses is maximized.

2. Address the public values of the political regime. Individuals should strive to let the warrants of office guide their actions and to translate their own values into values consistent with public discourse. Law, procedures, and constitutional values should remain the prima facie guides for action. Officials can also seek to change the interpretations of law and rules or extend the range of good reasons for action in an accountable manner.

3. Build institutions and procedures to achieve goals. Public officials are trustees of the legitimacy of the institutions as well as the durable capacity of the public for action. Legitimacy, deliberation, and rights are enshrined in the procedures when public officials act as trustees. Commitments and actions should result in institutional outcomes with clear accountability.

4. Ensure fair and adequate participation of the relevant stakeholders. Political legitimacy depends upon respect for others and their participation. The very idea of public integrity grows from a conception of self-respect and perspective of oneself as a citizen.

5. Demand competent performance effectiveness in the execution of policy. Government is not established to fail. Public officials have strong obligations flowing from the effectiveness imperative to focus upon gaining power and skill to overcome the obstacles to effective performance.

6. Work for efficiency in the operation of government. This supports the legitimacy of the institutions, flows from the purposes and sources of public funds, and buttresses conscientiousness and competence.

7. Connect policy and program with the self-interest of the public and stakeholders in such a way that the purposes are not subverted. This flows from the focus on respecting the rights and interest of the populace;

it addresses the tensions between the legitimate self-interests of officials and the obligations of office, and it builds the durability and legitimacy of the outcome.

These commitments should frame democratic responsibility and permeate the exercise of public discretion. They connect and reinforce the three domains of justification and define the initial range of public integrity. But the exercise of discretion and judgment cannot be overdetermined. Holding these domains in productive tension while facing the challenges of public life is a difficult task, one that constantly tests the integrity of individuals. It requires self-conscious reflection as well as sustained moral discipline. Public judgments cannot be dictated in advance or reduced to algorithmic deduction. In a complex and unpredictable world, public integrity should be conceived of not as rigid and determined, but as dynamic and accountable. Defensible public discretion is exercised by real human beings and sustained by personal integrity.

2

The Temptations of Power

If you aspire to serve the Lord, prepare for temptation.

Eccles. 2:1

I can't think of anything offhand that's as evil as politics. It turns good men into bad all the time.

John Dunning, *The Bookman's Wake*

DAVID, BELOVED OF GOD and greatest of Israel's kings, sinned. David had spied Bathsheba unclothed and had desired her. Upon learning that she was married to Uriah, a Hittite warrior in his army, David sent for the warrior and gave him a message for David's great general Joab. The message ordered Joab to place Uriah in the forefront of battle. There Uriah died a soldier's death, while David seduced his wife. Later David and his kingdom would pay grievously for his sin as Nathan the prophet had warned him. In his sin, David had not only violated the commandments and coveted his neighbor's wife but also abused the sacred obligations of his office. He had betrayed the trust of a loyal warrior for his own selfish desire. He had corrupted the integrity of his greatest general for his own selfish ends. He had risked the future of his office for his own selfish appetites. Earlier David had prayed with confidence to his God, "Let integrity and uprightness preserve me, for I wait upon thee." Later he would beg, "Have mercy on me, oh Lord, for I am weak. O Lord, heal me for my bones are vexed."[1] The history of the Hebraic kingship is fraught with such corruptions of office. The Israelites had seen their first king, Saul, grow querulous and paranoid. They would see Solomon, their most glorious and wisest, grow greedy and vapid. Throughout history humanity has been haunted by idealistic reformers who end as bloated, grasping tyrants clinging to tattered power. The history of Israel's kings recapitulates the lesson of political history that the power of office tempts people to use office for their own ends.

The exercise of public power tempts individuals to change their perceptions, beliefs, moral evaluations, and actions in ways that betray the obligations of office. These temptations strike at the heart of public integrity. They undermine honesty and liberal and democratic values and distort prudent decision making. The word *temptation* suggests that officials are tempted to depart from a morally desirable state and set of convictions linked to what David called "integrity and uprightness" and act in ways morally dangerous and reprehensible. Public integrity embraces the obligations, commitments and capacities, and prudent judgment that public officials in a democratic and liberal state should possess. These are the very characteristics tested by the temptations of power.

The exercise of political power in a democratic and liberal society involves great discretion. In theory, this discretion does not require any specific moral qualities. American political institutions depend upon the legal-institutional model of accountability and use "devices" such as separation of powers, oversight, hierarchy, rotation in office, and elections to ensure democratic control of officials.[2] The American system can assume that "since men are not angels," government should not try to make them so. With the exception of security forces and a few other agencies, the United States has eschewed formal political indoctrination and professional ethos for its political institutions. It relies upon informal socialization and professional associations to inculcate some virtues and commitments. In general, however, government practice assumes that official power can be held by self-interested individuals who are kept in line by oversight and the dispersion of power.[3]

Even with such limited expectations, a liberal, democratic system depends upon some integrity in its officials. It requires a high level of honesty and accuracy to make accountability work. Offices also assume a limited prudence in decision making: individuals should be capable of pursuing minimally satisfying strategies to political problems, and officials should have adequate foresight and a grasp of power realities and policy implementation. Finally, some respect and competence are necessary to sustain the trust and compromise necessary to run a democratic and liberal state with a reasonable level of coercion.

Traditional formulas, which minimize the role of ethical integrity in public officials, have several problems. The level of accountability is much lower than assumed given the low level of attention paid by most citizens to politics. The accountability that does exist tends to be very limited and oriented towards interest groups. As politics fragments, more public officials must rely upon ad hoc alliances of interest groups to sustain policy. Special interests, who expect clear return for support, scrutinize the actions of officials. Likewise, many officials find that their own account-ability is often enforced within subsystems of power that link the legis-lature to interest groups and bureaucracies.[4]

This means the moral discipline and integrity required of officials is higher than expected by economic and classical liberal models of gov-ernment.[5] The obligations of office need honest and truthful accounting but also require a commitment to the democratic process and due process guarantees. Officials should possess a strong sense of their responsibil-ity to act with efficiency and competence and to discipline personal desires to the standards of law and process. They should frame judgments within the context of constitutional and regime values, yet shape them in response to legitimate public demands. Officials have obligations to seek outcomes respectful to stakeholders within the demands of law, since they are trustees of the general good in a system dominated by private interests. Officials need courage to act with fairness in the face of special pleading and must be willing to fight for their views when opposed. As trustees of public institutions, they should attend to the long-term legiti-macy of their institutions. Additionally, these officials should be consci-entious in the use of resources and respectful of the law that legitimizes their power.

This democratic responsibility of public officials becomes a vital force in making liberal and democratic institutions work. These commitments of democratic responsibility cover the focal points of the public integrity of officials and citizens. Yet these commitments are the very ones tempted by the exercise of power. The pressures of exercising power can wear down these obligations, commitments, and capacities. They can erode the liberal and democratic values that inform relations to oneself, to office, and to others. They can transform relations to democratic institutions and can change officials in ways that incline them to abuses of power.

The Environment of Power

The temptations of power arise from the psychological experiences of holding power that can corrode liberal and democratic commitments, capacities, and virtues. These environmental experiences include stress and dissonance, frustration and resentment, deference and superiority, deindividuation and group effects. These experiences in office can drive people to moral and psychological reactions that, though understandable, are often undesired adaptations to the pressures of holding power.[6]

An archaic meaning of *temptation* was a "test" or "trial" of one's worth. This primordial sense highlights how holding power involves temptations. For in holding power, officials are committed to office and power in order to make a difference and achieve moral goals. They make promises and accept responsibility, and these actions link their integrity to their office. Only one of Plato's philosopher-kings or a total cynic could be detached enough from the environmental pressures to escape all temptations.

Most temptations occur in a situation generating stress or psychological discomfort and pain felt when people face a situation that involves significant stakes for them and conflicting social influences. This stress or psychological pressure can result in physical deterioration, a decline in mental alertness, depression, and myriad other difficulties. Politics aggravates stress by laying on intense responsibility, short time spans, and conflicting demands. Psychological pressure and stress increase when a person's integrity is linked to performing the obligations of office. When officials confront attacks, opposition, imperfect outcomes, frustration, or failure in office, they experience stresses that exact a high toll on the physical and moral stamina and discipline required by liberal, democratic office.

The most severe stress associated with the exercise of power comes with having to make decisions and then having to commit oneself to the decision. The need to make a decision in which personal integrity, self-esteem, official obligations, and perhaps one's career are at stake creates tremendous pressure to do the "right" thing.[7] Common adaptive strategies in such a situation are prematurely closing a decision before all the information is in, seeking only information that supports one's initial predisposition, taking cues from those around one, or "bolstering" the decision, that is, denigrating other options after the decision has been made. These tendencies, which seek to reduce the stress of commitment, always threaten prudent judgment. The public nature of political commitments aggravates these stresses because public disclosure will "trap" people, who will seek to avoid such stress and entrapment by relying upon secrecy.[8]

The stress of commitment also affects action subsequent to a decision. Personal integrity and self-esteem are now linked to a particular decision. People feel "bound" by implicit contracts to others when they come to a decision, and these binding forces keep them committed to policies. The more public the commitment, the more strongly it is held. The commitment "freezes" policy decisions and increases the pressure to reinforce one's moral evaluation with specific bolstering of the convictions that support the decision. These pressures also tempt officials to denigrate those who oppose their decisions. Likewise, individuals will be prone to select information that supports their decision and ignore any counterinformation.[9] During the Vietnam War when things began to go badly, W. W. Rostow displaced others as the prime national security advisor to President Lyndon B. Johnson. Rostow gained this access by constantly emphasizing the optimistic aspects of reports, culling out positive information, and downplaying negative information. In reports he would underline the optimistic sections, and Johnson tended to skim the reports, noticing this optimistic information to bolster his own troubled commitments.[10] Finally, individuals tend to harden commitments in the face of political attacks in order to save face or ride out the storm.

The exercise of power involves living up to obligations of office, set by the legal and role expectations and promises that go with the positions. With rare and psychotic exceptions, no neat correlation exists between the desires and convictions of individuals and requirements of a position. This means public integrity builds linkages between the obligations of office and personal commitments and capacities. Individuals in office must sometimes act against their personal convictions or self-interests to meet the obligations of office. This tension between personal commitment and capacities and the demands of office or prudence creates great strain in the triangle of judgment and leads to intense stress on people to keep moral coherence in themselves and see themselves as morally one.[11]

These tensions evoke a virulent form of stress known as cognitive dissonance. The result is acute discomfort felt when individuals possess simultaneously two cognitions that are psychologically or morally inconsistent. The simultaneous existence of two differing conditions can be either cognitive or emotional. People seeking integrity in their lives will seek ways to moderate the tension between their actions and self-image. This can be done either by changing an attitude or belief, especially a moral evaluation, to fit the behavior or by changing the behavior to fit the evaluation. People can also reevaluate the importance of a behavior or belief or choose to bolster new cognitions and information to support their belief about the preferred behavior. Over time the pressure of constantly balancing a public and private face takes its toll and gradually erodes honest self-reflection for individuals. The pressure invites self-deception,[12] in which individuals do not spell out to themselves the full implications of what they know, or they tell themselves stories about their actions that leave out vital pieces of information that would refute the story. They bolster this perception by changing the people around them and perceiving new information selectively.[13] Doris Kearns Goodwin describes the process for Lyndon Johnson during the Vietnam War:

> Most of Johnson—the outer man . . . remained intact, for most of the time. But in some ways, increasingly obvious to his close associates, he began to crumble; the suspicions congenital to his nature became delusion; calculated deceit became self-deception, and then matters of unquestioned belief. The President's will, once expressed, was not challenged. Advisers began to anticipate his reactions before they said or did anything; self-deceptions multiplied in this hall of distorting mirrors.[14]

Individuals with responsibility for the common good are constantly trying to accomplish something. Whether officials lead a war, implement an obscure regulation, or shepherd a bill through a committee, they have a goal. But no one accomplishes public purposes without encountering the resistance of people who question or oppose the goals. The democratic and liberal state permits—and indeed depends upon—such conflict. It attempts to legitimize and channel conflict and to achieve reconciliation. In contrast, one of the hallmarks of tyranny is the willingness to incarcerate or execute political opposition.

Not only will individuals meet resistance, but often they will be attacked. Allies or friends who feel betrayed at unfulfilled promises will often be the angriest, as were many of President Bill Clinton's liberal supporters when Clinton signed a welfare reform act or as were President George Bush's conservative supporters when he broke his "no new taxes" pledge to help reduce the budget deficit. Those who believe individuals' actions threaten basic values and interests will not only oppose initiatives but actively organize campaigns against officials. In face of this, democratic politics entails constant and incessant compromises in big as well as little things.[15] Officials will experience immense frustration from not living up to their own and others' expectations. The frustration can generate severe self-doubt and requires significant responses to protect self-esteem.[16] Political attacks engender great resentment, especially when officials believe the attacks are not in good faith or question their integrity. Media coverage aggravates this resentment and frustration.[17]

Individuals tend to respond to these attacks and the mounting frustration by shoring up their own self-images and protecting their sense of coherent integrity. This tempts them to condemn opponents to soften the criticisms. An aide in the Clinton administration described the response after disastrous midterm elections as "bunker-like": individuals tended to see the elections and criticisms of the administration as aspects of the "malevolency of an unjust world."[18] Over time the slowness of democracy can exasperate ambitious and committed officials. An oft-quoted statement by an aide to John Kennedy sums it up: "Everybody believes in democracy until he gets to the White House and then you begin to believe in dictatorship because it's so hard to get things done. Every time you turn around, people resist you."[19]

The world of resistance blends incongruously with the world of deference and superiority. An individual's sense of worth is influenced by images reflected from others. Most people validate their sense of self, at least in part, by checking it with those around them. But because powerful officials can help or harm the people around them, they often get distorted feedback. Most people approach them attempting to ingratiate themselves and gain favors. George Reedy describes the not-unusual state of the Johnson White House, where the atmosphere of deference was so pervasive that no one would tell the president "Go soak your head."[20]

Officials can thus get an exaggerated sense of their own worth and competence. Success accentuates this inflated self-worth, giving them a feeling of superiority, even over allies. It can intensify a related feeling, which denigrates the competence of opponents.[21] Constant positive feedback and success can combine to form a heady potion for anyone in office, leading him or her to ignore or subvert advice and undercut opposition.

Integrity in public office depends upon a firm sense of personal responsibility. One pressure on those in office, however, is towards deindividuation. Deindividuation is a state in which individuals feel released from normal internal moral inhibitions. It defines the experience so graphically portrayed by Plato in the story of Gyges' ring. Gyges, a shepherd for the ruler of Lydia, found a ring that could turn him invisible: "Having made this discovery he managed to get himself included in the party that was to report to the king, and when he arrived seduced the queen, and with her help attacked and murdered the king and seized the throne."[22] Socrates' student Glaucon argues that any person, just or unjust, who possessed the ring would have acted in the same way. Likewise, social psychologist Phillip Zimbardo argues that situations in which individuals lose a sense of personal identity and responsibility release "dark forces."[23]

Deindividuation occurs under conditions of anonymity such as among a crowd or in circumstances of secrecy. Individuals who believe they will evade identification and responsibility will often act in a manner less morally inhibited than if they were publicly identified with the consequences of their acts. In a group in which responsibility is diffused or is hidden behind a veil of secrecy, deindividuation erodes personal integrity and responsibility. I extend the notion of deindividuation to a number of conditions in which officials see their normal moral commitments and inhibitions eroded. In one kind of a case, documented by Stanley Milgram's studies, individuals performed actions that they believed hurt others because they viewed themselves as having "no choice" or "duty bound" to act when ordered to harm someone. Overscrupulous following of orders can lead individuals to scrupulously allocate positions in gas chambers. As discussed in Chapter 1, Milgram believes that an "agentic shift" occurs in which individuals reorient their sense of personal responsibility and abandon their judgment to some greater force such as "the experiment" or immediate superiors and absolve themselves of any clear responsibility. In another variant, people see themselves as an embodiment of a higher suprapersonal force—cultural identity, nation's necessity, or God's will. People then feel "freed" from ordinary human restraints, because such restraints do not apply to the culture, the nation, or God. People can also become consumed with identification with an office, and to protect "the office" they may act "officially" in manners that are forbidden to private persons.[24]

Group effects aggravate all of these tendencies. When decisions and commitments are made in groups, the bolstering is reinforced. Groups tend to exaggerate information distortions resulting from cognitive dissonance and commitment. Groups also provide insulated sources of warmth and commiseration when an official is under attack or confronting resistance. They can compound antidemocratic responses to frustration. The existence of groups, especially small cohesive groups subject to corporate sense of identity and "groupthink," worsens the dangerous psychological pressures and experiences of exercising power.[25]

The Distortions of Power

The temptations of power involve adaptations to the environment of power. These personal adaptations call to mind the second meaning of moral temptation: the enticement of people "to commit an unwise or immoral act by promise of a reward."[26] Adapting to the stress of the environment of power, officials begin to value the holding of power more than the performance of the duties and begin to justify actions that violate the democratic and liberal values to keep their power and pursue their goals.

The temptations induce changes in people's perceptions, and moral evaluations, of their own actions. These changes lead to disastrous consequences for democratic and liberal politics. Because they are moral changes, they involve changing the quality of people's relations at three levels: relations to themselves, to others, and to institutions.

The most insidious and important temptation involved in exercising power is the inflation of self-worth. This distorts the triangle of judgment, giving primacy to the inflated judgments of personal commitments and desires. Deference to an official, coupled with group feelings of superiority, leads to exaggerated notions of self-importance. The exaggeration of self-worth can be reinforced by the symbols of power. Law, office, and perks can lead officials to personalize office as a possession. An Air Force pilot once commented to Lyndon Johnson, "This is your helicopter, sir." To which Johnson replied, "They're all my helicopters, son."[27]

The elevation of office coupled with the urgency of its responsibilities can lead people to believe that a different standard of morality applies to them. As Machiavelli informed the Prince, he must learn "how not to be good." Officials can too easily assume that the importance of their responsibility can justify expedient action in the name of a privileged morality.[28] The illusion of excessive strength and competence compounds this assumption. Irving Janis has documented this as one of the primary characteristics, along with moral righteousness, that characterizes exercises of power afflicted by "groupthink."[29] Ralph White has documented that military overconfidence played a fatal role not just in the precipitation of World War I but on both sides during the Vietnam War.[30] In a similar manner Speaker of the House Newt Gingrich both overestimated his own power and skill and underestimated President Bill Clinton in their yearlong battle in 1995 over the Republican "Contract with America" and Gingrich's effort to transform the basic budgetary policy and budgetary priorities of the government. Gingrich's misperceptions lead him to lose control of the agenda and misjudge the consequences of his actions in twice shutting down the federal government. As Gingrich ruefully remarked, "People feeling confident of their own strength often fail to take the proper measure of their opponents."[31] The exaggerated sense of their own strength leads people to believe that they are beyond accountability and can act without fear of consequences.

Self-importance grows in thousands of ways, but one of the most important is the notion of one's indispensability. Given the successful exercise of power and the tendency to denigrate those whom one has successfully manipulated, people easily envision themselves, at all levels of office, as absolutely indispensable. Maintaining power becomes of critical importance, not for oneself, but to "save" the institution or the policy. For the most altruistic motives, the indispensable person does everything to keep power. In 1938 British Prime Minister Neville Chamberlain confronted the bankruptcy of his own policy of accommodation towards Nazi Germany after Germany invaded Poland and World War II started. Chamberlain remained paralyzed as England fumbled in the war. Even after the Germans invaded Holland and Belgium, he resisted resigning, demonstrating "how men in very high office can acquire the sincere conviction that their services are indispensable and that in moments of crisis they cannot be replaced."[32] During his attempt to transform the agenda of American government and push through the Republican Party's Contract with America, Speaker of the House Gingrich concluded that he had to become more like the Duke of Wellington and less like General George Marshall. He stopped delegating and injected himself in all aspects of the negotiations even when it was counterproductive and exhausted him.[33]

All office is surrounded by symbols of power and benefits. People can become attached to little things—their office space, the attention of others, the capacity to make a difference—or to bigger baubles—chauffeurs, notoriety, waiting jets, the scurry of others waiting to carry out one's slightest command.[34] The importance of Benjamin Disraeli's remark about why people enter Parliament should not be underestimated: "We came here for fame."[35] Even a minor official has a circle of peers and clients or interest groups who attempt to gain favor. Officials can take the excitement and center of interest for granted. They become attached to being part of the action and enjoy the attention of office and power and do not wish to part from them. Machiavelli, on losing his relatively minor post, described his life of retirement in his poignant letters as "sordid and inglorious," for "Chance has done the worst for me that she can, so that I am brought down to a condition enabling me to do little good to myself and less to others."[36]

The seductive advantages of power lead to the use of office for personal gain. Individuals can use office to amass wealth or to benefit family, friends, and allies, which becomes a further source of power and satisfaction. Office becomes a means to material ends, to "get rich."[37] Acquisition does not have to be great; small gifts and favors over time can add up to a changed perspective. Officials can also be tempted when they legislate on or regulate organizations that might later hire them. Individuals know the regulated organizations not only watch their competence but also see them as possible employees. The subtlety of conflict-of-interest temptations is complemented by more obvious gains such as bribery or extortion.

Power invites arrogance. The worlds of perks, attention, and excitement provide satisfaction and status but can easily engender a preference for arbitrary action. Winning and dominating others can reinforce the self-images of superiority to others and provide alluring satisfactions. These can motivate some people to keep seeking the satisfactions involved. Individuals, accustomed to having smaller needs met, live increasingly in a cocoon-like existence, expecting to get their way in larger matters. William Crossman describes the life of a top British minister as being like living in a comfortable, padded room where deferential bureaucrats come and go to ensure that all the minister's needs are met; he goes on to observe that the minister is quite controlled while possessing the illusion of control.[38]

People with more power at their disposal tend to use it more often to get their own way.[39] Power produces almost an itch to use it. Robert Moses, for years one of the most powerful political actors in New York City, held the titular title of head of the New York Triborough Bridge Authority. Yet he dominated New York City planning and politics for three decades, amassing immense power over New York state and city. He grew accustomed to living like a monarch in his own bureaucratic empire where he could viciously berate subordinates and attack enemies. He became habituated to capricious and arbitrary action, sometimes acting to prove to himself and others his own strength.[40] Similarly, when he was under pressure and angry, President Richard Nixon would order subordinates to "get someone" if that person stood in the way of one of Nixon's goals.[41] Arbitrary action, especially if a person becomes accustomed to its success in small and great things, can easily become a preferred mode of action:

> To lord it over others is a means of security, freedom, goods, and so on. But it is also a good in itself. A good which can overwhelm every other

good dictated by reason and conscience alike. It is strangely gratifying to make people come and go at our bidding, to overrule their minds and their wills, to take away their power, and virtually annihilate them. . . . There is a soul fulfillment in mastery over human beings. There is no pleasure quite like it, and for its sake men have risked every good and done every conceivable evil. It is well to remember these facts and take them seriously.[42]

The temptations to change one's relation to one's self and moral beliefs pose serious problems for prudential judgment. The sense of self-importance, moral privilege, preference for arbitrary action, seduction by perks and joys of the office—all can distort information assessment and a balanced judgment. They also encourage people to disrespect others and avoid democratic accountability.

A complementary temptation encourages officials to denigrate those around them. The play of official power involves two sets of critical relations—those with opponents and those with advisors and allies. The cumulative effects of exercising power, especially of frustration and resentment coupled with deference and commitment effects, induces changes in these critical relations. Opponents become enemies; advisors become sycophants.

Effective, stable, and minimally coercive policy requires compromise and the forging of consensus, or at least tolerance of solutions, by interested parties and the citizenry. To garner trust requires prudence, toleration, and a willingness to bargain hard, compromise honestly, and live up to promises made as part of a political deal. Individuals need to know that they can lose and fight another day for their cause without coercive penalties. This enables conflict to occur without constant coercion or defection.

This moral and political world requires the concept of "opponent." As Senator Robert Dole insisted during the bitter 1996 presidential campaign, President Bill Clinton was "my opponent, not my enemy."[43] "Opponent" identifies a person as an adversary but within the context of a contest played by acknowledged rules, in which everyone has a legitimate interest in avoiding reversion to violence. Individuals can vigorously campaign against one another, but once an election is decided, the defeated candidate pledges to support the winner. Individuals lobby on legislation or policy, but if they lose, they can go back and organize to influence policy without fear of reprisal. Officials can fight hard over the placement or design of a program yet accommodate and work with the final decision. The concept of "opponent" makes liberal democracy possible because conflict does not require resorting to violence and revolution as long as people perceive that they have an open and fair chance to organize and fight for their positions.

However, the cumulative effect of political frustration can slowly transform legitimate opponents into enemies. The "diabolical enemy" or "dangerous other" image reduces moral ambiguity and ambivalence and simplifies the moral and emotional universe of public officials.[44] Once opponents become "enemies," moral prohibitions are weakened. If someone is determined to be an enemy, that "explains" many actions, such as why the enemy would oppose good and clear policies or slander good intentions. It accounts for the enemy's refusal to "listen to reason," and it justifies the necessity of resorting to extraordinary measures that violate constitutional and democratic guarantees.

The morally simplified world of enemies reduces the stress on officials as well as reducing ambiguity and ambivalence. It paints the world in black and white. Officials can encourage "autistic violence" by cutting off dealings with the enemy and thus protecting themselves from challenging or conflicting data or recognizing the humanity of their enemies. They will denigrate their enemy's competence and good will. Finally, they will "blame the victim" in order to morally exculpate themselves.[45]

In the early 1970s, the stress of antiwar protests during the Vietnam War tempted the Nixon administration to define student and media opponents as enemies. This expanded to include Democratic Party opponents of the war. The cumulative costs of the protests, coupled with lack of success in the war, led to an angry and defensive administrative culture that spawned "enemies lists" and plans to spy on and subvert their opponents. When the FBI refused to do its bidding in this area, the Nixon administration created its own internal group, the "plumbers unit," to spy on and sabotage the Democratic Party.[46] All the normal rules had been superseded by a state of war. Presidential counsel John Dean provided a quiet narration of the siege mentality of the White House as the people hid in their psychological bunkers awaiting massive student marches on Washington. The Watergate scandals simply played out the consequences of an enemies mentality.[47]

In the late 1980s Speaker of the House Democrat Jim Wright came to power in the House of Representatives. Unlike his predecessor Speaker Thomas P. O'Neill, Wright demonstrated a fierce and uncompromising partisanship. He drove his own party leaders relentlessly, but he also violated a set of unwritten rules of comity: that the minority party Republicans should be treated with respect, consulted, and given reasonable chances to negotiate on issues. By violating these rules, Wright demonstrated his own disrespect for the Republican opposition but also undercut the existing moderate Republican leadership, who had relied upon comity in the House. This enabled highly partisan and ambitious members of the frustrated and angry Republican minority to rise to power.

In this charged political environment, Representative Newt Gingrich built his power and reputation through powerful rhetorical assaults. Responding to the outrage over the violation of comity by the Democrats as well as years of frustration as a minority member, Gingrich mobilized his party with a rhetoric that demonized the Democratic Party and all liberals. Further, he evinced a willingness to "destroy the institution in order to save it." He planned and masterminded a yearlong campaign to destroy the reputation and position of Speaker of the House Wright on a series of relatively minor ethics charges. In the course of the campaign Gingrich resorted to a regular flow of exaggerated and knowingly false plants in the media as well as the demonizing rhetoric. Gingrich's strategy succeeded in forcing Wright from the House.[48]

In 1993–94 Gingrich completed his campaign to destroy Democratic Party power by leading a national campaign based upon a nationwide attack on Democrats and the corruption of the House. The campaign was organized around a common rhetoric attacking the "liberal" and "corrupt" Democrats and a pledge to enact the Republican Party's Contract with America. Gingrich and his associates developed a vocabulary of vilification that infused a coordinated and nationalized attack upon the Democratic members of Congress. In 1995 when the Republican Party gained control of the House for the first time in forty years, Gingrich was elected Speaker of the House. In the congressional session after he had been elected Speaker, Gingrich initiated a yearlong contest with President Clinton to radically change the policy and budgetary priorities of American government beginning with the Contract with America. Intoxicated by his own power and success in a strategy based upon demonizing and denouncing opponents as enemies, he believed his own rhetoric about the Democrats' weaknesses, incompetence, and immorality. Gingrich came to believe in his own invincibility and "was supremely confident that he could outwit and outlast Clinton." Convinced that he could "break" a weak Clinton, "control" the entire agenda, and "move the whole country simultaneously," he overplayed his hand. Twice under his leadership, the Republican Party ignored history-making budget deals to protect a tax reduction and chose instead to precipitate a shutdown of the federal government, one of which lasted twenty-one days and brought the country to the edge of default. Despite the advice of his advisors, Gingrich personally participated in a series of budget summits to try to close the budget deal, but he failed.

In the end, Gingrich's rhetoric and style earned widespread blame for the Republican Party and undercut support for the Republican agenda. Underestimating President Clinton from the beginning, Gingrich found himself and the party boxed in on several issues and unable to reach the historic budget accord he sought. In the 1996 election, Clinton easily won reelection, largely by running on issues generated by Gingrich's failed drive to dominate the government.[49]

Not only are officials tempted to demonize and underestimate opponents, but they are also tempted to transform their relations with advisors. This relation is critical to prudent judgment and to getting honest and careful decisions in political life. The wisdom, rightness, and practicality of most political decisions depend upon the quality of an official's advisors and their honest and competent judgment. Advisors should be loyal but independent, not only providing expert advice but also sometimes serving as the official's conscience.[50] Yet under the pressure of attack, opposition, deference, and commitment stress, officials will often close their circle, thus undermining the quality of advice they get.

During the Vietnam War President Lyndon Johnson retreated to a select group of friends and advisors who mutually reinforced one another's misconceptions. Although the advisors tried to question the war and often doubted it, they could never break out of a basic set of premises that they shared about the need to contain aggression in Vietnam. Under such conditions dissenters find themselves ostracized or neutralized by group pressure. Although the competence level remained high, the distortions of small group dynamics encouraged conformity to group assumptions and tended to penalize individuals who questioned the group's basic tenets. Members of the group also felt more committed to policy that they themselves had helped formulate and were more likely to defend it outside of the group and to support it within the group.[51]

Advisors can also become sycophants. If the leader grows arbitrary and unwilling to brook any opposition, honest and strong individuals will be forced out of the coterie around the official, leaving only individuals willing to go along with the leader and say only what he or she wishes to hear. Albert Speer's portrayal of the circle around Adolf Hitler shows a world in which competence was devalued, information was distorted, and honesty was attacked. This environment produced a series of disastrous policy decisions based upon whim and misinformation. It was a world in which clarity of thought and moral integrity endangered one's life.[52] Robert Moses built his power base upon a coterie who demonstrated magnificent competence and dedication to building and engineering as well as loyalty to Moses. But as time went on, these individuals died or moved on, and Moses replaced them with individuals whose primary asset was their loyalty to Moses. His power increasingly displayed arbitrariness with less imagination and initiative.[53] More than one political machine has faltered when the first generation gave way to people less talented but blindly loyal to the boss.

The temptation to transform opponents into enemies and advisors into sycophants encourages the temptation to secrecy. Secrecy enables people to try out policy without public commitment, and it maximizes the freedom to keep options open. It allows necessary but distasteful actions to be accomplished as well as neutralizes resistance because people cannot organize to oppose what they do not know about. Finally, it permits policy to be made "rationally," in quiet, closed conditions and not on the street, with raucous and discordant voices raising "impractical" moral considerations.[54] Secrecy beckons as a perfect solution to overcome frustration, opposition, and resistance.

Consistent secrecy frustrates accountability, but it leads to closed decision making weakened by information distortion and groupthink. It can exacerbate opposition and distrust of government. It also accentuates the deindividuating dangers of power, because people with power are more likely to abuse it if they feel anonymous or secure in the knowledge that no one will know they are abusing power. Both Jeb Magruder of the Committee to Reelect President Nixon and White House counsel John Dean acknowledged that they helped abet the Watergate cover-up because they assumed they were protected by executive privilege. Secret power encourages people to believe that they will never get caught and never be called to account for their actions. People become less concerned with the harmful consequences of their secret actions.[55]

Lessened sensitivity to the human costs is another hallmark of the temptations of power. Most powerholders prefer social distance between themselves and those over whom they exercise power. The desire for distance increases if coercive power or harmful consequences are involved.

People buffer themselves with changes in bureaucratic language that dehumanizes those who are adversely affected, hides the real nature of actions, and reinforces the social distance. For instance, during the Vietnam War the military adopted body counts and body-count ratios to set goals and define whether the military were winning or losing the war. This language hid the real consequences and for many desk soldiers made the conflict feel like a war game in which to score kills. It also encouraged thoughtless killing and set up incentives not to differentiate between noncombatants and combatants. In implementing their "final solution," the Nazi government imposed elaborate "language rules" to hide the reality of the slaughter of the Jewish population from those who participated in it. Even the Watergate conspirators developed their own code to speak about their actions and hide the real moral import from themselves.[56] This use of language codes supports demonizing opponents and systematic self-deception among individuals who participate in a morally flawed policy.

The tendency to see opponents as enemies justifies actions that can undercut democratic process and civic community as well as violate due process and individual liberties. These characterizations deaden the conscience and reinforce moral insensitivity to the costs of actions. The reduction of advisors to sycophants destroys the basis of solid, critical decision making. Together, they generate an obsession with secrecy, which encourages unaccountable and irresponsible abuses of power.

The last temptation affects institutions. Institutions give substance to the exercise of power and define the scope of concerns and commonly accepted reasons for the exercise of power. Symbols, rituals, and institutions legitimize and channel the exercise of power. But institutions are impersonal; they exist before individuals come in and after individuals leave. Committed officials should be humble under the yoke of institutional knowledge and practice, but critical and active in making institutions responsive to goals and flaws and to the will of the people.

Three major temptations lurk in the institutional environment of a democratic and liberal state:

1. An official can become increasingly impatient and reject the democratic processes.

2. An official can overidentify with the office and confuse his or her own interests with the defense of office.

3. Within an organization, an official can be tempted to give up personal integrity for malignant obedience, accepting orders and practices regardless of their moral content.

The roots of impatience with democracy and due process lie in frustration, resentment, and the pressures of commitment. Stress generated by failure to accomplish goals, assaults upon personal image, and cognitive dissonance can undermine patience and integrity, both of which are needed if an official is to commit to the processes and to respect outcomes with which one disagrees. The pressure to succeed slowly undermines a commitment to fair deliberation and politics because the stakes are so high, and delays so costly. Many of the temptations associated with secrecy invite officials to evade democratic accountability in the interest of the speed and efficiency of action.

Because all office comes without sufficient power to accomplish its demands, officeholders are constantly searching for new sources of power. Officials can be tempted to use security forces to investigate opposition leaders as did Presidents Franklin Roosevelt, John Kennedy, and Lyndon Johnson with the collaboration of J. Edgar Hoover, the director of the FBI.[57] This temptation drove the demands of President Nixon and his advisors to undercut the Democratic Party during Watergate as well as the efforts of Col. Oliver North and CIA director William Casey to avoid accountability by creating an extragovernmental capacity to intervene in countries without congressional funding or oversight.[58] It can also tempt individuals to make allies with groups who can get things accomplished even if they do not share one's ideals. Early in his career Robert Moses watched his major reform initiatives die before the combined opposition of entrenched interests. He finally aligned with the power brokers who had earlier frustrated his visions of reform. This bought him some success but undermined the shape of many other progressive reforms.[59]

This temptation to violate democratic processes underlies most other temptations of power. Democracy demands that just decisions account for legitimate interests and be grounded in open participation. Stable and legitimate decisions need the effective participation of relevant people to get the highest level of voluntary adherence to policy and law. Resentment, frustration, dissonance, deindividuation, and deference all pressure individuals to hurry the process to overcome opponents and end the tensions of ambivalence, compromise, and incompleteness. The urge is to simplify—to solve the problems that need solving fast without the interference of "politics."

The second major institutional temptation undermines a prized accomplishment of western political theory and practice, the separation of office and person. Public office exists as an independent institution of power, responsibilities, and authority that individuals fill. Individuals may leave their stamp on the office by either adding to or diminishing its powers, status, and legitimacy. In a democracy, offices are not possessions of families but are linked to election, appointment, or competence and performance. Office also makes for a more peaceful political order because officials are not the office incarnate; they may be removed, but the office and powers remain. Individuals in the government aid a public official not because he or she is a particular person but because the official possesses the seal of office and has passed the legitimate qualifying tests. The notion of office makes nonviolent changes of regime and policy implementation possible. Changes of leadership do not involve purges, assassinations, or forced retirements.

People enter an office legally and morally charged to perform its duties. The responsibilities are already defined, although considerable latitude exists for discretion in interpreting goals and the methods of implementing them. The obligations also include the expectations that they maintain the powers gained and hand on the office in at least as good shape as when they occupied it. All office involves stewardship, not just for the duties of office but for its effective functioning. The protection of an office and its powers is a legitimate responsibility. If the office possesses a number of statutory and historically sanctioned powers, then it is legitimate for the officeholder to fight to keep those powers assigned to the office.

Individuals in office are also provided with a number of special excuses for action that serve as psychological and moral absolutions for actions. The hangman is an accepted member of the community who performs a vital if distasteful job. Likewise, the police officers and military officers who are trained to kill, the tax collectors, and the judges who sentence people to confinement are similarly excused. These offices are crucial to social peace, although they involve actions not normally permitted. Provided such officials are bound by due process, fairness, competence, and accountability, their performance is rewarded, excused, and sometimes praised. The power of the office invests a person with responsibilities but sometimes also with a special set of moral dispensations that regular citizens do not possess. Individuals must be clearly aware that the dispensations apply only to actions performed in pursuit of the office's functions, bound by procedures of fairness and accountability.

Possessing office tempts individuals to confuse their own interests with those of the office. Overidentifying can afflict anyone, but especially those who see the exercise of the office as intimately associated with their aspirations and satisfaction. The more closely the possession of an office intertwines with needs and desires, the more completely its holder will identify with it. This merging of identity will lead individuals to resist giving up the office or being accountable. Yet at its moral and political core, liberal and democratic government carries the exact opposite postulate: no one is indispensable in a democracy.

This personal identification collapses the triangle of judgment of public integrity that depends upon the self-conscious integration of the role of office into a broader sense of self. Overidentification with the office makes it impossible for officials to perceive which attacks are legitimate and which really do threaten the office. It also destroys any internal inhibitions born of personal integrity that serve as checks to abuse of power. When the personal aspects of self collapse into the office, the vital, conscious distinction between personal desires and public obligations is lost. The expectations that make democracy work are undermined. Offices are not a personal possession. In a democracy individuals leave office when removed or defeated; they leave without penalty and fear, but they do leave. An individual who refuses to leave or be accountable for office because of overidentification and who seems willing to bypass normal rules threatens everyone's commitment to the democratic process. The teetering suspense when it was feared that General Douglas MacArthur would not give up his military command as ordered by President Harry Truman demonstrates this fragility. Finally, overidentification with office can jeopardize accomplishments. If officials personalize all policy and personnel, they undercut the impersonal commitment to law and office of other officials. Leaving office then means that people cannot rely upon these professional, integrity-based commitments to continue a legacy.

J. Edgar Hoover embodies the archetype of a person who overidentifies with office. Over his years as director of the FBI, he gained personal control of the entire agency. Officials devoted immense time to attending to his personal needs and his personal policy agendas. Agents who questioned his priorities or the culture he enforced were harassed and forced from the agency. Any strong rivals found themselves shunted to the side. The agency amassed a vast reservoir of information on high-ranking government officials, making even presidents and senators unwilling to challenge Hoover's policies. Several presidents wished to remove him from office, but none dared try. As Lyndon Johnson so eloquently put it, "I'd rather have him on the inside pissing out than on the outside pissing in." In addition, in his later years, Hoover passed up institutional opportunities to take the lead in the battle against organized crime in order to protect his own institutional base in the agency. In his mind and in the minds of his subordinates, Hoover became synonymous with the agency and its mission.[60]

The problems of institutional imbeddedness and malignant obedience reveal the double-edged nature of the temptations of power. People in power, with very few exceptions, exercise power over others but under others as well. Additionally, they do so in the context of an institution with a culture, norms, practices, and authority structure. Many of the temptations take on a different cast depending upon the person's institutional position. Higher-ranked individuals might be tempted to surround themselves with sycophants; on the other hand, people in the subordinate position might submerge their own critical faculties to become loyalists. A division head can simultaneously operate as a loyalist to a superior and yet also be the center of another group of loyalists in the division.

When people become imbedded in an institution, they accept and internalize the institution's role expectations completely. They do not permit other dimensions of integrity to intrude into the demands of the role. They accept totally the definitions of the institution and the demands placed upon them by superiors in order to achieve both institutional goals and success and advancement.[61] In this situation, the triangle of judgment again collapses with the obligations of office overwhelming the personal commitments and capacities. The complexity of public integrity and the relation of the office to one's full integrity is denied. The role is severed from the other aspects of selfhood.

Malignant obedience carries institutional imbeddedness to its logical conclusion. It focuses upon the temptations involved in relations with superiors. Malignant obedience is the acceptance and enforcement of a superior's orders regardless of their moral content. People's motives may stem from advancement, a desire to be perceived as a loyalist, a need for money, or a fear of reprisal. The moral point reduces to the decision to follow orders even if integrity-based questions arise about their appropriateness. During the Watergate cover-ups, presidential counsel John Dean and others associated with the executive office followed "legitimate" orders to "protect the president." They violated laws, lied before courts, and abetted the violation of personal rights. Many of them, such as Dean and Herbert Kalmbach, questioned the morality and wisdom of what they were doing but followed orders anyway.[62] Similar obedience occurred among the bomber pilots who during the Vietnam War violated and falsified the fundamental reporting protocols of the Strategic Air Command in order to hide the illegal bombing of neutral Cambodia.[63] Stanley Milgram's experiments on obedience confirm the troubling willingness of common people to inflict what they thought was excruciating pain on others when an individual in a white coat assured them that "the responsibility is all mine."[64]

But institutional imbeddedness and malignant obedience resolve the tensions associated with power and office. Problems of commitment stress, dissonance, resistance, deference, and frustration occur because of the ego involvement of individuals and the acceptance of responsibility. Once individuals deny personal responsibility and transfer it to others or the institution, the tensions lessen. Individuals find it easier to respond to frustration and resistance with illicit means when they "have no choice." They can participate in policies, satisfy the demands of superiors, meet the requirements of competence and promotion, and still maintain a reasonable and humane illusion of integrity.

The rationalizations for such a situation are endless, but the consequences are clear for a democratic and liberal society. When individuals give up personal responsibility, this undermines effective internal checks to abuse of power. Any institution of bureaucratic secrecy that covers up policies causes ample problems. Many present mechanisms of oversight are too limited and rely upon the democratic responsibility and personal consciences of those who participate in the institution to check abuse of power. Officials willing to challenge and change policies and willing to end or mitigate the vicious consequences constitute a countersystem and an internal check. Another consequence is that without these internal checks, institutional imbeddedness and malignant obedience allow illegal, wrong, and inhumane decisions to be executed without accountability. Real accountability depends upon courage and dissent within institutions as well as informed and effective obedience to legitimate orders. Instead, a chain of irresponsibility undermines political responsibility and accountability. If individuals defer responsibility to superiors and if each superior defers responsibility to the one above in a chain of regression, then no one will claim responsibility for the decision. At the same time, individuals will be adding to the policy, changing and modifying it to meet the demands of their own careers, and exercising professional discretion. A policy becomes full and effective only when all individuals act and contribute their talent and energy to it, but no one will claim clear responsibility for implementation and consequences. The chain of irresponsibility becomes a parody of the chain of command.

Responding to Temptation

Tyrants and zealots should not exercise office in a democratic and liberal state. Both collapse the triangle of judgment and overwhelm the obligations of office with personal visions of the good. The experience of powerholding, however, erodes the democratic responsibility and balanced judgment of public integrity, which hold the impulses to tyranny and zealotry at bay within people and government. Officials experience commitment stress, dissonance, frustration, and resentment and suffer from the effects of group participation and deindividuation. This environment of power pressures and tempts individuals to adapt themselves in ways that disrupt the balance among obligations of office, personal commitment and capacity, and prudence of public integrity. Public integrity breaks down either when personal values and desires dominate office or when office conflates with the personal dimensions of self.

Temptations of superiority come easily to powerholders. Deference and success reassure individuals of their superior intelligence, their moral worth, and even their indispensability to the common good. Power can be enjoyed, and status and perks can seduce both the self-interested and the saint. People too easily use their public power to maintain their own power and increase worldly goods while believing that their stature and that of their office are the same. People can acquire a taste for domination and a preference for arbitrary action. The knowledge of power can seep into people's souls and lead them to confuse their own dreams and wants with the public good.

The Platonic tyrant was an individual without friends, and the committed zealot, as Lenin demonstrated, lives in a world in which there are no individuals but only pawns in the struggle. Neither tyrants nor zealots respect the constraints of institutions: their own wills take precedence over the laws, practices, and designs of regime and office. People under the stress of power are always tempted to simplify the moral universe of conflict by reducing opponents to enemies. Individuals seek solace, support, and unwavering loyalty from their advisors rather than honest criticism and good advice. Access is denied to all except those who flatter or conform; closed coteries not only make bad policy but also reduce the world to the forces of light and darkness. This combination tempts officials to resort to secrecy at the same time they are tempted to overidentify with the office in a way that releases them from moral constraints of integrity and conscience.

None of us can take for granted the public integrity of officials. This does not mean that officials are necessarily evil or dangerous. However, officials are human, and the exercise of power tempts all humans. A sometimes forgotten agenda of political concerns should be near the center of moral consideration. These concerns cover three levels: personal, institutional, and managerial.

Personal. The first concern begins with the Socratic injunction to know thyself. No one is immune from these temptations, and each person of integrity needs to maintain a disciplined awareness of the temptations as well as a healthy humility about office and power. This public integrity of individuals depends upon their self-reflective capacity to keep alive and move within the triangle of judgment. Individuals need to hold together in their judgments the obligations of office, personal commitment and capacity, and prudence and avoid reducing their judgments to any one domain. In addition, individuals need a full, private life outside of office to provide the space for reflection and perspective needed to resist the temptations. Citizens have the right and obligation to demand a degree of public integrity from their officials and to judge this integrity in elections and through supervision and accountability.

Institutional. The whole point of this chapter is that even strong, committed, and self-aware individuals will succumb to these temptations. Although internal devices and institutions cannot guarantee integrity, the traditional liberal obsession with demanding accountability and limiting power still should carry tremendous weight in institutional design and oversight. Internal checks on power, strict and regular elections, incessant institutional demand for accountability, a strong free press, and rotation of office all make continuing sense as bulwarks against the temptations. Additionally, imperfect devices such as conflict-of-interest laws, strong auditors and inspector generals, and postemployment limits can reinforce accountability and help minimize the predictable temptations.

Managerial. A strong managerial and leadership agenda follows from these concerns. Human safeguards can be circumvented by human ingenuity. Sometimes petty tyrants and zealots can be caught; at other times they can succeed in becoming nearly unassailable, as did J. Edgar Hoover and Robert Moses. Leaders and managers of public institutions should place the development of a moral culture and integrity at the center of their strategies and goals. Only unwavering commitment and modeling from the top down can offset the centrifugal tendencies of the temptations of power and create the cultural and institutional resources to sustain ethics in face of temptation. Leaders need to make sure that the culture aligns with the self-interests of officials to sustain it over time. This culture should be supported by monitoring and systems that attend to the predictable problems or reasonable temptations where the lethal combination of high stakes, protected service, secrecy, and access to those with resources can corrupt judgment.[65]

All power does not corrupt, but all power tempts. At a seminal moment in the formation of the western conscience, the following story was told: "And the devil took him up, and showed him all the kingdoms of the world in a moment of time, and said to him, 'To you I will give all this authority and their glory; for it has been delivered to me, and I shall give it to whom I will. If you then will worship me, it shall be yours.'"[66] If even Jesus could be tempted, certainly mortals will be. Although Jesus resisted, we cannot have the same confidence in ourselves.

3

The Moral Realities of Public Life

Truth uncompromisingly told will always have its ragged edges.

Herman Melville, *Billy Budd*

Outside I was my stolid, moderate decent self, a shoulder for weaker
souls to rest their heads on. Inside I felt a rampant incomprehension of
my uselessness; a sense that, for all my striving, I had failed to come
to grips with life; that in struggling to give freedom to others, I had
found none for myself.

John Le Carré, *The Secret Pilgrim*

TRYING TO DO THE RIGHT THING is not easy. Yet people of integrity
strive to do the right thing even against temptation and odds. In
public life it is difficult to accomplish the right actions with finite power,
limited information, and serious opposition. Public officials must also
navigate eddies of conflicting loyalties, temptations of power and rectitude, and demands of their own integrity. Often any action will involve
both good and bad. Confronting all of these realities of public life is crucial to acting with honest integrity.

Art can help in the quest for integrity. Good art can engage emotions,
stretch moral imagination, and influence judgment. Good fiction, especially, evokes empathy and identification with the characters. Such identification enables us to work through many levels of emotional and
cognitive understanding. The images, exemplars, and awareness that fiction and drama bring into consciousness can remain as strong insights.
For these reasons I believe that fiction can be a special help in working
through the quandaries of integrity in public life.

Most writing and teaching about the moral commitments of public
ethics focus on philosophical principles that govern policy or administra-
trative decisions.[1] As discussed in Chapter 1, the traditional approaches

to public ethics emphasize an individual's obligations of office and his or her loyalty and commitment to law and to the processes that shape official decisions.[2] Another approach stresses the importance of personal commitments and capacities and restores the role of responsibility and character in public ethics.[3] These approaches highlight two crucial domains of public integrity and should complement each other. Given their abstract orientation, however, they seldom address how individuals in office actually live and make decisions in the real world. They miss the complex undertow of personal life upon public life, the tragic dimension of public decisions, the hidden costs of rectitude, the problem of conflicting loyalties, and the way in which individuals play out their own quests for meaning and redemption within politics. Yet if we agree that personal responsibility and integrity are central to morality in public life, we must look more closely at the realities of public morality.

Fiction enables public officials to focus on their own individuality—their central web of commitments, capacities, beliefs, and models for comprehending the world. Fiction can lead individuals to focus on the self-mastery and self-knowledge that are critical to integrity. Self-awareness of the morality of public life, personal predispositions, and the implications of personal stances can surface as they engage good fiction. Through reading and reflecting upon serious fiction, individuals can learn from characters whom they admire, fear, care about, or wish to emulate or understand. Fiction allows them to model themselves after a character and "try out" different beliefs, commitments, and actions. The range of a person's intellectual and emotional responses can change through the act of engaging fiction.[4]

Fiction permits readers to experience and reflect on the emotional and moral complexity of a living character. Individuals experience the internal workings of the mind and passions of the character facing serious problems. Fiction brings out multiple points of view: various characters have their say and affect the story's outcome. Readers can assess differing thoughts, discussions, or actions. Fiction highlights the vital role of emotions—creative or destructive—in supporting life and commitments. Readers gain not just a cognitive response but an emotional one. Fiction also emphasizes the importance of the context and of relationships with others as well as with institutions in making decisions. In doing this, fiction does justice to a life's emotional and moral complexity. Characters have whole lives; they have friends, family, religions, enemies, loves, and hatreds that affect their public actions and the reactions to their actions.

Fiction exposes the relationship between personal and public with great power and insight.

I would like to explore the problems of real-world individuals seeking to act with integrity in public life through examining the stories of their fictional counterparts. I look at a wide and eclectic variety of humanist fiction (under which I include drama) that reveals the tensions and dilemmas of integrity in public life. Generally I choose texts set outside of contemporary American politics. Such texts highlight the consistent nature of issues and their moral structure and avoid the temptation to get lost in issues of verisimilitude. I turn to humanist writers who look with insight, sympathy, and mercy on human plight. They focus on individuals struggling for meaning in complicated lives and in their intimate relations with others. I try to avoid schematic or ideological fiction, which uses its characters as axes to grind in predetermined morality plays.

I believe that such fiction illuminates these moral realities and supplements both principle or character-based conceptions of public ethics. It deepens the sense of challenge and respect for those who seek to act with public integrity. This chapter discusses four aspects of morality that this fiction highlights: (1) the moral balance of selfhood, (2) the role of decision and redemption, (3) relations with others, and (4) the ironies of rectitude. It concludes by examining a moral stance that individuals of integrity can achieve as they learn to live with moral imperfection.

The Moral Balance of Selfhood

Humanist fiction concentrates on the qualities of selfhood and integrity, which is often ignored in formal moral theory. Most official decisions are made by individuals, yet thinking about public ethics seldom addresses the dynamics and strains upon selfhood when people try honestly and carefully to act properly in public life. This becomes doubly important because individuals must hold together multiple roles and commitments within their integrity.

In humanist fiction, as in life, taking office poses a problem for the self. Office requires some estrangement from personal commitments and personal life. The promises individuals make when entering office expand their obligations and set them apart from personal loyalties to family, friends, community, or religion. Individuals promise to frame their judgments by official or legal standards and to discount the ties of friendship and family as well as the pull of racial, ethnic, religious, or gender identity. Yet this sundering of the personal from the public is easier promised than done. Fiction is uniquely suited to showing us characters whose public actions are entwined with personal imperatives.

Taking public office involves putting on a mask. Few works show this more clearly than Shakespeare's *Henry IV, Parts I and II,* and *Henry V.*[5] Prince Hal, the fun-loving, witty, bright, and cynical hero of *Henry IV,* develops a deep affection for and commitment to his friends, especially the great braggart Falstaff. Yet upon a troubled ascension to his father's throne—an office he both desires and despises—Hal must not only abandon his friends but also reject and punish them. In a very profound way, the personal life he lived in *Henry IV* must die along with his friends. Hal turns into the hero of *Henry V* who has almost no inner life, no real friends—only counselors. Although he might reflect upon the burden of kingship the night before battle, the mask of kingship, once he assumes it, suffocates his life. The burdens and demands of his office fill his whole life. His old self is hidden even from himself as the obligations of his office drain his personal life and self; even his marriage becomes a pawn to the demands of office and power. The charming and inward character of the two earlier plays disappears beneath the heroic figure of the last.

Taking on a mask and changing oneself for a role is a necessary part of taking office, but it does not have to be wrong. Another Shakespeare play, *The Tragedy of Coriolanus,* illustrates the tragic costs of refusing to accept the demands of political roles.[6] Coriolanus, a proud, courageous, and noble military leader seeks the Roman consulship. But he has no use for the niceties of politics. He hates flattery, despises the populace, and refuses to submit to time-honored and cherished political rituals. He demands power on his own terms and seeks recognition of his own prowess without theatrics. In all this, he misunderstands the role of ritual and deliberation in taming and legitimizing power. He has little use for the tact required of public office, and so his pride and self-confidence are seen as insolence. Envious tribunes fan the people against him, and Coriolanus adamantly refuses to listen to friends and family who urge him to "play the part." He refuses to compromise on policies that he feels pamper the plebes. Instead, his temper erupts, and he berates his opponents rather than conciliates them. His intransigence causes him to lose the consulship, and he is expelled from Rome as a traitor. With aggrieved pride and a raging thirst for revenge, he turns to Rome's enemies, the Volcii, whom he has previously defeated, and takes command of their armies. Under Coriolanus, the Volcii rout the Romans and ravage the

Roman lands. Outside the gates of Rome, however, Coriolanus's mother convinces him to spare the city and establish a just peace. His personal loyalties override the obligations of his office, and he makes peace. When he returns to the Volcii city to announce his treaty, the Volcii see him as having betrayed them and execute him.

The play illuminates the dangers, temptations, and necessities of public office. It demonstrates the reality that competence and even nobility do not necessarily translate into effective political power and accomplishment. Politics and office, for good or bad, require unique skills and unique masks. These skills tame and direct the power and passion so central to political life and make possible the negotiation and accountability so vital in public life. Pride and passion can be harnessed, as in Coriolanus's military operations, to achieve great things. But undisciplined, they breed disaster.

The mask of office and the requirements of public achievement do not guarantee isolation of the personal life from the official. Instead, humanist fictional portrayals usually affirm the inextricable connection between the personal and the public. No political authors make this intertwining of personal and official clearer than John Le Carré and C. P. Snow. For both novelists, personal needs, ambitions, and passions erupt into public deliberation and influence many decisions.

The basic plot of Le Carré's *Tinker, Tailor, Soldier, Spy* hinges on the thwarted ambition and personal grudges of a cadre of administrators in British Intelligence.[7] These welling personal concerns lead them to band together to stage an internal coup against the longtime head of the Intelligence agency who is known as Control. The same self-interested ambitions of the cadre members lead to their self-deceptions: they never critically examine the tainted pipeline of information that is the source of their bureaucratic credibility and power. Yet their acceptance of the source, called, appropriately, "Witchcraft," subverts the entire British Intelligence network. When George Smiley, who is Le Carré's protagonist and a protégé and ally of Control, questions the source, the others impugn his motives as envy. More important, the cadre's friendships or class affiliation with the traitor, Bill Haydon, who set up the false information source blind them from the truth of Haydon's betrayal. Even Smiley finds his own uncanny judgment blinded by his repressed jealousy over Haydon's affair with his wife.

In Snow's two most overtly political novels, *The New Men* and *Homecomings*, driving personal ambition deeply influences the actions of the characters.[8] The novels are narrated by Lewis Eliot, a barrister and ambitious and successful British administrator. In *The New Men,* set during the Cold War red scares in England, the government launches a massive drive to uncover possible Soviet agents in nuclear research. Martin Eliot, Lewis's brother, works at a major research lab and faces a choice between trying to protect his colleagues and the integrity of their work or ferreting out possible traitors by turning on colleagues and disrupting their work. Martin chooses to aid the investigations both from patriotism and from career ambition. His willingness to cooperate gives him the edge over his major rival to run the nuclear labs, Luke Davidson. Davidson moves much more slowly against possible spies out of genuine concern for the scientific enterprise and for the accused individuals. Davidson's humanity costs him a promotion to run the nuclear research lab. Yet, in a final twist, Martin Eliot turns down the job as head of the labs to return to a university lab, even knowing that he is a better administrator than pure scientist. His refusal is motivated by a desire to save his troubled marriage and to distance himself from the influence of his own brother, Lewis, who had gained significant power in the ministry. He and Martin had come to disagree on several crucial policy issues, and these disagreements were poisoning their relationship.

Even as these works insist that the personal and passionate will erupt into public life, they illustrate the necessity for a disciplined separation of the personal and the public. Only this distancing enables individuals to achieve actions with any semblance of fairness or competence. In Snow's *Homecomings,* despite grievous personal problems at home, Lewis Eliot maintains his self-discipline and functions at a high level as a civil servant contributing to some important results. In Le Carré's *Smiley's People,* George Smiley achieves his greatest success for British Intelligence by distancing himself from his personal entanglements with his family, his friends, and his agency, while he funnels his personal frustration and anger into setting a trap for Karla, the Soviet spymaster.[9] In Le Carré's *The Honourable Schoolboy,* Smiley sets aside his deep-seated distaste for bureaucratic politics and his personal concern for his field agent to design and implement, over significant bureaucratic opposition, a masterful strategy to uncover a far-flung Soviet plan to infiltrate China.[10]

Just as important for the moral balance of integrity, actions in public office react upon and profoundly affect personal identity. Even when protected by masks, people change into different people—a fact they assiduously hide from themselves—in the exercise of public responsibility. In

Snow's *The New Men*, Martin Eliot finds his scientific humanism corrupted by the power plays motivated by his desire to head the nuclear lab. Yet, ironically, his more humane counterpart, Luke Davidson, takes the job as head of the lab and finds himself forced to act more like the unfeeling and calculating bureaucrats he despised and opposed when he fought them during the spy hunts. This slow change of the core of oneself occurs at all level of public office. No more stunning portrait of such transformations of people by power and office exists than in *All the King's Men* by Robert Penn Warren. Like many tragic political leaders, the impassioned leader fighting for social justice finds himself succumbing to the allure of power for its own sake. Not only the central character but almost everyone in his entourage, including the "outsider" news reporter, sacrifice their most cherished personal beliefs, often without noticing, to seek and maintain power.[11]

Humanist fiction highlights how individuals struggle to make sense of their lives. It demonstrates how those for whom integrity is important are the most tempted to hide this change from themselves. In Dostoevsky's "The Grand Inquisitor," the Inquisitor explains in clear but tortured logic why "love of humanity" leads him to keep people ignorant and docile and to burn those who question his authority.[12] But Alyosha Karamazov, the naive listener to this tale of justification, somewhat hesitantly claims that the Inquisitor is lying to hide his desire to maintain a priestly monopoly on power. The irony is that both are probably true.

The humanist imagination maintains that people take on a mask when they take office and identifies the inescapable tensions and costs of doing so. No clean philosophical solutions exist for these dilemmas. As individuals struggle to maintain their integrity, they can take two stances towards their commitments that can help preserve their humanity in office. First, individuals must recognize the effects of ambition, passion, and conflicted loyalties on their actions. Second, they can balance and harness these to support public good and personal integrity. People live contradictions; that is not the issue. The issue is how we resolve them in decision and action.

Decision and Redemption

In the end, keeping one's integrity, even with an awareness of the obligations of office, may require dangerous and painful decisions and actions. Two of Anthony Trollope's political novels, *Phineas Finn* and *Phineas Redux*, follow the story of a charming, intelligent, penniless, and extremely ambitious Irishman who aspires to climb the social and political ladder in Victorian England.[13] Utterly ambitious but without resources, Phineas needs money and sets out desperately seeking to marry a rich woman. With charm and connections, he wrangles himself a safe parliamentary seat in a rotten borough while wooing well-off English ladies. After several failed romantic adventures and slavish job hunting, he gains a minor position in the Foreign Office that carries a reasonable income.

During those tumultuous years the issue of Irish tenant's rights comes up in Parliament. To Phineas's consternation, his mentor and role model, Mr. Monk, chooses to resign from the cabinet in opposition to the government's slow-moving reform efforts. And to Phineas's surprise, he discovers convictions about the oppression of his homeland. He frantically tries to repress them. In a conversation with Barrington Erle, his friend and a party hack who has backed him, he complains, "What is a man to do, Barrington? He can't smother his convictions." Erle replies,

> Convictions! There is nothing on earth that I'm so afraid of in a young member of Parliament as convictions. There are ever so many rocks against which men get broken. One man can't keep his temper. Another can't hold his tongue. A third can't say a word unless he has been priming himself half a session. A fourth is always thinking of himself, and wanting more than he can get. A fifth is idle, and won't be there when he's wanted. A sixth is always in the way. A seventh lies so that you never can trust him. I've had to do with them all, but a fellow with convictions is the worst of all.

"I don't see how a fellow is to help himself," says a resigned Phineas. "When a fellow begins to meddle with politics, they will come."

Phineas tries to stay in office and ably dispatches his duties, but he ultimately decides to resign, regretfully, and follow his mentor. Before he leaves office and Parliament, he proves his continuing loyalty to his party and balances the scales of how he got to Parliament when he votes to abolish his rotten borough. He returns home to Ireland and marries his estranged sweetheart, who carries no dowry. In later novels in Trollope's Palliser series, Phineas returns for other adventures and political conflicts. But in these two novels Trollope illustrates with a sure and wry hand the tensions among integrity, ambition, and political achievement. The political actors make many good and bad compromises, but his characters also illustrate clear and graceful resignation as well as principled and prudent opposition.

Trollope, like Snow and Le Carré, demonstrates that under the weight of decisions, selfhood and integrity can grow or erode. These changes are most prominent in crucial decisions such as the ones Phineas faced, but the balance in personal integrity builds and sustains itself over time. Often characters do not realize that their soul is at stake until a critical choice faces them. Even then, the moral balance can be righted and integrity can be regained by redemption. The erosion of selfhood as well as the capacity for redemption is well illustrated in the Le Carré novels. In *Smiley's People*, George Smiley illustrates the redemptive possibilities when he risks becoming like his enemy and cuts himself off from all institutional commitments to trap the Soviet master spy Karla.

Karla is the Soviet spymaster who recruited the traitor Bill Haydon and planned the ruse that ruined British Intelligence. Karla illustrates another facet of fictional portrayals of public life. Humanist fiction reminds us that individuals live whole lives. People cannot cut one part of their life off from others without a day of reckoning and balancing. In the Le Carré novels that focus upon George Smiley, Karla is portrayed as a cold and distant spy who masterminds the fall of British Intelligence. He ruthlessly uses and discards people and knows how to discover and exploit the weaknesses of individuals. He uses this skill to lead the traitors who infiltrate British Intelligence.

Yet in *Smiley's People*, Karla is trapped by his one poignant attempt to keep some humanity alive in his soul. Smiley learns that Karla illegally protects his mentally ill daughter. Karla's estrangement from his wife because of his political commitments has lead to her death and caused his child's mental illness. The treatment of mental illness in the Soviet Union is primitive, and he seeks a better place to care for his daughter. She ends up in an asylum in Switzerland under an assumed name secretly supported by Karla. But this act makes him vulnerable both at home and to Smiley for entrapment. The individual who had sacrificed his entire personal life to his cause and destroyed the lives of all who cared for him is betrayed by his one act of redemption.

Louis Auchincloss's novel about family, commitment, and service, *Honorable Men*, highlights many of the same issues of wholeness in a life.[14] Chip Benedict, the protagonist, has insulated himself throughout his life from personal feeling and commitment, even as he marries and fathers children. His success in business and public life has been driven by a hard notion of duty and honor. Deeply enmeshed in running the Vietnam War, he finds himself estranged from his family. His daughter uses her trust fund to support antiwar causes, his son becomes a drug addict and draft dodger in Europe, and his wife sinks into alcoholism. For some time none of these events deeply affects him, but ultimately the pressures of the war and the collapse of his family do seep into him. At the same time he meets a woman who pierces his armor with her own care and commitments. His relationship with her reawakens his own principles and commitments. In an act of redemption, he chooses to oppose the war he helped wage, effectively ending his political career. He honestly faces the wreckage of his family life and seeks to rebuild what connections he can. At the same time, he marries the younger woman and starts a new family life, both more caring and humbled. In these actions, he feels oddly free from a cold, ambitious duty. For the first time, he experiences a real connection between heart, commitment, and action.

The reality of wholeness in a life opens the possibility not only of redemption but also of destruction. In the Phineas Finn novels, Mr. Robert Kennedy—austere, rich, and impeccably moral—marries the woman Phineas Finn first courted in England, Lady Laura Standish. Kennedy's austerity and cold moralism contrast sharply to Phineas's more fallible warmth and commitments in the novels. Kennedy has little success as a cabinet minister and even less in an aloof and loveless marriage. He withdraws from social life, grows dangerously jealous of his old rival, and lives in gloomy isolation. Friendless and abandoned by his wife, he dies.

Humanist fiction strives to see life and integrity as a complex whole; it explores the multiple loyalties involved in each decision and lays bare the difficulty of balancing within public integrity. Each decision not only entails judgments but also often forces betrayals of other commitments in cases in which people must deny their families or friends time, energy, and warmth in their pursuit of public achievement. The intricate wholeness of life means that people make no decision in isolation: each action echoes throughout their lives.

Good fiction shows the satisfactions of decision and integrity as well as their costs, which can be considerable. John Hersey's fine administrative novel *A Bell for Adano* tells the story of Major Victor Joppolo, an Italian-American from the Bronx.[15] He is ordered to take command of a ruined Italian town during the American occupation in World War II. Joppolo restores a sense of dignity and community to the town and helps it regain its livelihood as a fishing village. He astutely delegates authority, mobilizes residents to take control of their destiny, and cheerfully ignores the rules to achieve these ends when he needs to. He even restores the town's bell—and its self-respect—by borrowing a bell from a U.S. naval vessel. He succeeds by fighting his leaden and rule-bound careerist subordinate, Captain Purvis, who opposes his actions at each point. At one point, Joppolo countermands a general's angry order to shoot all the donkeys in the town because one donkey cart had gotten in the way of his car; Joppolo knows such an act would destroy the town's economy. The general would never have known that Joppolo countermanded his order except that Purvis, in a time-honored bureaucratic technique, slips the decision into the general's reading pile. In the end Joppolo is exiled to duty in Algeria.[16]

Sir Thomas More in Robert Bolt's play *A Man for All Seasons* sums up the humanist credo on the moral integrity and decision. Bolt's play is written around the historical story of Thomas More, who served as Henry VIII's chancellor when Henry broke from the Roman Catholic church. In the play More is pressured by Henry to break with the Roman church and support Henry's divorce from his barren queen, Catherine of Aragon. Henry also wants More's support for his subsequent marriage to his mistress, Anne Boleyn. More, who is the king's chancellor as well as his friend, demurs. He knows he cannot abandon his church and his basic commitments. He tells his daughter Meg, "When a man takes an oath, Meg, he's holding his own self in his own hands. Like water. And if he opens his fingers, then—he needn't hope to find himself again."[17] More has no wish to become a martyr and desperately searches for legal and personal ways around his predicament. He resigns from office, maintains silence, and refuses either to participate in open opposition or to align himself with a revolt. He uses the law to protect himself but ultimately, knowing the costs to himself and his family, he cannot give the king the confirmation and, in a sense, the absolution, that Henry demands. More is convicted of treason in a rigged trial and beheaded.

Relations with Others

An individual seeking to know and act rightly in public life does not think or act in splendid isolation. The ability to achieve goals and keep integrity hinges upon the support and friendship of others. Most defeat, failure, or temptations flow from the actions of others. Good political fiction never forgets that the world is inhabited by human beings with beliefs, commitments, ambitions, interests, passions, hates, and loves. People's relations with others will profoundly influence their integrity.

All individuals beyond oneself exist as others with their own uniqueness and inscrutability as well as their own passions, commitments, and beliefs. Too often political theory and ethics assume that those around us exist with a sameness of interest or affect. Yet all other people exist independently from oneself or the protagonist in fiction. Friends, brothers and sisters, spouses, strangers, and enemies—they are also humans with their own unique passions, desires, interests, and issues. These others and a person's relations with them lie at the center of moral life in fiction. These relations account for both success and failure. They also account for the multiple loyalties bedeviling each decision.

The most important political relation is friendship. Any accomplishment, including integrity, needs friends and allies. If Coriolanus had listened to his family and friends, he could have avoided his fate. Chip Benedict's new love gives him the perspective and strength to reform his life and his politics. Despite Smiley's penchant to see himself as alone and unaided, he constantly relies upon support, loyalty, and love from those around him, including, in particular, his often straying and betraying wife. Lewis Eliot and his brother Martin find themselves and their family central to each other's consciences and decisions.

The quality of relations with others is influenced by a person's emotional capacities. The importance of friendship emphasizes how central the capacity to care is to integrity. Both Lewis Eliot and Smiley find the strength to endure the frustrations and defeats of public life because of their capacity to care. In Snow's novel *The New Men*, after he has chosen to resign the post he sought, Martin Eliot tells his brother Lewis, "I'm colder hearted than you are. I care much less for the people around me. . . . If it weren't so, I couldn't have made this choice." Martin explains that facing the issues surrounding making a nuclear bomb, he had no clear way to stay engaged. He had to resign or "struggle on . . . and take our share of what had been done and what might still be done, and hope that we might come out at the end of the tunnel . . . being well-meaning all the time, and thinking of nothing worse than our own safety."

Martin Eliot knows that office requires a distancing and rationality that can distort human judgment and ambition. He isolates a basic point of humanist fiction that the capacity to care offsets that distancing and is vital to maintaining integrity and balanced judgment. He adds to Lewis, who chooses to stay on in the ministry and fight for his beliefs, "For a warm-hearted man who's affected by the people around him perhaps it's the only way. It's the way you're going, though you're more far-sighted than they are."[18] Martin can escape responsibility because he cares less about people; Lewis is trapped in responsibility by his care. Similarly only after Auchincloss's Chip Benedict could feel passion and connect his compassion to his actions could he see and feel the limits of his cold, hardened honor in confronting the casualties and breakdown of military service in the Vietnam War.

The relation between care and commitment infuses the moral responsibility central to public integrity and reinforces the balance among the domains of public integrity. Care can determine the quality of relationships with others. As the previous examples hint, the relationship between care and concreteness looms even larger. Most humanist novels distrust ideology because it reduces humans to surrogates for an idea. Real-life relations and friendships lead to durable commitments and defensible action. A focus on real people infuses action with attention to detail and the real costs. More interestingly, friendship creates the basis to help sustain integrity intact because it provides a refuge for honesty. Additionally, political friendship can become the basis of power and achievement. No novel better illustrates the importance of friendship and its limits than Edwin O'Connor's *The Last Hurrah*. Here warmth, affection, and self-interest all blend into abiding relationships that ensure political alliance and success. But the book also tellingly portrays how affection can lead individuals to hide the truth from those they care about. At the same time, it chronicles the attrition of friendship because of changes that undermine old relations and create new avenues of power and interest.[19] *All the King's Men* also portrays the interlocking of power, trust, and friendship, as well as the capacity of office and power to corrupt the qualities that underlie friendship.

While care may be central to maintaining friendship and integrity, ambition drives much political life. Human ambition motivates many political actors and will influence all political relations. This ambition means no safe havens exist. All power and accomplishment are contingent and questioned. Neither office, authority, nor honors are secure in a world of restless ambition. Leaders need to accommodate and subordinate ambition or harness that of others. Any public official needs not only to attend to his or her own ambition but also to deal with the ambition of others. Ambitious enemies—or, worse, ambitious allies—may become jealous. Or they may be restless, even contemptuous, knowing they could have done better and wanting their own power.

These realities haunt Le Carré's and Snow's novels but are highlighted with peculiar brilliance in the work of Shakespeare. The concisely drawn ability of jealous tribunes to use Coriolanus's weakness against him and destroy him embodies a theme central to all of Shakespeare's political plays. *Richard II* manifests the issues in their purest and most interesting political form.[20] A relatively quiet and ineffectual king sees himself as the embodiment of the medieval ideal of rule in which he reigns and provides the principle of order to his country. He is, however, overthrown by a talented and ambitious cousin, Bolingbroke. *Richard II* highlights how fragile an office, even one surrounded by great authority and ritual, is if the officeholder finds his talents mismatched with the job. The character of Bolingbroke is a masterful study of how one official's weaknesses can justify another's pursuit of his ambitions. The play also clearly shows how friends and allies melt away under pressure from failures, incompetence, and the threats of another's success.

Yet *Coriolanus* reminds us that even success is no guarantee against usurpation. Regardless of one's accomplishments, politics never cease in office. In the Smiley novels, George Smiley is twice thrown from his position at the moment of his greatest triumphs. In both cases, cabals, allied by ambition and bureaucratic aggrandizement, take over. Good political fiction highlights the unceasing realities of power seeking, ambition, and self-interested gain that go on without regard to accomplishment or the dictates of office. But it also reminds us that friendship and loyalty of others define to a great extent our own possibilities for integrity and accomplishment in public life. We must learn to balance the roles of friendship, opposition, and above all ambition in public life and to remember always the humanity behind the masks.

The Ironies of Rectitude

Humanist fiction recognizes the importance of principled integrity. As in taking office, it also recognizes that principled action involves a narrowing of human sensibilities and focus on judgment that can be harsh and cold. More important, principled rectitude usually involves putting aside the reality of individuals' suffering to pursue long-term gains that clearly benefit the general public. But the people that benefit are not the living, breathing, and suffering individuals we meet in fiction.

No one isolates this humanist fear of rectitude better than John Le Carré. Each of his novels embodies an adversary who is unflinchingly committed to a grotesque historical utilitarianism. The thoughtful Fiedler who interrogates the captured Alex Leamas in *The Spy Who Came in from the*

Cold summarizes the logic to this, the moral equation: "Afterwards I would draw the balance—so many women, so many children, so far along the road."[21] In each novel, the adversaries devalue the human suffering and loss entailed in their decisions by focusing only on their long-term goals. In Le Carré's adversaries the warmth of passion and faith transform into unfeeling calculation. They make the cabal of self-serving bureaucratic schemers of Le Carré's Smiley novels pale by comparison given the harm the adversaries do.

In Auchincloss's *Honorable Men*, Alida Benedict refers to her husband Chip Benedict's "cold gleaming armor of honor." Chip Benedict needs this armor to fight the evil he finds in himself and throughout the world. One of Benedict's best friends explains that he possesses "rules without faith" and that "there is nothing to moderate the rigidity of their logic."[22] Such moral coldness cuts off most human emotions, especially warmth, empathy, and mercy. Care turns into ambition.

Pure principled rectitude distances people from their immediate attachments, muffling and denying feelings about consequences of actions. Seemingly without remorse, Benedict instantly cuts off his best friend, Chessy Bogart, for a moral lapse in law school. He chooses the moral clarity and hard risk of war over the messy entanglements and emotional demands of his family. The family ends in ruins amid the emotional and moral chaos of Vietnam and Benedict's own detached, honor-bound commitment to fight.

Dostoevsky's "The Grand Inquisitor" depicts the link between moral rectitude and political oppression. The Inquisitor, exhausted and exhilarated from a day of burning heretics, is called upon to interrogate Christ, who has returned to sixteenth-century Spain. During the questioning, the Inquisitor berates Christ for his utopian and dangerous dream that humans can live and love on their own. According to the Inquisitor, people are too weak to live Christ's message. When they try to live freely, they create chaos, war, and hell. Acting from "love," the Inquisitor and those morally strong enough to see the truth have "corrected" Christ's work. Building upon "miracle, mystery and bread," they have tamed the weak and ill-fated mass of humanity. They provide the masses with meaning, bread, and community, which makes them happy on this earth and innocent enough to pass to heaven in the next life.

The Inquisitors believe that they alone possess the wisdom to recognize the moral hopelessness of Christ's message. They justify their authority by their superior knowledge and moral strength. Additionally, they risk their own eternal damnation in the interests of the welfare of weak and fallible humans. Those strong enough to question their cruel but necessary rule, they either invite into their ranks or destroy. No rebellion can ultimately succeed because every revolution fails due to the weaknesses of the masses. At the end of the Inquisitor's speech, Christ remains silent, kisses him, and walks out the door, never to return.

The Grand Inquisitor conflates love, moral superiority, sacrifice, and moral domination of others. But in a twist from the coldness of a Fiedler's pure ideology or Chip Benedict's puritan honor, the Grand Inquisitor justifies his power by his fate as a suffering servant to others. In this way, he balances the moral equation for the suffering he imposes by the suffering he internalizes to better others' welfare. Few more pernicious moral strategies justify power and domination and eliminate sympathy and mercy.

Such rectitude always subverts other personal loyalties. Jean Anouilh's *Becket* covers this dilemma with great insight.[23] Thomas Becket, Saxon, confidant, and best friend to the Norman king Henry II, serves as King Henry's trusted friend and chief advisor. Time and again, Becket teaches Henry that the requirements of office must take precedence over personal desires. At the same time, Becket strips bare the essentials of power and manipulation needed to sustain office; he ruthlessly destroys illusions Henry has about his own kingship, popularity, and office. Witty, amoral, and dedicated to the king, Becket makes a perfect friend.

Surrounded by sycophants and power seekers, Henry II trusts Becket and appoints him Lord Chancellor, somewhat to Becket's chagrin and certainly to that of Henry's jealous barons. Then, when the Archbishop of Canterbury dies in the midst of a political conflict with the King, Henry, against Becket's advice, makes him archbishop. Becket, uncharacteristically somber, adamantly opposes the idea: "If I become archbishop, I can no longer be your friend." Later he tells the king, "This is madness, my lord. Don't do it. I could not serve both God and you," to which the King replies, "You've never disappointed me, Thomas. And you are the only man I trust."

But upon ascending the episcopacy, Becket resigns the chancellorship, gives away his gold and finery, and distances himself from the King. Becket tells a confused Henry that he, Becket, must now serve "God's honour." An anguished Henry feels betrayal and anger. He accuses Becket, "Only I loved you and you didn't love me . . . that's the difference." In anger and sorrow, Henry discovers how his office affects all relations and how friendship alone cannot sustain institutional relations. He must learn "to be alone."[24] Later, when Henry seeks to consolidate the king's power over the church as Becket had urged him, Becket now upholds the institutional independence of the church by defending the right of monks to be tried only in church courts. Acting upon precepts of power that Becket has taught him, Henry engages in full institutional war with Becket. He strips Becket of office and fortune, declares him a traitor, and forces him into exile. Becket, abandoned by his pope and bishops, returns for a reconciliation. Yet Henry desires and hates Becket as only a betrayed lover can, and the reconciliation is brittle. Embittered, one night, Henry demands of his assembled barons, "Will no one rid me of him? A priest. A priest who jeers at me and does me injury?" Inspired by his anger and eager for advancement, several barons sneak off to kill Becket as he says Mass.

During the course of the play, Becket, to his surprise, as often happens in fiction and life, discovers himself and his honor only when his personal emotions and official obligations match. Prior to entering the church, his other commitments and friendships were disconnected, leaving his integrity fragmented and dangling. When he discovers the fit between self and office in God's honor, he finds his integrity but ends up the enemy of his former friend and king; he cannot avoid it.

No comment on the ironies of institutional authority would be complete without a reference to Herman Melville's *Billy Budd*.[25] The young seaman Billy Budd exemplifies natural goodness in his honesty, hard work, and natural leadership. His commander, Captain Edward Vere, comes to love him as a son. Yet John Claggart, the ship's master-at-arms, envies and hates Budd. When Claggart frames Budd by charging before Vere that Budd has fostered mutiny, Billy Budd becomes tongue-tied from fear and frustration; he lashes out spontaneously, fatally striking Claggart with his fist. On a warship far from home, in the middle of the Napoleonic Wars and haunted by recent mutinies in the Royal Navy, Captain Vere puts away his humanity and demands an immediate trial for Budd. Killing an officer challenges the entire authority structure of the navy and is punishable by death. During the trial Vere bullies his junior officers into sentencing Budd to death in order to protect the safety of the ship. Vere himself oversees the hanging, and Budd's last words are "God bless Captain Vere!" Vere acts upon what he believes are necessary imperatives, yet the decision breaks his heart. From that time on he lives a bleak and diminished career, and his lingering death after a successful battle only formalizes the earlier death of his soul. He dies murmuring "Billy Budd, Billy Budd."

For all of these writers the holding of power or office narrows and distorts humanity even as it achieves good ends. In this light, integrity resides as much in the way in which we hold and balance our beliefs and commitments as the beliefs and commitments themselves because all rectitude involves betrayal.

Coming to Terms with Moral Imperfection

Good art does not give final answers, magic algorithms, or techniques to guarantee good judgment or personal integrity. The authors I examine catalog a host of moral realities that individuals must confront in public life, realities usually ignored in discussions of ethics in public life. Attending to selfhood and the tensions between one's self and one's role form the beginning of any insight into integrity. Actions in office demand an estrangement, a balanced narrowing of judgment, a tension between office and affiliations, and the moral character of integrity. Individuals' actions in office change the individuals themselves. The personal and the public intertwine, for good and bad, and self-deception beckons anyone exercising power and authority.

Life and integrity play themselves out through decisions. Life is a flow of decisions; most are minor and require little reflection, but they possess a cumulative consequence for action and selfhood. Most choices are not crises of conscience. Although many people compartmentalize their lives for the sake of ambition or convenience, the humanist imagination urges that we remember that life is a whole, even if we sunder ourselves. Individuals discover their integrity as much as they construct it. People often gain integrity through a redemptive decision to recover meaning in a life gone amiss through lack of reflection or misguided goals. Yet decisions not only provide for possible redemption but also come at a cost—a real, human cost. No public figure should ignore the costs of integrity or its advantages. But neither should anyone equate integrity with martyrdom or rigidity. Flexible, imaginative, and committed judgment provides the balance needed to sustain public integrity.

Yet we live in a world of other people who often impose themselves on us. These others can be friends, allies, compatriots, family, or enemies. Life and integrity are inextricably linked with others. No moral course makes sense unless it takes account of people's ambition, as well as the possibilities and limits of friendship and enmity. Finally, integrity and moral commitment can be a two-edged sword. Acting on principled commitment involves betrayal and a narrowing or cauterizing of human sensibilities. Integrity does not exist without costs, and they should not be hidden. Additionally, how people hold their commitments matters profoundly. Ideologues, cold, detached masters of honor, tortured but secure denizens of moral superiority can twist any moral commitments into human suffering and degradation.

In the moral world of humanist literature paradox, imperfection, and tragedy insinuate themselves into all aspects of life. The fictional world is thereby surely more honest and true-to-life than are most theories of ethics. None of the authors examined here provides a certain answer. I discern, however, a particular stance towards self, commitment, and power that emerges from these reflections on public life. It provides an angle of vision for individuals to pattern their integrity within the tensions of politics. Two public servants who were also gifted writers came to the same conclusion more than four hundred years apart.

In the first book of his *Utopia*, Thomas More begs his wise and well-traveled fictional companion, Raphael Hythloday, to join the government and help the king rule more wisely. Hythloday adamantly refuses. He cites cases in which wise counsel has been ignored and insists that "there is no place for philosophy in the councils of princes." His belief is that anyone who tries to help will find his own beliefs and commitments corrupted and will be forced to participate in and support decisions he morally abhors. More finds such a conception of integrity inflexible and too selfish. He responds:

> If evil opinions cannot be quite rooted out, and if you cannot correct habitual attitudes as you wish, you must not therefore abandon the commonwealth. Don't give up the ship in a storm because you cannot control the winds. . . . You must strive to guide policy indirectly, so that you make the best of things, and what you cannot turn to good, you can at least make less bad. For it is impossible to do all things well unless all men are good, and this I do not expect for long time.[26]

Hythloday is unconvinced. More, however, entered into Henry VIII's service shortly after he wrote the dialogue.

At a similar junction in Snow's *Homecomings*, Lewis Eliot wrestles with whether to leave or stay in government service. He has seen both good and injustice: he has participated in both. He decides to carry on: "People of my sort have only two choices in this situation; one is to keep outside and let others do the dirty work, the other is to stay inside and try to keep off the worst horrors and know all the time that we shan't come out with clean hands. Neither way is very good for one."[27]

The stance More advocates is not without dangers, as his own life shows, but it provides a way to anchor judgment and decision. Snow's Lewis Eliot comes to a similar conclusion. Snow also makes clear that beyond the dangers lies the satisfactions of accomplishment and commitment. Snow also emphasizes that integrity needs to be supported by the warmth of affection for people and institutions. More and Snow both share a sense of not just the moral risk of office but the moral importance of office. The risk is worth taking because humans of integrity create a society in which people of integrity can flourish.

4

Character and Moral Attrition

> "One does rather run the risk of becoming nothing to oneself," he [Smiley] confessed sadly. "Please don't ever imagine you'll be unscathed by the methods you use. The end may justify the means—if it wasn't supposed to, I dare say you wouldn't be here. But there's a price to pay, and the price does tend to be oneself."
>
> John Le Carré, *The Secret Pilgrim*

THE DEFENSE OF THE REPUBLIC always poses moral dilemmas for individuals. The dilemmas exact a high cost on the integrity of public officials. Plato identified a central one when he argued that the guardians of the state must be trained as if they were great guard dogs: the dogs should be fierce and violent towards enemies yet gentle and respectful with citizens. This analogy identifies two dimensions of this dilemma: first, the Guardians must live a contradiction; second, the Guardians are set apart, unable to live the life they defend—they are treated like animals and used as a means to an end. In a liberal democracy, this dilemma takes on a special urgency, because the society is pledged to mutual respect for the dignity of individuals—people should not be used as a means to an end. Yet defending citizens from enemies and criminals requires a number of professions, such as soldiers, police officers, prison guards, and spies, in which individuals must sometimes use methods that violate the core values of liberal and democratic life. Dealing with these dilemmas, people create distance between their professional lives and their personal commitments or fall into self-deception in order to avoid burnout or have their work corrupt their personal lives. These psychological strategies place immense strains upon the moral responsibility and internal balance required by public integrity. The tensions exist most profoundly in the defense professions of a liberal democracy. This chapter examines the most pernicious and troubling of these defense activities, espionage, to explore the costs to the integrity of the people who must do wrong to achieve right and some possible responses to their dilemma.

In a world of putative peace, espionage agents carry on a continuous war against ruthless adversaries. With the end of the Cold War, the need for espionage may grow rather than lessen as more conflicts flare throughout the world and large multinationals and crime syndicates become targets for spying. These conflicts have no boundaries, few rules, and no negotiated ends. Officials in the clandestine world end up using, hurting, betraying, seducing, or corrupting other human beings. In these very personal and close conflicts, no one maintains purity or untainted principles or ideals. In the bitter phrase of George Smiley's co-worker Connie Sachs, it becomes a world of "half-angels fighting half-devils." These activities highlight and accentuate all the tensions of individuals engaged in defending a political order against adversaries who will resort to violence and manipulation.[1] As John Le Carré's major protagonist George Smiley puts it, people must "be inhuman in defense of humanity . . . harsh in defense of compassion . . . single-minded in defense of our disparity."[2] Judgment and character become all-important when a moral exception becomes a way of life.

The moral attrition to integrity involved in espionage has been brought home with resounding clarity both in fiction and in fact in the last several decades. Le Carré's novels were partly inspired by the phenomena of Kim Philby and other British traitors who tore the British secret service apart. In the United States during the last decade members of the National Security Agency, the Central Intelligence Agency, the Federal Bureau of Investigation, and Naval Intelligence have been convicted of selling state secrets, while rogue CIA agents have aided the country's enemies. Almost fifty other espionage convictions have involved American citizens who betrayed defense secrets motivated by personal needs and desires. These facts should remind us that such activities cut to the heart of the moral identity of liberal democracy and pose profound problems of maintaining commitment and effectiveness. In institutional life where officials commit normally forbidden actions and discretion pervades decisions, the quality of the person, in terms of both commitments and character, takes on much more importance. Leading and managing such institutions requires a strong focus upon establishing and supporting a strong sense of internalized ethics and culture as well as technical skills.[3]

In response to abuses in activities such as espionage, legalistic reforms are usually enacted specifying prohibitions or requiring more oversight and monitoring. More incorruptible technology is used to replace human discretion. But technology has severe limits. In Le Carré's novel *The Secret Pilgrim*, sensors misread oxen urine as exhaust fumes of convoys or children's chatter as military commands during the Vietnam War. These mistakes lead to the bombing of innocent people. Recounting the story, one of Le Carré's spymasters observes, "Unfortunately the sensors are not as well informed as Hansen is." Smiley's spy Hansen must struggle with the complexity of that misbegotten war to provide the judgment and intelligence to pinpoint the bombing.[4] Legal and structural reforms cannot eliminate both the discretion and moral attrition inherent in the means officials must use in their encounters with ruthless adversaries bound by no such limits. To address these concerns in recruiting, training, and leadership, we must reflect upon the type of character and quality of judgment needed by individuals who are asked to live moral contradictions.

Finely drawn studies of the moral and psychological pressures, discretion, and dilemmas of an activity provide the best insights into the character required in realms of political and moral life.[5] The novels of John Le Carré—most tellingly in the Smiley novels and Karla trilogy *Tinker, Tailor, Soldier, Spy* (1974), *The Honourable Schoolboy* (1977), and *Smiley's People* (1980), their brilliant precursor *The Spy Who Came in from the Cold* (1963), and the contemplative coda *The Secret Pilgrim* (1991)—explore the moral tensions and costs of covert defense with a depth found almost nowhere else, and they are the basis of this discussion. These novels illuminate a world of moral capacity, commitment, and character, not laws or neat theories.[6]

For citizens and leaders in a liberal and democratic state, espionage and like activities pose some powerful moral challenges, which focus our attention on issues of institutional culture, leadership, and staffing such organizations. This focus on moral character complements concerns about institutional design or oversight. This chapter addresses the questions central to Le Carré's writing. What kind of person can pursue this activity who will not be destroyed by it and who will remain true to the reality and values of liberal democracy? Le Carré's gallery of characters provides three models of character: moral absolutists, careerists, and committed humanists.

The Moral Attrition of Espionage

Moral attrition afflicts all the characters in Le Carré's world. What they are asked to do tears at the fabric of their lives. The strains among various roles rends the central web of values and commitments by which people maintain integrity. The ugliness of professional life threatens to rip into their personal lives, and efforts to isolate their personal lives leave them deadened to human emotions and isolated from relationships. This constant tension inside them undermines not only their humanity, but also their professional competence, their commitment to liberal democracy, and the balances required by public integrity.

In absolutist societies, many of these issues do not arise. In *The Spy Who Came in from the Cold*, the ideology of the regime eliminates the moral tensions. The moral power of the ultimate goals answers all questions about the end. Alec Leamas's captor, the committed East German Communist Fiedler, makes the comparison explicit: "Christians may not draw the balance. They believe in the sanctity of human life."[7] In a very early Smiley novel *A Murder of Distinction*, Control, Smiley's mentor and the head of the Circus, British counterintelligence, explains that "intelligence work has one moral law—it is justified by results."[8] This tension between a monstrous utilitarianism that dismisses all human costs as means to a greater good and western respect for individual worth runs through all the books.

Machiavelli formulated the challenge almost five centuries ago when he argued that the end justifies the means, and that individuals must learn how not to be virtuous in a world of not-so-virtuous people. Modern utilitarian thinking accentuates the issue. Utilitarianism can, in practice, disregard all moral responsibility for the wrong or harm incurred to attain an aggregated good. Individual worth or intrinsically wrong actions do not matter in the moral equation. All "wrongs" done drop out of the moral equation or are transmogrified into a "good" that contributes to the end.[9] Fiedler pushes the difference to the breaking point when he baits Leamas in a telling exchange: "Would you kill a man, an innocent man. . . . Would London do it?" "It depends on need . . ." "Ah," said Fiedler contentedly, "it depends on the need. Like Stalin in fact."[10] Two questions haunt Le Carré's books: Are there any significant differences between the moral quality of the action of the absolutists and those of the West? As the differences narrow, what characters minimize the degradation and dangers to democracy and those placed in harm's way?

At the core of liberal democracy and of George Smiley's character—for in Le Carré's books he embodies those values and tensions—lies respect for the worth and dignity of individuals. Liberal democracy justifies itself by the quality of humanity it allows to flourish in its citizens. Its political system exists in dialogue with the consciences of its citizens and must earn legitimacy through accountability. In the end, the government's actions should both model and comport with the moral values and integrity of the citizens. A society of individuals with an accountable government requires tolerance, openness, and honesty in social and political relations. Without these, intimacy, creativity, and democracy cannot thrive. The society is built upon Kant's injunction not to use individuals as means and the acceptance of personal responsibility for the consequences of one's actions.

National defense highlights these problems because the high stakes of communal defense and the aggression of adversaries constantly pressure the defenders. George Smiley's mentor Control sums it up: "I mean you've got to compare method with method, and ideal with ideal. I would say that since the war, our methods—ours and those of the opposition—have become much the same. I mean you can't be less ruthless than the opposition because your government's policy is benevolent."[11] In the Smiley novels, western spies use deceit, betrayal, blackmail, bribery, illegality, and force as well as exploiting other people's love, friendship, and loyalty to achieve their ends.

The humanity and integrity of all who participate are eroded by espionage. Capacities for honesty, commitment, and friendship are undermined. Feelings are numbed while agents learn to disconnect parts of themselves from the tasks of lying, killing, seducing, and betraying without remorse. As Ned, a fine agent and one of Smiley's protégés, ruminates, "When we are exhilarated, or drunk—or, even as I am told, make love—the reserve does not dissolve, the gyroscope stays vertical, the monitory voice reminds us of our calling. Until gradually our very withholding becomes so strident it is almost a security risk itself."[12] In the name of "personal security," each agent develops a reserve so deep that humanity becomes almost irretrievable. Agents submerge themselves in lies in order to survive and use false identities and emotions to create false friendships. As in Webster's play The Duchess of Malfi, so dear to Smiley, the characters genuinely love and care for individuals even as they betray them, because unfeigned love gains them better access. These psychological and moral distortions undermine professional skill because individuals must numb sensitivities and expose vulnerabilities. Their integrity dissolves as agents are reduced to a collection of unrelated tasks and roles floating in the same body and mind. This life can make individuals unfit to thrive in the society they defend.

Alec Leamas, the eponymous *Spy Who Came in from the Cold*, defines Le Carré's tragic archetype. He is a committed and commonsense agent. At the end of his mission, he has been deceived by Control, his superior, has had his love manipulated, has been forced to protect Mundt, the very man who destroyed his network of agents and friends, and has had to betray the thoughtful and committed Fiedler, who interrogates him. Leamas does not break, nor does he betray the system or turn moral renegade. With desperate dignity, he refuses to escape over the Berlin Wall. Instead, in an act of redemption, he recommits to the only humanity left him, climbs back down his escape ladder, and dies while defiantly holding his dead lover. His death symbolizes the spiritual grave waiting at home.[13]

Espionage depends upon absolute secrecy and deception. Political accountability, oversight committees, and superiors simply increase the possibility of leaks and betrayal. It is a world of shifting alliances and loyalties in which "the oldest maxim of the trade" is "spy on your friends today, they're certain to be your enemies tomorrow."[14] The integrity and humanity of others become the targets, for the integrity of individuals must be subverted before they will betray secrets. Most officials prefer blackmail to bribery because it hooks a victim's integrity more deeply.[15]

Agents must practice a self-deception so deep and profound that it seeps into their souls. In *The Spy Who Came in from the Cold*, Alec Leamas must pretend to be a traitor. Once he is captured, deception becomes "first a matter of self-defense. He must protect himself not only from without but from within, and against the most natural impulses."[16] All of Le Carré's agents exercise such plasticity, but it has a high cost. The strains upon integrity and a coherent moral life are immense. Smiley muses that "treason becomes a matter of habit."[17] Control warns Leamas, "We pass so quickly out of the register of hate or love—like sounds a dog can't hear. All that's left in the end is a kind of nausea; you never want to cause suffering again."[18] Emotional fatigue, needs for friends or love, temptations to gentleness, they are all the "kiss of death."[19] In the end, Smiley's protégé Ned concludes that the isolation and denial can drive good agents to such a "hunger for connections" and they become vulnerable to exploitation and can have a "nervous breakdown in place." Such an agent continues to "go through the daily motions—naturally, he was soldier—but his mind wouldn't play any more."[20]

People in a liberal society reconcile moral dilemmas by adopting roles and organizing loyalties in a way that gives some coherence to personal integrity. Roles involve personal loyalty to rules, practices, techniques, and authority embedded in a profession or organization. Roles link "immoral" actions with the moral goals and sanctions of society. Through them, individuals can carry on "dirty work" without necessarily gaining "dirty hands." Individuals in an office separate and balance personal and professional lives even as their personal lives provide buttresses and support for the official life. In many of the defense and police occupations, people build a wall between the two moral universes or sever one role from all others. But pure role disconnection from the rest of life subverts integrity and can lead to the ultimate perversion: the "banality of evil" chronicled by Hannah Arendt. Adolf Eichmann, caring family man, ruthlessly and efficiently oversaw the slaughter of innocent Jews and excused himself by believing that he was simply obeying orders.[21] Integrity drives people to make sense of their moral world, to demonstrate and feel the connection between their personal lives and deepest values and what they do. In reality, the wall does and should break down. But when the agent's work does reconnect with personal life and the wall breaks down, it too often poisons the life of the agent.

In a telling motif, almost no one in Smiley's world can sustain personal relations or marriage. The distrust, secrecy, and plasticity of identity that characterize their work undermine their ability to sustain personal commitments. Peter Guillam, Smiley's friend and factotum, thinks that his own insecurities warp his affections for women. He sees his needs as weaknesses and hounds his lovers for signs of imminent betrayal, driving them to betray him. Ned, Smiley's friend and protégé, goes through a series of meaningless affairs in a desperate attempt to rediscover a capacity to love. Smiley leaves and returns to his wife throughout five books, even as she loves and betrays him with astounding regularity. Lesser characters such as agents Ricki Tarr and Toby Esterhase have several wives and mistresses around the world. Control's wife never knows his real occupation. In a sad coda, after her death, Control lives a secret life with a woman—a typical bourgeois life of the kind he has always mocked in the office. When Smiley informs her of Control's death, she demonstrates the unease at the core of all relations with agents by demanding reassurance that Control had not returned to his wife.[22]

Le Carré refuses to hide the moral waste of this activity or the core moral dilemma of means and end. But he does not simply suggest that no real moral distinctions exist between absolutists and liberal democratic officials. The novels are obsessed, as Smiley is, with how to avoid the law of emulation that states that people come to be what they most hate in their enemies. Control sums it up: "The ethic of our work . . . is . . . that we are never going to be aggressors. Thus we do disagreeable things, but we are *defensive*."[23] When Control and Smiley run the Circus, the quality of deliberation differs. They insist on accounting for all the real costs to humans. They seek to limit the costs to innocents and try to minimize violence. Their deliberations result in real but not absolute differences in the long-term results of policy. The liberal democratic services ultimately remain more tolerant of mistakes, while a Russian agent can be killed by his own people for a mere indiscretion.[24]

What kind of people can keep their integrity and maintain the inner balance that enables them to avoid the moral attrition of the task? Espionage and defense in liberal democracies requires individuals who can live and struggle with these contradictions while not losing their humanity, competence, or commitment. Their integrity, or "private faith" as Smiley calls it, must remain alive and connect the commitments and domains that both inform their decisions and constrain their judgments. It involves a capacity for honestly facing the real costs, minimizing them, and living with the responsibility for the harms done. Smiley expresses the nub when asked to help the service out of his loyalty and duty: "Duty to what? Smiley wondered, with that part of himself that sometimes seemed like a spectator to the rest. Loyalty to whom?"[25] Le Carré portrays three character types who try to resolve these answers.

Absolutists

Le Carré's novels indict absolute loyalty to a cause as the most dangerous threat to the values of a liberal democracy. Such absolutist loyalty fits perfectly the requirements of espionage, since it justifies the use of any method to attain the goal. The authority granted by the goal exonerates people from individual responsibility and erases any guilt for action. People act as agents of a higher power or moral necessity, and the tension is abolished. No tensions exist within the self because all aspects of selfhood become absorbed and subordinated to one overarching goal and the authority structure demanded of it. Balanced public integrity collapses into one commitment. Fiedler sums up the moral equation: "Afterwards I would draw the balance—so many women, so many children; and so far along the road."[26]

Le Carré's books present this pattern of loyalty as the enemy from the beginning. In the first chapter of the first Smiley novel, *Call for the Dead*, George Smiley contemplates the "stamping and shouting" of Nazi students burning books. Smiley, "watching and hating, triumphed that he knew his enemy."[27] In an anguished double-edged statement to Smiley, Elsa Fennan, a Soviet spy and survivor of concentration camps, summarizes the dynamic: "Give them one theory, let them invent one slogan, and the game begins again" (95). In *Call for the Dead*, Dieter Frey is a brilliant and flamboyant East German spy, originally recruited by Smiley. In the novel, which is a complex story of double agents, Frey is committed to building a perfect world. He ruthlessly kills anyone who stands in his way, including his own friend and accomplice Elsa Fennan. He is the exemplar of a "man who thought and acted in absolute terms, without patience or compromise" (124). Smiley learns to hate Frey and the "fabulous impertinence of renouncing the individual in favour of the mass. Dieter cared nothing for human life" (130).

Each Smiley novel has such characters, but the dark eminence of Karla, the Soviet master spy, dominates the three central ones and exemplifies the danger of absolutism. Karla places moles in deep undercover in foreign governments and creates an independent commissariat within Russia. He recruited Bill Haydon, the mole who "turned the Circus inside out" in *Tinker, Tailor, Soldier, Spy*. Karla's picture sits eternally upon George Smiley's wall in *The Honourable Schoolboy*, in which Smiley traces a trail of gold payments Karla had initiated to its source in a Soviet double agent in China. Karla precipitates the quest in *Smiley's People* by killing an old and valued friend of Smiley's. Known as "the sandman" because those he touches have a way of "falling to sleep," Karla uses superb craft and merciless violence in the service of his unswerving commitment to the progress of the Communist state.

Karla has submerged his identity into that of the revolutionary march of history. He possesses a "philosophic repose" in his certainty that Smiley both envies and fears. His life remains austere like that of a monk or priest.[28] Unlike Dieter Frey and Bill Haydon, he seems to have no ego and no moral self-consciousness to question himself. The sketchy details of his personal life reflect the same scrupulous subordination of humanity to cause. We learn his first wife "killed herself when he was sent to

Siberia."[29] Smiley's abiding friend and longtime ally Connie Sachs recalls that Karla had one lover in his life. Karla educated her, "had her all got up to be his ideal hag." Then his lover "mixed with the bloody intellectuals" and asked the great forbidden question "Why?" Karla "had her shoved in the slammer." His "love turned to hatred and he had his ideal carted off and spavined: end of story . . . he destroyed all records of her, killed whoever might have heard, this is Karla's way, bless him, isn't it, darling, always was."[30]

Bill Haydon serves as Karla's mole in the Circus, betraying his country, friends, and class for the cause. But unlike Karla's or Fiedler's austere commitment, Haydon's loyalty flows from his flawed ego. He acted with daring, disdain, and brutality. His self-promoting exploits made him a role model for many younger agents.[31] Smiley sees both Haydon and Dieter Frey as "out-of-scale" men who need a cosmic drama to justify the girth of their selves.

The imperial reality of prewar England could satisfy the ambitions of a Haydon. At that time an Englishman could commit to both England and Communism. The Spanish Civil War and the rise of Hitler urgently demanded that people choose between two great cosmic choices—fascism and Communism. Many, like Smiley, would choose to oppose fascism; others would also commit to Communism. After the war, a shrunken England proves a squalid contrast to the world Haydon assumed he would defend. He is appalled at its crassness, mediocrity, and ugliness. America dominates the western alliance, and, like Dieter Frey, Haydon hates and envies the "fascist puritans." He cannot abide being an appendage to them. In his "heroic" guise, Haydon is always "creating plans to reassert British power, none of which ever reached fruition" (150–55).

At the beginning, his vestigial love of England keeps him from passing information that would harm his country; he only wants to hurt America. But Haydon needs to be a hero at center stage, and England can no longer provide a sufficient cause, so he stays with Communism. The historical drama of East versus West provides an apt background for his daring and violent style. He confesses to Smiley that he had sided with the East almost as "an *aesthetic* judgment as much as anything else. . . . Partly a moral one, of course." In the end, Haydon betrays his best friend and former lover Jim Prideaux in Czechoslovakia in order to discredit Control's suspicions about himself. His once dynamic art ends as "cramped" and "condemned. " He is reduced to bragging about Soviet medals he has never seen and worrying about the tailoring of his clothes when he arrives in Russia. His life epitomizes of the life of espionage: "in every capacity, Haydon had overtly pursued one aim and secretly achieved its opposite" (342–45, 353; emphasis added).

Bureaucratic Careerism

Haydon's dissatisfaction demonstrates a nagging challenge in the Smiley books. Liberal democratic life offers no utopian goals, absolute ideologies, or certain authorities. Consequently, it cannot offer the moral certitude, romantic vision, and exoneration that absolutists know. Although some are always trying to construct ideological clones to offset this "disadvantage," the play of self-interest, materialism, and inequality undercuts such pure idealism among defenders of the liberal democratic faith. Most modern defectors and traitors act for money, drugs, and sex rather than robust commitment. Roy Bland is an old colleague of Smiley's who sides with Haydon when Haydon stages his coup to take over the Circus. Bland sums it up to George Smiley: "it's the name of the game these days: You scratch my conscience, I'll drive your jag, right?"[32] Smiley's friend, collaborator, and sometimes conscience Connie Sachs provides him with a faint answer to the dissatisfied ambition of his colleagues: "We're fighting for the survival of the reasonable man."[33]

It takes a very different, almost chastened faith to accommodate such a real world and defend it. But without absolute idealism, it becomes very difficult for agents to accept and tolerate the squalor of espionage. In *Smiley's People* Oliver Lacon is the liaison between the Circus and the ministry that oversees it. He must convince Smiley to cover up an old general's murder, but Mostyn, the young agent who guards Lacon, watches this scene and later "resigned of his own accord a few months later, part of the wastage rate that gets everyone so worried these days."[34] The end of the Cold War and dissolution of the great war of good and evil makes it even harder to sustain durable moral commitment among agents. In *The Russia House* not only the Russians have a difficult time making sense of the new world, but so do western agents.[35] Barley Blair is an agent recruited by Smiley's protégé, Ned. Blair arranges for the transfer of information that would shatter all understandings of the nuclear balance of power between Russia and the western alliance. Yet, disillusioned by both systems, Blair double-crosses both the Russians and the British. He strikes out to create a new life with a Russian woman with whom he has fallen in love. He finds the thread that enables him to reconnect a life of integrity in a world in which ideologies no longer seem to matter.

Bureaucratic careerism too often fills this vacuum of disillusioned idealism. Le Carré's novels excel in capturing the dynamics and perversions of institutional life. His stories are alive with the pressures on subordinates to distort their skill and information to satisfy the interests of superiors. The sense of how informal networks and understandings subvert the institutional structure pervades his stories. The displacing of the real goals of the organization for self-interest and organizational survival is shown as the norm of life in institutions under stress. Institutional norms and groupthink blind members to obvious situations and inhibit creativity and craftsmanship. Le Carré's novels portray with telling force what organizational theory warns: that in a world of budget, promotion, and status mongering, the skills of pleasing superiors, building networks, and playing bureaucratic games are often rewarded more highly than is competent craftsmanship.

In the first chapter of the first Smiley novel, *Call for the Dead,* we meet Maston, "the career man." Knighted, mannered, and regretful of his empire building, he excels in the "efficiency, bureaucracy and intrigue of a large government department."[36] Vague, flexible, insincere, and ruthless, he exemplifies this central character type in all the novels. Such characters are spawned within any institution; they are more concerned with their own promotion, power, and status than with the actual results of the craft or welfare of their agents. The entire plot of *Tinker, Tailor, Soldier, Spy* hinges on the collective blindness of bureaucratic careerists who sacrifice their craft and integrity in exchange for promotion based on the fake "Witchcraft" file.

George Smiley must battle the world of careerists in all the novels; he meets it head-on in *Tinker, Tailor, Soldier, Spy* where a group of careerists stage a coup in the Circus and gain their power by means of a special pipeline of information called "Witchcraft." Trying to head off the coup and believing the "Witchcraft" file to be tainted information, Smiley meets Toby Esterhase, a Hungarian émigré he had originally recruited. Esterhase refuses to admit that there might be a conspiracy. Instead, he carps on his offended dignity and lack of promotion under the old regime. Disgusted, Smiley tries to bribe Toby with a promotion but fails. Roy Bland, another East European émigré and Smiley protégé, meets with Smiley. In response to Smiley's attempt to call on past loyalty, Bland callously responds, "So what's the deal?" Bland has burnt out in the field and nursed his own personal grievances that no ideology could soothe: "I've paid, see, George. You know that. I don't know what I've bought with it, I've paid a hell of a lot. I want some back. . . . There must have been a reason why I fell for all that spiel, but I can't quite remember what it was."[37] Without ideals, bureaucratic spoils satisfy both Bland and Esterhase. They stay with the Witchcraft group and gain a chunk of the bureaucratic empire. Years later after many changes of administration, we again meet Esterhase in *The Secret Pilgrim*, where he is still thriving in the bureaucratic game. To build up his base in Vienna, where he is now chief, he sponsors a broken, useless agent, Professor Teodor. Teodor, knowing he is ineffectual and about to lose his sinecure, arranges to have an actor friend fake an assassination attempt. Toby knows this, but the faked assassination affirms the professor's worth and enhances Toby's own position in the service. Esterhase with the collusion of his superiors arranges to save money and have the Americans pension off Teodor. Esterhase's survival depends upon his own capacity to use and rely upon the self-interested gains of others without regard to competence.[38]

If Esterhase and Bland were competent craftsmen whose loyalties were corrupted by burnout and aggrieved ambition, Percy Alleline, Control's successor as head of the Circus, represents the quintessential distortion of craft by careerism. A consummate egoist, he lacks Haydon's genius or commitment. A Maston protégé with a perpetual sense of undervalued worth, he succeeds primarily by his social ease in the "smart set" and a blunt and vigorous style that periodically produces results. In India he preaches loyalty to his agents and "when it suited him—sold them down the river." Elsewhere he joins the Americans in their favorite activity—a failed coup—and discredits himself. All Percy wants is a "place at the top table," and, as Control quips earlier, he "would sell his mother for a knighthood and this service for a seat in the House of Lords."[39] Karla and Haydon dupe him into believing that he has actually discovered Witchcraft and use him to lead the coup that maximizes Haydon's power and betrayal.

Two careerists, Oliver Lacon and Saul Enderby, stand out in the novels as leaders. Lacon connects the Circus and the ruling government. The Circus is Lacon's bureaucratic and political base, and he must get results from his bailiwick. In fine Madisonian tradition, his ambition should serve the common good, but he succumbs to the charm of Witchcraft and Control's failings. He purges Smiley and Control and replaces them with the Alleline coterie. Driven in equal parts by duty and ambition, Lacon merges the two into a self-effacing priggishness combined with a great capacity to manipulate people and bureaucratic budgets and process. Twice he brings Smiley back to save the Circus; twice he throws Smiley out after Smiley performs his dirty work.

Despite his pomposity and self-deception, Lacon can make hard points and decisions.[40] He recognizes Smiley's insight and competence, even as he manipulates him. When a whisper of a mole in the Circus is heard, he moves decisively to give Smiley plenipotentiary power to ferret it out. He saves Smiley from dismantling the entire Circus and fights stoutly for Smiley's position when the Circus is rebuilt. When he removes Smiley from command at the end of *The Honourable Schoolboy*, he does both Smiley and the service a favor. Smiley hated the bureaucratic politics, even as he excelled at them, while Smiley's replacement Saul Enderby, not at all incompetent, could better defend the service in the new political world. He could even apologize when required.[41]

Lacon's smarmy style also recognizes, however bluntly and unattractively, the dilemma of civil servants in a democracy. He understands that the agents had to "live by rather different standard. " He knows that for Smiley morality resides in "aim" and not "method." But the Circus does not make policy; elected governments make policy, and Lacon sees to it that the Circus carries them out. Lacon must delicately shift and address the leaders of conservative or reforming socialist governments and keep the service intact under both. It requires sophistry, and "sophistry was Lacon's element."[42] It isn't Smiley's cup of tea, but in that difficult borderland between professionals and elected representatives, Lacon does well.

He does so at a cost. Lacon genuinely cares about the service and its role, but he loses his energy and ideals. This disconnects his office from his integrity and compromises his choices to run the agency. He angrily tells Smiley in *Smiley's People*, "We are pragmatists, George. We adapt. We are not keepers of some sacred flame. I ask you. I commend you, to remember this."[43] He possesses no finesse in his assessment of the agency and falls prey to Karla's trap because he cannot really understand the craft. He ages in defense of the agency and loses his young wife. Yet Lacon holds the service together and does not betray its functional integrity, even if he never understands its operational soul.

At the end of *The Honourable Schoolboy*, Oliver Lacon replaces Smiley with Saul Enderby. Blunt, aggressive, and insightful, Enderby revels in bureaucratic infighting. He can preen: "Nice little meeting. Lot achieved. Nothing given away. Nicely played hand."[44] He will defend the service well. Unlike most administrators in Le Carré's novels, Enderby sees through the careerist haze around him. He recognizes Smiley's superior talents and can take risks. In *Smiley's People* when Smiley broaches his plan to catch Karla after he has found out about Karla's daughter, Enderby agrees to violate every new law of the reforming government. He is quite clear: "I want his body, George, hear me. Hand me a live, talking Karla and I'll accept him and make my excuses later." But if Smiley fails, Enderby will blame "a ludicrous piece of private enterprise by a senile spy who's lost his marbles." Enderby has enough sense to give Smiley the room to maneuver that a great field agent needs. He is "thick-skinned" enough that he can wryly admit his past errors.[45]

But he possesses an underside. At the end of *The Honourable Schoolboy* he hands over Nelson Ko, whom Smiley had captured at great cost, to the Americans in order to get American support for his promotion to head of the Circus. In doing this he sacrifices what Smiley believed would be major bargaining leverage against the American "cousins."[46] He goes to meetings surrounded by a phalanx of smart and "doglike" yes-men and uses burnt-out agents to extend his domain.[47] He represents the triumph of bureaucratic rationalization over craft and art and prizes "cheap killing" or blackmail for their efficiency.[48] Enderby represents the future. His ideals are manufactured and self-serving, his vision cramped, and his craft crude and limited.

Bureaucratic rationalism and moral absolutism unite in the disquieting vision of the American services, "the cousins" as they are referred to by the British in the novels. Jim Prideaux dismisses the Americans as a bunch of "greedy fools fouling up their inheritance."[49] The novels abound with references, usually tinged with envy and frustration, to the arrogance and wealth of the Americans. But the real problems arise from the combinations of bureaucratic rationalism with self-righteousness. Most office bureaucrats care little for the gentle and patient activity necessary to get good information. Americans perfect this bluntness and play a "rougher game."[50]

Whenever Americans arrive on the scene, they bring too many people and too many guns. In *The Honourable Schoolboy*, Sol Eckland of the Drug Enforcement Agency demonstrates the American approach when he tries to pry control of the Nelson Ko case away from Smiley. He excoriates the British because they refuse to "go for the jugular": "Jesus, if we'd been handling this thing, we'd have had that bastard trussed over a barrel long ago" (268–69). Had the Americans acted as they wanted, Smiley would have lost Nelson Ko and a treasure trove of information about Soviet and Chinese activities.

The American approach leads the CIA to the bizarre byways of selling opium for the tribes they armed during the Vietnam War. But Jerry Westerby, the eponymous *Honourable Schoolboy* and a Smiley agent, pins down the Circus's disdain as opposed to envy for the Americans. Working with the Americans in Vietnam, he speaks with an embittered American captain when they hear the news of the pullout from Vietnam. During the conversation Westerby notices that "the windows overlooking the airfield were smoked and double-glazed. On the runway aircraft landed and took off without making a sound. This is how they tried to win, Jerry thought: from inside sound-proof rooms, through smoked glass, using machines at arm's length. This is how they lost."[51]

The Committed Humanist: George Smiley

George Smiley, the overweight, cuckolded, "failed priest," is Le Carré's major protagonist and exemplar. Unlike the absolutists and careerists, Smiley manages to remain true to himself, his service, his craft, and his country, although he comes to doubt this in the end. Smiley holds within himself a balance between his humanity and his profession. He embodies public integrity that plays out in the complexity and balance of his loyalties and makes him, however rare and flawed, the model for a public official struggling to achieve integrity in a liberal and democratic society.

Smiley is a humanist and individualist. He lives by commitments to concrete reality—the tools of his craft, his marriage, the Circus—and invests his loyalty in concrete practices and institutions in stark contrast to Karla's ideology. He possesses no absolute ideals that justify all actions, nor can he take solace in a God or in a historical utopia that excuses responsibility for violence. In *The Secret Pilgrim,* he speaks to a new class of agents whom his old protégé Ned is training. In his last words in the Smiley novels, he states, "I only ever cared about the *man.* " He adds:

> I never gave a fig for ideologies, unless they were mad or evil, I never saw institutions as being worthy of their parts, or policies as much other than excuses for not feeling. Man, not the mass, is what our calling is about. It was man who ended the Cold War in case you didn't notice. It wasn't weaponry, or technology. . . . It was just man. Not even West-

ern man . . . but our sworn enemy in the East, who went into the streets, faced the bullets and the batons and said, we've had enough.[52]

He considered himself "weak" compared to those like Haydon and Karla, because he was unable to "live a self-sufficient life independent of institutions." But these concrete relationships grounded his moral strength and restraint. At one point in *Tinker, Tailor, Soldier, Spy,* Smiley succeeds in capturing Karla and confesses his beliefs to the now imprisoned Karla: "Did he [Karla] not believe, for example, that the political generality was meaningless? That only the particular in life had value for him now? That in the hands of politicians grand designs achieve nothing but new forms of the old?"[53]

In a sense, the story of Smiley and his adversaries play out Max Weber's famous dichotomy between the "ethic of ultimate ends" and the "ethic of responsibility." Karla and his minions exemplify the former and Smiley the latter. The bureaucratic careerists also capture quite accurately Weber's fears for the brittle fate of institutionalized norms and responsibilities. The Smiley novels, however, demonstrate the richness and ambiguity of the categories by focusing upon the personal reality of living these different approaches—something neither Weber nor the numerous citations of his overused distinctions address.[54]

Smiley's conservative individualism makes him "rational" and "protective" of his world for "Everything he admired or loved had been the creation of intense individualism."[55] But integrity requires honest self-reflection, and Smiley is not so embedded in concrete practice that he loses the capacity for critical self-reflection. He retains his own "private faith," which enables him to step back and assess his actions and balance his domains of commitment. Several times he leaves the Circus to gain intellectual and emotional distance. He returns because he chooses to "serve" and he feels a moral obligation to pay a debt to society. In his view, the "secret road" "seemed to lead straightest and furthest toward my country's goal." His self-consciousness enables him to judge himself and others, hold complex loyalties together despite the tension, and maintain immense moral discipline and restraint. It also protects him from self-deception and makes him acutely aware of his own responsibility. When a colleague tries to escape responsibility for the death of an innocent man the Circus was blackmailing, Smiley rebukes him: "I ordered this initiative. I refuse not to look at the consequences merely because they are ugly. Put it on my head. But don't let's deceive ourselves."[56]

This sense of responsibility flows from Smiley's abiding care for the world. He does not love an abstract humanity as Karla does; nor does he seek the holy grail of romantic love as does Ann, his wife. He cares for existing people and things in a real world. The same care he feels for the intricate beauty of his porcelain figurines extends to the world and the people around him. In *Smiley's People* Olga Ostrakava has been pursued and wounded by Karla's men to silence her about his daughter. She is hiding and terrified but unbolts her door for Smiley because "she sensed in him a passionate caring for herself that had nothing to do with death, but with survival."[57] Because his care centers on the real and not ideals, he could know a surge of resentment "against the institutions he was supposed to be protecting . . . the Minister's lolling mendacity, Lacon's tight-lipped complacency, the bludgeoning greed of Percy Alleline,"[58] and still remain loyal. Imperfection did not lead him to Haydon's betrayal or the cynicism of Esterhase and Bland.

The counterpoint story of young Bill Roach and Jim Prideaux at the boarding school in *Tinker, Tailor, Soldier, Spy* also establishes the critical relation among care, selfhood, and a sense of responsibility that is a hallmark of Smiley's character. Round, bespectacled, and shy, Roach was abandoned by his divorced parents at the school. He is Smiley's prototype. A "loner" and a "watcher"—"best damned watcher in the whole damned unit"—Roach cares deeply about and feels responsible for his parents, the world, and Jim Prideaux. This care and responsibility motivates Roach to spy on Prideaux and others as a way to protect them.[59]

Smiley always remains acutely aware of the moral costs of his actions and could never reach an easy reconciliation of the means he uses with the ends he pursues. He weighs the costs of human life and dignity in every equation, but he can act even when he knows the cost. But unlike Fiedler, Karla, or Haydon, he could not simply draw up a satisfied balance and ignore the moral harm. Each novel reaches a critical denouement at which Smiley acknowledges the costs of his own actions without moral balances to exonerate him. In *Tinker, Tailor, Soldier, Spy,* Smiley waits to catch Bill Haydon in an act of treason; he reflects on friends and broken loyalties and sees "great things dwindling into a small, mean end. . . . It worried him that he felt so bankrupt: that whatever intellectual or philosophical precepts he clung to broke down entirely now that he was faced with a human situation."[60] Smiley never achieves morally pure victory.

Too much self-consciousness of ambiguity has paralyzed better people than Hamlet, but it has made Smiley a better agent. Good professionals know the strengths as well as the limitations of their materials. By probing his own motives, Smiley can understand those of others. His empathy extends his awareness of the complexity of others' worlds and enriches his sense of nuance.[61] His calibrations of costs inspires his meticulous planning of each operation. His care and responsibility torture him, give him no untainted triumph, but anchor his skill. People he trained and mentored like Ned also develop these hard and painful skills.

Smiley's care infuses his loyalty to his craft. He admires "thoroughness and precision" and respects individuals, even enemies, who succeed with cool skill.[62] Gentleness, patience, and deftness characterize his work. He distrusts egoistic agents and the flamboyant violence of Bill Haydon's "scalp-hunters."[63] Like Karla and unlike Haydon, he practices a hard-won humility before his craft and doesn't know the distinction between "business" and "pleasure." His successes in the novels hinge upon Smiley's hours of painstaking labor to discover patterns. This humility and care makes him a superb listener—the archetypal skill of an agent and a skill that is lost to larger or more cynical egos.[64]

Smiley practices a profession of an older craft variety that emphasizes personal skill and responsibility, not bureaucratic manuals, blunt method, and results at all costs. At heart, he remains a "case man." The Circus he rebuilds resembled a close family with idiosyncratic individuals, many of whom had been discarded by the bureaucratic climber Alleline. Smiley hated the interbureaucratic battles necessary to win money and turf for his policy, even as he mastered them. Retreating to a café one evening, he muses, "Did Karla have to scheme in committees? Fight cabals, deceive the stupid, flatter the clever . . . all in order to do the job?"[65] Le Carré hints that Smiley may actually have welcomed his replacement by Enderby. He steadfastly ignores Peter Guillam's warnings about a bureaucratic coup and laments to Ann prior to the coup that he now interprets "the whole of life in terms of conspiracy": "Such is the sword by which I shall die as well. These people terrify me, but I am one of them. If they stab me in the back, then at least that is the judgment of my peers."[66]

Smiley's care and humility give him the strength to commit and endure in the world of espionage without losing his humanity or honor. He does not betray his country, friends, or even institutions and craft, but he suffers immense personal anguish. He maintains his poise at tremendous cost as he tries to be the "oak" of his times. His brutal repression of his feelings of anger, repugnance, and concern brings on self-deception and a constant depression based on his own misdirected and repressed anger at himself, something that also afflicts his protégé Ned. We get few glimpses of the passion that seethes within him and gives him the energy to carry on. Tightly controlled and overlaid with irony, his passions sometimes surprise him and come out in unpredictable ways as in his long, late-night London walks, sometimes to spy on Ann, or his unreasoning anger at Karla's sloppy craft.[67]

Only his wife, Ann, genuinely senses the passion at Smiley's core. She loves Smiley and returns to him as "her law" because of that deep passion and commitment, even when his rigid control and humility stultifies his ability to return her passion. She draws out and tests his passion. She finally forces him to admit his own superiority to Haydon and urges him to return to the Circus and expose the plot that overthrew him and Control.[68] She keeps alive his passion and refuels it with her own passion and energy so that he could channel it into his superb craftsmanship. But in the end, she is not enough. Despite Smiley's convoluted denials and because of his own unwillingness to face his anger, Ann's affair with Bill Haydon had permanently poisoned their marriage for him. Smiley could still live with imperfection, but at the end, he finds himself almost unable to commit, unable to love, only to grieve. He "had forborne," others had not. He "toiled in backrooms," but shallower men still held the stage, and Smiley knows that "I have invested my life in institutions . . . and all I am left with is myself."[69]

The Uncertain Triumph

A double tragedy haunts Le Carré's novels. First, the quality of humanity that justifies liberal and democratic life cannot be sustained in the life of espionage. Second, espionage institutions seem unable to accommodate the agents who possess the very qualities of character they need. As a moral exemplar Smiley embodies the liberal democratic respect for individuality and carries the real burden of proving that the liberal democracies can pursue the activity without totally degrading themselves. The books hinge on the dialectic between the methods of the absolutists and the goals of the liberal democracies: the tension between Karla and Smiley. The fate of George Smiley's soul matters not only for instruction on integrity but also because Smiley's character represents the best hope of learning how to live with the moral ambiguity of flawed means.

Smiley's People is the last novel of the brilliant Karla trilogy and presents the dilemma in its darkest form. When Oliver Lacon calls in Smiley from retirement to cover up the death of an old and discarded émigré ally,

Smiley discovers Karla's plan to keep his mentally ill daughter in a Western sanitarium in violation of all Soviet laws. Smiley deliberately disobeys Lacon's charge to limit his investigation. He coaxes his old friend Connie Sach's last dying remembrances with lies and alcohol. He convinces Saul Enderby to juggle the Circus's books and violate all of Whitehall's new prohibitions on spying. Last, he uses Karla's love for his daughter to trap him and purchase his betrayal. At the end, as Karla crosses the bridge into West Germany, Smiley reflects in anguish that "the very evil he had fought against seemed to reach out and possess him. . . . On Karla had descended the curse of Smiley's compassion; on Smiley the curse of Karla's fanaticism. I have destroyed him with weapons I abhorred, and they are his. We have crossed each other's frontiers, we are the no-men of this no-man's-land."[70]

Smiley is not perfect, and his own self-reflection made him suffer from his own scruples in being a too "stringent critic of his own motives."[71] This fired his discipline to maintain his humility, restraint, and humanity amid the moral corrosion but inflicted immense and sometimes self-deceiving suffering upon him. He was more accurate in his self-appraisal when he rejected Connie Sach's taunting comment that George and Karla were "two halves of the same apple."[72]

Very little new occurs in the way of methods in *Smiley's People*. In *The Honourable Schoolboy*, Smiley's agent Gerald Westerby had used affection to blackmail a man named Frost, and Smiley had blackmailed his friend Toby Esterhase. Funds had been juggled in pursuit of Nelson Ko, and Peter Guillam had been forced to lie and spy on his old friends in the Circus. Connie had been seduced with alcohol to gain information many times. In *Call for the Dead*, Smiley had resigned and illegally pursued a case that Maston had ordered closed. But the irony of Smiley's earlier prediction that he would catch Karla because "he's a fanatic . . . that lack of moderation will be his downfall" haunts the novel.[73] Smiley exploits Karla's weakness and love for his daughter, the same humanity Karla exploited in Smiley. But Karla was caught because his "sandman" signature of violence alerted Smiley to his presence. Karla's fanaticism gave him away, but not in the way Smiley anticipated.

George Smiley does not become Karla. Smiley never kills his lover or his agents. Nor does he kill to cover his tracks. His agents are not destroyed for errors, and he still abhors violence and minimizes its use. To the end, his goals remain reactive and specific. He accepts responsibility for his actions, maintains accountability, and acts only after Lacon calls him in to investigate a killing. He initiates the case, gets approval, and organizes the plan. His craft "had never been better," but the case still remains one case with a specific and reactive goal pursued by the normal messy methods with a minimum of violence.

The real danger for this "old spy in a hurry" comes from the obsessive quality of this quest, not the content or the methods. Ann says that Karla is Smiley's "black grail." Yet Smiley's pursuit of Karla differs from Ann's anarchic preference for eros or Karla's commitment to a historical utopia. It even differs from Enderby's half-laughing suggestion that Smiley resembles Captain Ahab seeking the white whale without concern for the entire ship, maybe Holmes and Moriarty on the ledge at Reichenbach Falls, Enderby's other comparison comes closer to the truth. Whatever the correct analogy, Smiley's final chase of Karla remains an obsession, neither moderate nor caring, but narrow, complex, and consuming. His "determination" alone gave sense to his moral life, and Smiley bitterly resents the change in himself.

In the final case what so disconcerted Smiley was his aloneness and moral nakedness. Every institution had betrayed him, and all his loyalties had been shattered. He was left with himself. He was terrified of himself and stricken that "faithless, I am pursuing another man's convictions." Smiley realizes the only "restraints upon him were those of his own reason, and his own humanity." He refuses Ann's call for reconciliation, takes leave of Lacon and the Circus, and strips his life down to its bare essentials. He pursues the case knowing that he is only "responsible to himself" and his "private faith."[74]

Yet Smiley, like all individuals of integrity, had always been ultimately alone with his "reason," "humanity," and "doubts"—that remains a secret he hid even from himself. The capacity for self-reflective judgment and self-disciplined action on those judgments remained his moral core. That part of himself that seemed a "spectator to the rest" had always mercilessly questioned, balanced, and directed his motives and loyalties, just as he had handed on this capacity for "secret questioning" and a "heretical heart" to protégés like Ned.[75] His self-consciousness made him a moral agent, not someone subsumed by a role or vision. His loyalties found their reality in institutions and the fabric of a life. But the institutions served as trustees for his faith, a faith and care that humanized the institutions and made him a craftsman, not a bureaucratic clone. He entered the service because it seemed the best way to give "service" and pay moral debts. In the end, he acts to pay debts to an old friend, the old service, and his old marriage and atone for the "tortures, killings and endless ring of corruption" traceable to Karla.[76]

His quality of deliberation and decision ultimately differentiate him from Karla. He knew that his "enemies" were humans and that the death or betrayal of another human could never be ultimately justified by any moral purpose. Individuals of integrity must always accept responsibility for the pain they cause, minimize it in action, and know remorse for actions. In *Smiley's People*, he, like Alec Leamas, longs for death, but he remains intact and carries on. He can barely love, but he can infinitely grieve.

For all his aloneness, however, Smiley also leaves a legacy. He leaves a legend, an ideal for others to follow. He protects and nurtures people like Ned and saves them from destruction by Haydon. He supports and mentors young agents in the Circus. In *The Secret Pilgrim*, we learn that he contributes to its future leadership cadre by recruiting the brilliant, energetic, and restless Leonard Burr from All Souls College. In the Circus Burr becomes "Smiley's Crown Prince" and heads a division of the service after Smiley leaves. Finally, Smiley returns to teach. The entire structure of this last novel in which Smiley appears is built around Smiley's lecture to a class of trainees taught by Ned. Each of Smiley's comments inspires Ned to reveries upon the dilemmas of a career. The legacy itself continues even within the flawed world of the service. Burr is willing to take chances and picks Ned to break a hard and dangerous case outside of normal channels. He does so because "you're done some good things in your time. You've a heart too which is more than I can say for some of the capons in this outfit."[77]

No one escapes the moral attrition of war and espionage. With the end of the Cold War, it seemed possible that the moral landscape of Le Carré's world would disappear—it will not. At the very end of *The Secret Pilgrim*, Smiley's friend, student, and protégé Ned sets out to do one last favor for the service before he retires. He meets with Sir Anthony Bradshaw, a knighted arms dealer and entrepreneur, whose fortune was launched by Percy Alleline when Bradshaw provided illegal arms to clients the British were secretly supporting. Bradshaw has turned rogue. He uses the status and skills the service gained for him to make another fortune running arms to stoke ethnic civil wars. Ned asks him in the name of his country and conscience to cease from such action. Bradshaw asks if Ned is "appealing to my *conscience*?" His response to Ned is succinct: "*I don't give a fart*. . . . If I don't sell 'em the goods, some *other* charlie will." Bradshaw points out the savage power and moral immunity of drug cartels as well as the tobacco companies who do "creative selling" to foist cancer on children. He laughs at Ned's weak appeal to a conscience.

He points out that he is "rather proud" of being British, but it has nothing to do with his interests. "When people get in one's way, I break 'em. Or they break me." Echoing Fiedler's historical utilitarianism he states, "I'm Pharaoh, right. If a few thousand slaves have to die so I can build my pyramid, nature." The Bradshaws of the world suggest a new "wrecking infant" in the "real world" that Ned hardly knows anymore. He had spent his life fighting "an institutionalized evil" with a place and purpose. This new world suggests that evil resides "not in the system but the man." The cold war is over, but the need for defense, police, and espionage are not. As Smiley observed "spying is eternal" (330–31, 174).

Ethnic wars, regional rivalries, disintegrating countries and empires, transnational corporations competing for world dominance, international drug cartels—all inhabit a new/old world in which the safety and security of citizens will still need to be guarded and policed. Older loyalties and allegiances have been dissolved by new lures of identity and interests. The hard and morally dangerous work of using means that conflict with the ends of liberal democracy will remain. For this work Smiley's conserving humanism represents a strong character model. The dangers of the excessive egoism of Haydon and Alleline, the absolutism of Karla and Haydon, or the cynical or satisfied careerism of Enderby or Lacon— all threaten the success of the undertaking and the person's humanity. This type of character suggests the goals for institutional culture, training, and modeling that must complement the necessary structures of command and oversight.

The ambiguity of Le Carré's stories, however, gives us cold comfort. Smiley endures, but for his humanity's sake he can no longer commit to the institutions he formally served. Once he discovers a mole at the core of the service. Twice he is purged from the service he saved. Once he risks a trusting friend to recover the credibility of the service, only to have his gains sold out to the Americans. In *Smiley's People* he rescues the honor of the service by ignoring his leaders and violating the laws of a reforming government. Time and again the absolutists or self-interested careerists carry the day. And yet, he leaves a legacy: not just Smiley's people, but his legatees like the insightful and energetic Leonard Burr or the humane and effective Ned. Smiley himself returns to teach, and in his last appearance he reminds the new generation that "it is really essential in a free society that the people who do our work should remain unreconciled. . . . All I'm really saying, I suppose, is that if the temptation to humanity does assail you now and then, I hope you won't take it as a weakness in yourselves, but give it a fair hearing" (246–47).

When a moral exception becomes a way of life, we must search for characters who can live in the world without betraying the humanity that justifies us. Laws and institutional design will get us so far. In the end, however, only the complex integrity of real human beings will sustain the tensions at the core of the defense of democracy. But even the best will not escape untainted.

5

Staying In

The Ethics of Commitment in Office

> You can't fall on your sword every time you disagree with a policy.
>
> General Colin Powell, *My American Journey*

I CAN DO MORE GOOD by staying in than by getting out" has been a
classic justification for public officials to resolve crises of conscience.
Individuals of integrity enter public service in order to make a difference.
Successful public officials know how to influence policy. They take right-
ful pride in their ability to function in the complex mazes of public institutions. When they face moral dilemmas and problems, their first instinct
is usually to continue in the institutions and try to work through the
issues. A number of ethical and empirical assumptions need to be vali-
dated to justify this course. Experience, however, suggests that these very
assumptions are often undermined by the act of dissent. What begins as
a strong ethical justification for continued participation in government
can end as a rationalization for staying in power.

Political biographies and memoirs, the revelations of whistle-blowers,
and the apologias of Watergate and Vietnam War participants chronicle
numerous episodes in the lives of people who came to an awareness of
their moral responsibility in unacceptable policies or abuses of power.
This awareness galvanized their integrity, and they became dissenters.
However, once people become dissenters, they hold a minority position
from other policy makers who are at least publicly committed to the problematic actions. Bureaucratic interests and momentum, group-conformity
pressures, genuine commitments to the policy, and complex webs of personal loyalty lead people to defend the policy or abuse of power both in
government discussions and in public defenses or cover-ups.[1] The entire
language of justification and "tacit knowledge" of the decision-making

world supports commitment to the policies. Lawrence O'Brien provided one of the clearest statements of this case when he defended his decision to remain in President Lyndon Johnson's cabinet rather than join Senator Robert Kennedy's antiwar candidacy. Although opposed to the Vietnam War, O'Brien confided to Robert McNamara: "I still hope it can be changed by pressures from within the administration." Later, speaking directly to Robert Kennedy, he argued:

> You know I share your concern, but I can't ignore the political realities. The only hope I see is that the men around the President can ultimately change his policy, that he has to be impressed by the opposition not only from you, Bob, but from people who have worked with him and have been loyal to him. . . . If the President doesn't change his policy, I, too, will face a hard decision down the road, but until then, I will remain loyal to him.[2]

O'Brien's statement illustrates the moral and empirical assumptions that underlie these defining moments for integrity. Here I examine these assumptions to clarify the strengths and the weaknesses of this commonplace justification. Too often the argument can become a moral rationalization, because the very process of "staying in" after a disagreement has emerged and fighting for change can undermine the assumptions that make staying in and doing good a valid moral claim. To raise one's "voice" and accomplish good presumes both that people keep their commitments intact and that they remain effective.[3] The dissenters must present their position to relevant policy makers. They must change the opinions of leaders and either change the policy or end the wrongdoing. If the policy cannot be changed, individuals can at least hope to mitigate the consequences. As Thomas More reminded Raphael Hythloday in *Utopia*, "What you cannot turn to good you must make as little bad as you can."[4] Paradoxically, however, the process of moral dissent often undermines personal commitments or effectiveness. This means that individuals will often not be able to influence things to the good and may end up becoming more deeply implicated in actions they abhor.

The Moral Basis for Dissenting

Public officials do not operate in a moral vacuum. Their public integrity is connected to the domain of obligations of office. The obligations in office comprise a set of commitments that delineate democratic respon-

sibility. These are the moral promises expected from citizens who participate in politics, and these promises anchor the integrity of public officials:
the obligation to honest and accurate accountability within the structures
and values of the constitutional regime; a fidelity to the warrants of office
and law as well as to democratic decision making and constitutional values; respect for individuals, due process guarantees, and equality of citizens before the law; a concern for the safety and legitimacy of the political
order and the integrity of law; and a commitment to competent and efficient performance.

These commitments generate an activist imperative that motivates
individuals to use prudence to achieve concrete results flowing from one's
obligations. For example, people do not simply desire world peace; they
seek to end a particular conflict or to minimize bloodshed in a specific
country. What Thomas More called "the duty of all good men" leads individuals in politics to seek influence, to want effectiveness, and to make
a difference. In doing this they balance their obligations in office and prudence with the quest for policies that are reasonably congruent with their
personal convictions.

If public officials possess no sincere loyalty to democratic values, then
few moral dilemmas will arise for them. If they ambitiously seek only self-
aggrandizement, then no clear concerns for the rights of others or constitutional integrity will set boundaries to their deliberations. Likewise, if
they possess consuming loyalty to a person or an ideology that admits
of no compromise, then they will acknowledge no limits set by democratic rules of the game, due process, or accountability since the leader's
success or the dogma of the ideology override all other ethical considerations.[5] For such people there will be no crises of conscience in politics,
only narrow, self-interested calculations of power or clear-cut imperatives
for action justified by infallible leaders or revealed ideologies. For such
people there are no dilemmas, only tactics.

An informed conscience in politics, however, poses its own problems.
As Hamlet reminds us, an overly scrupulous conscience can "make cow-
ards of us all."[6] Nor is Hamlet's paralysis the only problem. Individuals
who are too scrupulous can lose all effectiveness or threaten the daily
operations of government. Political leaders obsessively complain that dis-
sent-inspired leaks and bureaucratic resistance unravel policy formation
and disrupt policy implementation.[7] Government institutions require personnel who are willing to implement policies with which they might
disagree, especially when the policies are legitimated by democratic

deliberation and when possibilities of debate and change exist within the institution. Public servants must, over time, be willing and able to adapt to the changing mandates of democratic politics and to serve in good faith. Without such basic loyalty and personal compromises, enduring and professional public service would be impossible.[8]

Realistic personal compromise not only undergirds the effectiveness of public organizations but is a central moral tenet of the democratic political process. In a world in which there are no final victories, different individuals or groups have diverse self-interests and varying power; furthermore, they have various conceptions of the common good. To avoid resorting to killing or coercing their opponents, people must respect others' power and goals and must constantly persuade, bargain, and build coalitions.[9] Constitutional restraints and democratic politics guarantee that personal ideals and commitments will inevitably face attrition. No policy will ever be perfect; no implementation will be flawless. A merciless strain on personal integrity is built into the practice of politics as people enter into preexisting universes of power and commitment where others stand ready to oppose or aid one's own efforts. To paraphrase Justice Brandeis, the real issue is what concession to make and when.

The daily balancing among personal commitments and capacities, obligations of office and prudence rarely poses profound moral dilemmas. In the cases examined here, the individual has arrived at that rare moment that Karl Jaspers would call a "limit situation." Here a person has uncovered or is participating in policies that fall into any of the following four categories, each of which strains or transgresses the bounds of acceptable ethical compromise in government: (1) criminal conduct such as murder, theft, acceptance of bribes, or venality or negligence in procurement of equipment upon which security and lives will depend; (2) actions that undermine democratic accountability of the system of government such as illegal campaign contributions, electoral bribery or fakery, use of government agencies or paragovernmental groups to intimidate or hurt political opponents or suppression of information necessary to make informed choices about vital policy choices when the suppression has no plausible national security justification;[10] (3) actions that violate the civil liberties of individual citizens or undermine the governmental rules that make democratic decisions possible and accountable;[11] and (4) actions that violate one's central moral convictions or standards of justice and that have no clear moral justification or excuse.

Finally, just as there are no dilemmas when individuals possess no liberal and democratic convictions, the dilemmas are quite different if people do not live in a democratic republic or a political order with some means of nonviolent accountability. The following discussion assumes that the country possesses both a free press and a multiparty system or its equivalent, that it honors democratic and liberal principles, and that citizens expect decisions to be democratically accountable and seek popular review of decisions. If none of the above conditions exist, then the moral responsibilities and options of a public official are quite different. In a tyrannical or totalitarian state dissent outside the government may be extraordinarily dangerous or impossible, and therefore the threshold of staying in the "only game in town" will be much higher. Likewise, in a world in which dissent, even inside the government, might result in severe threats to one's life or to the lives of friends and relatives, the obligations to dissent may be severely limited.

The Integrity Assumptions

To make a difference in the moral consequences of a policy in an environment in which most policy makers and superiors are committed to the wrong actions, individuals must make some strong ethical assumptions about themselves. Public officials fighting internally against policy or wrongdoing must believe that they possess the moral commitments and capacities as well as the integrity to endure and fight for their position. They might have to carry the battle alone as did Bill Moyers, the last "dove" among Lyndon Johnson's closest advisors during the Vietnam War. Or they might try to either create a network of dissent among less-courageous or less-visible colleagues or become a conduit for dissent percolating from lower ranks, a role Moyers also took on when he opposed both the bombing and escalation in Vietnam.[12]

The strength to stay presupposes personal moral integrity and strength, yet individuals can be broken for their opposition. When Lyndon Johnson's Vice President Hubert Humphrey openly fought against the escalation in Vietnam, he was peremptorily frozen out of decision-making circles; despite lingering doubts, he later became both a public and a private defender of the escalation and bombing.[13] The pressures for "team play," the concern for promotion and access, the webs of loyalty—all pull against open, consistent dissent; yet if individuals change beliefs or cave in, the whole rationale for staying in breaks down.

A more subtle danger to strong commitments based on integrity is posed by self-deception. Confronted with qualms of conscience and the cognitive dissonance that arises when they must act in ways inconsistent with their private beliefs, individuals will be tempted to "persistently avoid spelling out some feature of his engagement with the world," even when it would be "normally appropriate."[14] The psychological stress associated with making and following up on commitments causes even more personal distress.[15]

As in many temptations of power, calculated or unconscious self-deception can resolve the cumulative stress and qualms of conscience. Individuals might subtly change moral beliefs to justify what was once illicit; they might change their evaluation of the actions and intentions of others to make the world seem more morally consistent; they might simply discover or ignore certain aspects of reality that enable them to "rectify" past mistakes of information evaluation. Once having embarked upon a morally problematic course, people are tempted either to live with the pangs of conscience or to transform either their perceptions of reality or their moral beliefs to reduce the stress. Self-deception then represents "a policy not to spell out certain activities in which the agent is involved. . . . Once such a policy has been adopted there is even more reason to continue it, so that a process of self-deception has been initiated. Our overall posture of sincerity demands that we make this particular policy consistent with the whole range of our engagements."[16] Although most people strive for a consistent self-image and are vulnerable to self-deception, those most concerned with integrity are the most vulnerable: "The less integrity, the less there is motive to enter into self-deception. The greater the integrity of the person and the more powerful the contrary inclination, the greater the temptation to self-deception."[17]

Self-deception in this context means that individuals convince themselves that they are doing good and making a difference when in truth they are only enjoying power and contributing to the wrongdoing, wrong policy, or cover-up. John Dean's easy assurance to himself that as the president's lawyer he was acting to "protect the president" enabled him to calmly help initiate and further the Watergate cover-up and "contain" damage for months. He had ignored, slighted, and bent the law until he impulsively mentioned the "obstruction of justice" to H. R. Haldeman. Shocked by his own words, he retired to his office and pulled out his dusty law books. After a "sweaty tour through the obstruction of justice laws," he saw it in "black and white. We were criminals. We had skated this far on the president's power. How had I doubted it?" Two months later while destroying the "Hermes" notebooks that contained lists of Howard Hunt's illegal operatives, the last of his self-deception was stripped away: "Destroying the notebooks was only a small addition to a whole string of criminal acts I had committed, but it seemed to me to be a moment of high symbolism. This direct, concrete and sweaty act had also shredded the last of my feeble rationalizations that I was an agent rather than a participant—a lawyer defending guilty clients, rather than a conspirator."[18]

To hold strong moral convictions and act upon them, to resist the pressure to cave in, and to avoid self-deception are all morally necessary to justify staying in. But one more important condition must be met: a participant must not contribute more significant harm than possible good. Many participants possess influence because of their special competence in policy areas, and this condition poses special problems since they are often directly involved in executing the abhorred policy. Albert Speer, Adolf Hitler's minister of armaments, helped prolong the conduct of World War II for almost two years through his own organizational skill and drive; he vainly argued that this was to some extent offset by his ability to prevent Hitler's scorched-earth policy at the end of World War II or his attempts to save European Jews from extermination camps by placing them in forced labor camps.[19] This condition clearly involves subjective judgment, but to keep their moral commitments and capacities intact, individuals involved need to make honest and accurate assessments and be free of self-deception. They must also avoid the temptation of the "suffering servants" who, like Dostoevsky's Grand Inquisitor, know they are guilty of more harm than good but embrace a secret martyrdom. They believe they are doing all they can and that their own intense pain both offsets the harm and expiates their guilt. Lyndon Johnson, as tormented as Lady Macbeth, haunted the situation rooms of Vietnam War late at night, internalizing and justifying the suffering inflicted even as he strengthened his own resolve to go on.[20]

The Paradox of Access

Assuming an individual protects their moral commitments and capacities and avoids moral collapse, self-deception, and complicity in greater evil, the rest of the justification for staying in hinges upon prudence and effectiveness. People must make a difference inside the government by influencing the opinions, decisions, and actions of relevant policy makers. Effectiveness has special moral import because people who stay in to fight deliberately eschew other routes such as resigning, leaks, and working with the press or outside political opponents.[21] People staying in should be able to accomplish more inside than they could outside by using other means to actively change the policy. Such personal effectiveness is in direct proportion to access. Access may consist of one of two things: the opportunity to make decisions that affect policy, or the ability to persuade relevant policy makers of a course of action with a reasonable chance that one's opinions will make a difference. If individuals have no power to act or speak and are ignored, then all their good intentions and tortured integrity will accomplish little good and probably abet harm.

People maintain access with leaders and decision groups through unique amalgams of proven competence, loyalty, and trustworthiness. They must also keep access amid the constant competition from other talented people scrambling for influence and power in a world of limited time and entree. George Reedy captures this world in his portrayal of the White House: "For White House assistants there is only one fixed goal in life. It is somehow to gain and maintain access to the President. . . . There are few fixed rules and playing consists in laying down alternating counters in patterns that permit flexibility but seek to deny flexibility to the opponent."[22]

Individuals inside institutions are heeded because others believe that they are not only competent but also loyal to the leader or the group and sympathetic to their values and goals. Individuals of exceptional competence or those who represent a needed power base might gain initial access to power without proven trustworthiness. As Richard Nixon warily remarked about Henry Kissinger early in his administration, "I don't trust Henry, but I can use him." From that inauspicious entry, Kissinger earned Nixon's respect and trust by proving his own loyalty and shared commitment and by discrediting other major competitors.[23] Many other powerful individuals have not been so fortunate. President Nixon's Secretary of State William Rogers was effectively excluded from foreign policy making, and Vice President Lyndon Johnson was almost completely exiled from influence in the Kennedy administration in spite of his proven skills, needed power base, and official position; neither of these officials could cross the intangible line of trust and access.[24]

The dangerous paradox is that the process of moral dissent undermines the access of people and destroys the effectiveness upon which the whole justification depends. Too often the competition for power and access places a premium upon personal loyalty. Leaders need individuals whom they can trust, not only for their competence, but for their concern for the leader's own well-being and plans in a world in which betrayal is not uncommon. Additionally, executives and appointees become part of an administration and owe most of their power and position to the principal who appointed them. This creates a special set of obligations to further the administration's and principal's goals and protect that principal's position.

Political advancement often depends upon finding patrons and proving loyalty and soundness to them. The patrons in turn would recommend a "sound" person for further advancement. Individuals who seek access must constantly prove their competence and loyalty to leaders or groups and are constantly pressured to conform or acquiesce to the needs and will of patrons, leaders, and groups. The group nature of many decisions aggravates this tendency to conformity. Groups often impose initiation costs upon individuals to prove their own commitment to the goals of the group. Most groups possess informal rules that encourage a strong group consensus and limit comments or actions that might threaten or affront other group members. Almost any administration over time freezes out individuals who do not "go along" or "fit in." Even the Kennedy administration, supposedly noted for its openness, excluded Chester Bowles and Adlai Stevenson from significant foreign policy making, despite their experience, position, and power bases, because they were considered too "soft."

These pressures discourage overt dissent in government. The complex webs of access can distort dissent into perceived disloyalty or weakness, which can disqualify one from power. When the stakes are high and moral ambiguity surrounds a policy, overt emotional coercion and threats of ostracism mute most effective dissent. Individuals fall into what James Thomson describes as "the effectiveness trap:" "The inclination to remain silent or to acquiesce in the presence of great men—to live to fight another day, to give on this issue so that you can be effective on later issues—is overwhelming."[25]

To bring up touchy questions of conscience that might prick others' consciences could easily lead to quick banishment or gradual easing out—a process hastened by ambitious people who will use another's expressed moral qualms as stepping-stones for their own advancement into inner circles. To retain access, people tend to keep quiet. As General Earle

Wheeler reminded a recalcitrant aide before one of President Johnson's policy lunches, "You just don't go in there and piss in the President's soup."[26]

Individuals can rarely do good by staying quiet in the face of wrong, but conscious moral dissent over time can undercut access and influence. Robert McNamara, Secretary of Defense in the Johnson administration, increasingly began to question the Vietnam War. He did so first in private with the president and with friends, but later in meetings in which he questioned new escalations of the war and argued for pauses in the bombing to try to spark negotiations. Although Lyndon Johnson could and did bully and dominate most people, he had developed an abiding affection and respect for McNamara and trusted what McNamara called his "candid loyalty." Besides, Johnson himself remained deeply troubled by the war and its intractable continuation, so he permitted individuals like McNamara and George Ball to provide honest dissent. Yet over a course of three years, McNamara grew increasingly disillusioned and found himself fighting a rear-guard action against each new escalation of the war. His greatest victories consisted in limiting the size of escalations and the range of new targets, but he was unable to move the administration towards serious negotiations. By May 1967 he found himself increasingly at odds with most other senior advisors and with the Joint Chiefs of Staff. This isolation finally lead to his loss of influence and access until Johnson appointed him head of the World Bank. McNamara himself was not quite sure "whether I quit or was fired."[27] Similarly, Attorney General John Mitchell slowly lost access as Richard Nixon's oldest and most trusted advisor when he balked at the stream of aggressive and illegal suggestions emanating from the White House staff. The more Mitchell ignored or curbed the excessive zeal of the White House staff, the more H. R. Haldeman and John Ehrlichman alienated him from the president and excluded him from the reelection campaign and domestic policy.[28]

The slow or direct loss of access does not befall all dissenters. Some may dissent on one policy, yet remain effective in other policy areas that they value highly. George Ball, Undersecretary of State in the Johnson administration, became a major dissenter on Vietnam but stayed in the government because his focus of responsibility remained Europe.[29] Similarly McNamara believed that his actions in many other areas justified his staying in, even suggesting that the pull of many other responsibilities often made it hard for him or the administration to give the focus needed to Vietnam.[30] The weight of other responsibilities, especially in other areas, can carry great moral weight.

On the other hand, people may keep access but lose effectiveness on the important issues, or, more insidiously, they may incur additional moral burdens as the cost of keeping access while they ineffectually dissent. These patterns of access vary but result in institutionalizing dissent so that it becomes ineffective. In one variation, an individual becomes a "dissent specialist" who is allowed to question a specific set of concerns. Sometimes such individuals may succeed, yet usually they fail to make a difference; but more important, they are not allowed to stray beyond the one area of allowable dissent. William Safire recounts how dissent specialization worked:

> Certain members of the Nixon group, their loyalty proved over the years, were indulged as iconoclasts, encouraged to have their own non-group set of assumptions in certain areas, and were expected to present their objections at meetings so that the devil would not be denied an advocate . . . but the self-censorship did take place in areas outside of one's iconoclastic "specialties"; when I volunteered a suggestion in a Vietnam speech that no more draftees be sent to fight, I was promptly taken off the speech entirely, and was less inclined to do that again.[31]

In a second, more common variation, people become tagged and even accepted as the "house moralist" or "conscience" of the leaders. James Thomson describes the process as "the domestication of dissenters." The dissenters feel as if they have discharged their conscience-bound duty, and the other decision makers can congratulate themselves on being open-minded and fair by having listened to all sides. Bill Moyers, one of the last Vietnam dissenters in President Johnson's intimate circle of advisors, may have suffered such a fate. While he actively worked to cultivate a network of informed dissent, he became increasingly frustrated at his inability to effectively change anyone's mind. Typically, Johnson would greet him with "Here comes Mr. Stop the Bombing." Other policy makers had their "favorite dove" whose ineffectual dissent assuaged their mutual consciences but accomplished little, and they enabled the dissenter to remain in government.[32] Such dissent, as in Safire's example, is entirely predictable and nonthreatening, almost a form of role-playing. Other policy makers can prepare for it and discount it.

In face of these dynamics, one way to regain leverage is to maintain an "exit option" and be ready to resign or threaten to resign. Individuals who forswear the exit option fatally wound their effectiveness.[33] When individuals are already marginalized on an issue, one of their only remaining sources of leverage in discussions is the implicit threat that they will resign and "go public." If exit is ruled out, there is even less reason to take the dissenter seriously. Individuals might also decide that even if they cannot influence the policy, at least they can act like Deep Throat during Watergate and leak critical items of information to outside parties. Assuming the individuals can avoid taking a central role in the illicit activity, this option has considerable merit as long as individuals can maintain access to the information and leak effectively without getting caught. Unfortunately, such critical leaks usually inspire intensive counterintelligence action within the government and aggravate all of the dangers associated with secrecy fetishes. Finally, the access of leakers is extraordinarily tenuous. Once suspected of leaking, an individual can lose all access and can even become a conduit of "disinformation" to the outside in addition to facing all the difficulties of trying to keep access when suspected of disloyalty.[34]

In the most insidious variation, individuals suffer the terrible irony of increasing contributions to the very policy they oppose. Few policy makers must pay the price of the sixteenth-century Florentine Francesco Guicciardini, who executed his friends and allies and publicly defended a tyrant he hated. With this he "proved" his renewed loyalty after he had vacillated in his support of the Medici rulers.[35] But for many the moral cost of dissenting access is high. Once people are suspected of lukewarm loyalty and moral qualms over a policy, they are asked to continuously prove their loyalty in order to keep access. After John Dean had helped stop Charles Colson's plan to firebomb the Brookings Institute, he was passed over for the job of running the "plumbers unit." Informed that he had "some little old lady in you," Dean became an ardent exponent of "toughness" and using the government apparatus to harass political opponents.[36]

During the Vietnam War a number of officials who opposed aspects of the war chose to abide by the standard political rule best articulated by Lyndon Johnson describing his relationship with President Kennedy: "I did not always agree with everything that happened in his administration. But when I did disagree with the President, I did so in private, and man to man."[37] Secretary of Defense Robert McNamara reserved his doubts about the war for private meetings or memos to the president or a few close advisors. Yet in loyalty to the president and his policy, McNamara felt impelled to work doubly hard to destroy internal government opponents of the war. In policy meetings he devastated dissenting officials, especially attacking George Ball's powerful memos. Sometimes he used questionable statistics, and at other times he pressed dissenters for lacking any viable alternative to losing Vietnam with all its perceived consequences. At the same time, he privately encouraged them to keep up the bureaucratic fight against the war. He personally helped dismember all effective bureaucratic opposition to the war in order to prove his loyalty to Johnson and save his private channels.[38] Vice President Humphrey after his return to the fold again had qualms about the war but mentioned them only in private to President Johnson. Within the government and in public, he even more avidly defended the war that he increasingly opposed in private.[39]

Some dissenters pursue vigorous internal dissent rather than confine their disagreement to private chats. George Ball, like Bill Moyers, actively tried to change Vietnam policy within government circles. To maintain his access, even with his thwarted dissent, Ball was called upon to become a major public spokesman for the policy he opposed. At one point he was dispatched to Europe as the major public defender of American policy to skeptical allies.[40]

Whether the chosen route of dissent is private conversations or inner governmental battle, either tactic requires protective actions to maintain access. These almost inevitably demand deeper complicity in the very policy or crime one opposes. The complicity is greater for many such as McNamara who possess access because of their high competence. The more skilled they are, the more disproportionately they contribute to the questionable policies.

The Attrition of Integrity

The problems of access and effectiveness ensure that many attempts to do good by staying in will end in loss of effectiveness or increasing complicity in morally problematic actions. Sustained dissenting participation faces inexorable pressures towards self-deception. The cumulative strain of violating their basic convictions and their self-image tempts people to change their perception of reality or their values. Both John Dean and Jeb Magruder recount such experiences in their ambitious climbs to power in the Nixon administration.[41] Similarly, even as President Lyndon Johnson

remained tortured by the costs of the Vietnam War and doubtful of its outcomes, he gradually hardened his commitments even in face of his deep
doubts. As he was increasingly attacked by opponents of the war, he hardened his beliefs and his response to opponents.[42]

The lure of self-deception is increased by the policy language trap and
the erosion of independent moral and social contacts. To persuade others,
individuals must use the language and categories that their opponents
will understand and accept as valid. Bureaucratic momentum reinforces
the reliance on commonly shared notions and language and often formalizes rote justifications. When Thomas More chides Raphael Hythloday in *Utopia* about not participating in government, Hythloday responds
that no politicians would listen to his utopian harangues: "Deaf indeed,
without doubt . . . neither . . . do I think that such ideas should be thrust
on people, or such advice given, as you are positive will never be listened
to. What good could such novel ideas do, or how could they enter the
minds of individuals who are already taken up and possessed by the
opposite convictions?"[43]

But once individuals have accepted the bureaucratic definition of the
terms of the debate, it becomes almost impossible to significantly change
a policy while using the very rationales developed specifically to defend
that particular policy. Robert McNamara points out that all the major decision makers accepted the credo that once committed to Vietnam, the
United States had to stay. They believed that American credibility to
maintain containment in other parts of the world depended upon it and
that if the United States left Vietnam, the rest of Southeast Asia would fall
under Chinese Communist hegemony. This meant that, even as they saw
the South Vietnam as lacking the institutional and political capacity to
defend itself, they felt increasingly trapped by the rhetorical claims, with
no way out of the quagmire.[44] McNamara's own data had created the
bureaucratic justifications for the escalation and bombing in Vietnam and
had discredited the CIA and other reporting that contradicted his own
estimates of the effectiveness of the war. The Pentagon Papers reveal his
intense problems when he tried to change the course of the war in 1967.
Forced to use his own data, he also turned to the now-discredited CIA
analysis to buttress his case, as he hopelessly tried to demonstrate to a
skeptical Senate Armed Forces Committee that while the past bombing
had succeeded, the present bombing could do no good and that future
escalation would be counterproductive. Similarly, he opposed the Joint
Chiefs of Staff's requests for massive new escalation and for increasing

troop levels to 200,000 men. The Chiefs relied upon McNamara's own justifications: protecting American credibility, avoiding a domino effect in
Southeast Asia, and preventing Chinese Communist hegemony in the
region. Whipsawed by his own logic, McNamara's "victory" lay in keeping new troop commitments to only 50,000 and limiting the increased sor-
tie level to only 12,000—hard victories for a man now opposed to the
war.[45]

As the pressures on integrity mount, individuals find themselves isolated from friends and independent social support for their own dissenting convictions. Outside friends and contacts with possible opponents can
easily undermine access and trust in tense political situations. Like
McNamara many of Johnson's other officials had to circumscribe their
friendships. Their families were under pressure to homogenize their
social relations and relinquish any social or moral contact outside the
closed decision circles.[46] At the same time, many officials during Vietnam
found their own family lives disrupted as other family members grew
opposed to the war.[47] William Safire and Henry Kissinger both found
themselves mistrusted because of their connections with those Nixon
regarded as "liberal"; Safire lost access several times and had to curtail his
press contacts, while Kissinger found it necessary not only to limit some
contacts but also to constantly assert his own toughness to compensate
for his outsider friends.

The strains of cognitive dissonance and nagging conscience coupled
with the immersion in the bureaucratic language of justification and the
steady isolation from friends and outsiders pose a lethal combination for
public integrity. The end result is best summed up by Albert Speer's
acknowledgment of his own guilt in spite of marginal adjustments he
made to save lives: "I did not see any moral grounds outside the system
where I should have taken my stand."[48]

As is always the case, if the good do not govern, the zealots and the
avaricious will. The preservation of democratic and liberal institutions
requires capable and committed individuals who can act—and compromise—with integrity. Yet the moral eddies of politics can swamp the
strongest, and the murk of political twilight can confuse the best. When
public officials are confronted with actions that violate basic purposes or
norms or threaten the foundations of a liberal and democratic order, the
choice is simple—be quiet or act. Having chosen to act, people must
choose between staying in or getting out, and this choice becomes a defining moment of their integrity. Staying in often involves as much courage

as leaving, especially when individuals leave quietly. But to justify doing good by staying in requires a clear assessment of the moral and practical assumptions involved. Individuals can accomplish no enduring good unless they keep their integrity, avoid self-deception and complicity in greater evil, and, above all, maintain effectiveness. Yet such dissent is haunted by a paradox. Active dissent all too often undermines access, relentlessly reduces effectiveness, often requires greater complicity, and insidiously encourages self-deception. Doing good by staying in can become done in by staying good.

6

Getting Out

The Ethics of Resigning from Office

Damned if you do, damned if you don't.

Folk saying

GET OUT OR STAY IN? This choice marks a defining moment for a person in public life. Most decisions in office are woven into a fabric of habit, experience, and professional judgment. Difficulties may require "judgment calls," deliberation, and more time. But these too are expected and woven into the fabric of life and office. Only a few rare decisions threaten the fabric of integrity and unravel the texture of a life or an office. At these frayed edges of selfhood, at which people decide to stay or resign, is their integrity defined.

Staying in, as we have seen, is fraught with significant moral problems, but very little has been written about resignation despite its importance to moral life within an institution. Staying in is usually the norm; resigning remains the forgotten moral option because of the combined personal costs of leaving and the social pressures to stay.[1] The few analyses of resigning focus upon the high moral drama of resigning over principle.[2] The standard account argues that participating in actions or policy with which one morally disagrees requires resigning from office to protect personal integrity; it usually adds that people who resign should publicly oppose the policy. These high moral dramas, however, are not typical cases, and they are seldom helpful to people trying to decide whether to resign. For someone in such a quandary, the moral reasons bound with public integrity are more varied and often more prosaic because the moral landscape of participation involves more than principles.

This chapter presents a moral theory of resignation that accounts for the ethical complexity of life in office and can help guide individuals in their deliberations. Like the examination of staying in in the previous chapter, it relies upon case studies, biographies, and interviews. They reveal that the moral landscape of resignation is more complex and subtle than merely resigning over principle. Unlike the analyses that focus exclusively upon the rigid obligations to act from principle and either oppose or leave, my analysis builds upon the three domains of public integrity. Each leg of this tripod supports public integrity in office. Each domain builds on the assumption that the moral status of holding office can best be understood as a promise by an individual to live up to the obligations of office. This promise presumes three separate domains of integrity. Individuals possess the personal moral commitments and capacity to make and keep promises, the competence to live up to obligations of office, and the ability to act prudently and effectively in office. I will explore the range of reasons to stay or resign that can arise from each of the three domains of integrity. If an individual fails to meet any one of these standards, he or she has a strong moral reason to resign.

The Ethical Importance of Resigning

Resigning has a profound role in the moral life of a person. First, resignation supports integrity. Integrity matters because it enables people to claim life as their own and enables society to allocate responsibility on the assumption that individuals can in fact act with consistency and discipline on behalf of promises. Our integrity involves the capacity to take a reflective stance towards roles and actions and make sense of how they cohere. Through self-reflection individuals move across roles and actions and assesses their compatibility or consistency with each other and with an individual's reflective commitments. This reflective movement across roles, obligations, and actions spins the threads that stitch together selfhood and creates a wholeness, even a beauty, across the quilted fabric of a person's life. Personal integrity emerges when individuals sew the roles, obligations, and promises together into a life quilt that possesses durability, wholeness, and coherence.[3] Personal integrity also means that people can direct and revise actions on the basis of belief and commitment. People of integrity can keep promises and play by the rules because they have the self-discipline and character to overcome temptations, opposition, and problems.[4] They can seek greater compatibility by revising actions or roles to restore moral coherence. If all else fails and a role threatens the fabric of life, then people may sever the role and resign.

Second, resigning sustains moral responsibility. Individuals in public office possess responsibility for their actions, and resigning is a basic moral resource of responsible people. Although the level of personal responsibility may vary, individuals above the most ministerial levels possess some co-responsibility for institutional actions because they materially contribute their competence to the outcomes. Too often individuals respond to moral conflict by denying responsibility with excuses such as "following orders," "no choice," or "not my job." The existence of the option to leave office prevents them from escaping responsibility and exculpating themselves with such excuses.[5] Although most examples in this chapter refer to appointed and senior officials, the broader case applies to all officials, including those in the career services, especially as they enter senior management positions. The issues of maintaining personal moral capacity, competence, effectiveness, and access apply across the board. The option of resigning means that the theoretical linkage of personal responsibility and position is real.

The resignation option complicates the moral and psychological temptations to save integrity yet deny responsibility. The knowledge of this option means that a person cannot escape responsibility by pretending he or she had no choice. Participation becomes a matter of choice, not force or inertia. This matters because the social and psychological pressures of office push individuals to live by group norms. Everyday organizational life impels people to stay and blinds them to the resignation option. I want to make clear that I am referring to a robust notion of integrity and responsibility. This is not a call for hair-trigger resignations. In public life, no one gets all they want all the time. Most officials lose more battles than they win, and victories are almost always imperfect. So public officials find themselves compromising and contributing to imperfect outcomes. Moral effectiveness does not flow from innocence or scrupulosity, and a responsible public official cannot resign over every conflicted principle but has to learn to live with moral imperfection while keeping his or her moral compass and integrity intact.[6] As British Minister Aneurin Bevan said in his resignation speech, "No member ought to accept office in a government without a full consciousness that he ought not to resign it for frivolous reasons."[7]

Third, resignation can help ensure accountability to democratic institutions. As Albert Hirshman made clear in his classic study on "exit" and "voice" in organizations, exit from an institution can signal to the public the existence of a debate over deeper or more serious issues than had been exposed in public deliberations. A public resignation with "voice" adds information and credibility to dissent. Like any human action, however, resignation cuts both ways and can also harm accountability. If everyone opposed to a policy exits, the institution loses its capacity for internal reform. Exits of dissenters narrow the range of options within an inner circle, encourage groupthink, and undermine the internal trust and communication needed for honest policy discussion.[8]

The willingness to resign buttresses the moral and psychological core of integrity and responsibility. If people become so wedded to office that they will not resign under any circumstances, they risk violating their integrity, the norms of office, and effectiveness. A classic case demonstrates how facing resignation is crucial to keeping integrity. As Secretary of State for President Ronald Reagan, George Shultz fought the plans of the National Security Council and the CIA to trade weapons to Iran in exchange for the freeing of hostages. In November 1986 the administration's actions exploded in the press, and the Iran-Contra scandal was born. Officials such as National Security Advisor Admiral John Poindexter and director of the CIA William Casey pressed to continue the exchanges. Shultz believed the actions to be fundamentally wrong because they encouraged more hostage taking, undercut administration policy, and damaged President Reagan. He also feared the policy would curtail efforts to end the Cold War with Russia.

Shultz faced considerable pressure to resign from White House staff who viewed his opposition as disloyal. At this point, Shultz made a vital moral decision. In August 1986, he had submitted a letter of resignation to the president, but Reagan had refused the resignation and encouraged Shultz to stay.[9] In November 1986, when the story broke, Shultz told President Reagan that the president could accept his resignation at any point: "My credibility with the president could only be enhanced by his knowledge that I was the easiest guy in Washington for him to get rid of." Shultz began a very rough and public effort because "I had to stop completely any further arms-for-hostages deals. I know my job was on the line, but proud as I was to be Secretary of State and conscious as I was of possible achievements of great significance, *I knew I could not want the job too much*" (emphasis added).[10] The resignation in the drawer liberated Shultz's integrity to begin the arduous and ultimately successful struggle to change policy and not conform.

While extremely important morally, resignation remains only one moral resource for public officials facing moral conflict. For example, in October

1973 President Richard Nixon ordered Special Prosecutor Archibald Cox to cease his attempts to subpoena any more tapes from Nixon concerning the Watergate cover-up. President Nixon believed that this order would force Cox to resign. Cox did not. As he explained, "I don't think there was ever any thought in my mind or talk in the office about resigning—it was so obvious it wouldn't be the right thing to do. . . . You were rather expected to fight. . . . You had to go about doing what your job was. To resign would be to run away from it."[11] Nixon chose to fire Cox and ignited the firestorm that contributed to his downfall. Career public officials have additional obligations both to protect their institutions and to work with policies about which they have moral qualms as long as the actions are legal and accountable.[12] These officials may choose to stay in such circumstances for moral reasons and pursue a number of defensible strategies such as internal dissent, ameliorating the problems in implementation, waiting out the policy, or mobilizing external allies to oppose it. Resigning is an essential moral resource, not a panacea.

Holding Office

I believe the moral relationship between a person and an office is best seen as a promise to live up to the obligations of the office.[13] This promise joins the person's integrity and responsibility with the obligations of office. While the range of discretion varies for appointed, career, and elected officials, the moral structure of the promise and its base conditions remain the same. This promise requires key assumptions about the individual and his or her relationship to the position. For persons in office, the violation of these assumptions provides very strong reasons to resign.

The promises made in taking office are complex and cover two broad areas. The first covers the substantive promises presumed by all public officials—to obey the laws and respect due process. In addition, they promise good-faith performance of the skills and technical demands of office. These obviously apply to all executives—career, appointed, and elected—but also to legislators. The second range of promises involves the pledge to be accountable to principals. This becomes more complex in American politics because of the varied number of principals—those individuals to whom persons pledge to account for performance. At the clearest level members of an official's staff promise to competently promote the interests of the principal whom they directly serve within the law. The principals served are usually elected, appointed, or career executives.

These staff members will often serve at the pleasure of the principal in a hierarchical relation. They promise not just competence but also loyalty to the principal's interests and agenda.

At the next level, individuals may be appointed by principals, often executives, but also boards or other entities, to serve as heads of offices on behalf of the principal. Sometimes these appointments require approval of a legislature or an oversight body. In these cases the appointed officials have multiple obligations and promises. In addition to their legal and technical obligations, they also promise their principal to serve within the framework of the principal's policy agenda and protect the administration's legitimacy. They may also owe reporting and responsiveness to oversight bodies and consultation and respect to the stakeholders that cluster around their agency and are often necessary for its success and protection.

Career officials who become appointed officials in an administration take on these same complex promises. Nonpolitically appointed career officials have strong obligations to promote institutional integrity, competence, and legality. As they rise their own promises become more complex. They must attend to the directions of administration's policy, the demands of legislative oversight, and the opinions of groups clustered around their organization's policy and budget. As career officials rise in responsibility, the complexity of their promises resembles the complexity of appointed officials. All senior leaders whether appointed or career serve in an administration and for a principal with broader responsibilities. These officials have special obligations to protect and support their principal and administration as the mechanisms of democratic accountability in government and have strong implicit obligations to stay within the policy framework of the administration and not undermine their principal. Finally, any office involves responsibilities to build political capital, institutional competence, and legitimacy for their office.[14] The complicated nature of promises and patterns of accountability means individuals must weigh the relative importance of their obligations in making decisions and seldom have absolutely clear lines of accountability.

Regardless of its complexity, any promise has certain basic assumptions. First, a legitimate promise assumes that people possess the moral and personal commitments and capacities to make promises and perform the required tasks. This presumption of good-faith competence means persons should have the self-discipline, commitment, and professional or technical competence to do job. Second, they need the time, physical and emotional health, focus, and energy to carry out the daily demands. Finally, they should be independent and not beholden in such a way that they would sacrifice the integrity of the office for their relations to others. These personal commitments and capacities of self exist prior to taking the job and are often the very reasons one is given a job. To the extent a position involves significant pressures, complexity, or discretion, the personal qualities of an individual will significantly influence performance in office.

Second, the promise presumes that the individuals agree to live up to the obligations of office. These are defined by the web of expectations created by rules, law, and process. These laws define the purpose and often specify the technical and policy directions of the job. The political processes and environment shape accountability and interactions with the public, superiors, and subordinates. Additionally, an office lies at the center of a web of reliance in which other people and institutions rely upon the correct and consistent performance of tasks.

Third, holding office demands that people be politically effective in performance. This seems a truism; yet more than one public official has entered office with commitment, skill, energy, and technical competence, has taken his or her promises and legal obligations seriously, and has succeeded in the technical and routine matters, but in the end has failed. Such officials fail because they do not pay attention to political prudence and master the political dimensions of the office that elude legal, technical, or organizational description. These prudential dimensions involve the capacity to marshal the political resources and power to influence the political environment and the principals and to protect the organization.[15]

Integrity-Based Reasons to Resign

Personal moral commitments and capacity, obligations of office, and prudent effectiveness represent the three moral domains and reference points of the triad of public integrity. They determine the moral "fit" between an individual and an office. Individuals move among the three domains to find the right actions. When the three mesh and reinforce each other, a moral synergy exists that enables individuals to perform official responsibilities with commitment, competence, energy, and style. The web of reliance is fulfilled; the legal and authorizing demands are satisfied; the institutional and political dimensions support the office. Here I examine and illustrate the range of moral reasons to resign from each domain and demonstrate how this range extends far beyond the standard arguments from principled dissent.

Personal Commitment and Capacity

The ability to bring critical self-reflection, discipline, energy, focus, and insight to the job depends upon integrity. Personal capacities enable individuals to endure the routine, hassles, and the physical and emotional strains of office as well as provide the moral backstop for periods when legal or institutional directives may be vague or in conflict.[16] They are also the capacities that give strength to a person's ability to judge and act upon principles. When these basic capacities of integrity erode, it is time to resign.

Such erosion can occur in various ways. At the most prosaic level—usually ignored in moral discussions of office—the daily stresses of official life undercut personal physical or emotional health and endurance. When people exhaust their physical capacity given the required demands of office, then they have a moral reason to leave. This applies to all offices. When Representative Morris Udall resigned from the House after a distinguished thirty-year career, he cited the affects of cumulative illness that prevented him from meeting the "rigorous demands and duties" of his office.[17] When George C. Marshall resigned as Secretary of Defense in the Truman administration after an exemplary career of public service stretching over fifty years, he cited his "exhaustion" and inability to carry on the tasks of the office. He resisted President Truman's entreaties to return to office for the same reason. Marshall recognized the often overlooked but obvious point that people must possess the physical and emotional capacity to do moral justice to an office's responsibilities.[18]

At a different level, persons can lose their emotional commitment to the job. Emotional commitment provides the energy to carry the heavy burdens of office. Senator Sam Nunn of Georgia hinted at this when he decided in 1995 not to seek reelection to his safe seat by explaining, "I didn't want to stay beyond my capacity for enthusiasm."[19] When energy diminishes or burnout occurs, people "go through the motions." In an interview, a public official described her decision to resign this way: "Each night before work, I had nightmares. In early morning, my stomach churned. By the time I reached work, I felt hollowed out inside. I knew it was time to leave." The job may "get done" in a formal routine sense, but at deeper levels, performance decays. Little things do not get done. Extra time or effort is not expended to ensure that things are right. No new initiatives begin and moral issues are not pursued. When colleagues or superiors need to be persuaded by commitment and example, neither manifests itself. The quality of officeholder's performance goes down but, more insidiously, his or her low-quality, low-commitment actions undercut morale.

Confronting moral conflict in office can also result in diminished moral capacity. As we have discussed, officials who participate in making or implementing a policy with which they morally disagree may choose to stay in office despite their qualms. The disagreement might be a relatively minor moral concern, or they might believe that other policies to which they are morally committed outweigh the disagreement. Career officials possess strong independent moral obligations to stay and accede to legal changes in policy as they respond to democratic accountability and defend the competence of their office. They also have a wide array of responses to illegal or morally offensive orders. They can go to external allies to rally support; they can delay or subvert the policy in the implementing details; they can slow down implementation until a more sympathetic superior comes along. Yet such patterns of resistance if applied to legitimate and legal policy initiatives can pose significant problems for a democratically responsive government.[20] Individuals might also believe they can ameliorate the wrong, leak or whistle-blow, or work to create a counter-system and change in the policy.

These are reasonable and defensible approaches to moral dilemmas in positions. They can, however, threaten integrity and moral capacity. Individuals who experience two contradictory moral imperatives experience cognitive dissonance. This dissonance, as we have seen, pressures individuals to self-deception or tempts individuals to reinterpret reality to ignore moral problems. Yet it is one thing to be consciously persuaded to change because of argument and quite another to have one's position erode over time without self-conscious reflection.

Organizations aggravate this temptation by providing persons with excuses or rationalizations that permit them to "live with" the unacceptable state of affairs. Going along with a troubling action might be "customary practice" or something "everybody does." Being implicated in the wrong policy can be acceptable because "one person really can't make a difference."[21] As these rationalizations keep individuals in office, they find that they still participate but fail to change the policy and also lose influence. This dilemma demands resignation. It can end with a moment described by one official who resigned when he realized "I was becoming someone I despised."

For the justification of staying in under moral duress to make sense, persons should meet three conditions. First, they maintain their own beliefs intact under the stress of opposition, and any changes are reflective and self-conscious. Second, they are able to demonstrate some progress in making a difference in the policy or actions that they oppose or they are able to show moral success in other vital areas. Issues of principle or ethics seldom present themselves with such clarity as to be trip wires that demand resigning. Rather, the fight for principles involves difficult conflicts over time to make a meaningful difference in degree. The capacity to engage in moral conflict depends upon personal moral capacities as well as commitments.[22] Third, people maintain a reflective balance in which they keep alive the tension and remain alert to the wrong involved, even as they work both to change and to implement policy. In this case, they may have strong obligations to resist resigning, as Shultz and Cox did, in order to purse moral goals from their unique position of influence.

A final reason for resignation comes from outside the office. Individuals may experience turmoil or disgrace in their personal lives that could profoundly limit their ability to live up to the symbolic and ritual aspects of an office. It can also hurt their actual performance on the job and tarnish their principal or institution. Media coverage and political attack worsen this dynamic. This scenario would provide a strong ethical reason to resign.

Obligations of Office

Officials have an obligation to perform the functions of the office. These are warranted by law and process and can range from clear and exact technical operations to matters of broad discretion. Success in these involves the perceptions of those in the political environment who oversee and depend upon the office. In office, some actions will have a rationalized or routine dimension, while others will require more sophisticated judgments and discretion. In this world, officials must be able to prove to their relevant publics and principals that their actions satisfy the basic institutional requirements as well as sustain those who depend upon them for competent execution. For this reason many senior leaders spend immense effort managing the perceptions of their actions.[23]

Two broad classes of reasons to resign arise from the promise to live up to the obligations of office. In the first class, individuals fail in the routine or technical competencies required by the position. In the second, they confront demands to participate in actions that violate legal or professional norms or the basic moral conditions of the office. Persons have a number of options facing these problems since living in a world of moral incompleteness and insufficiency is one of the obligations of public officials. They also have obligations to respect the legitimate outcomes of democratic processes. This means that many of the decisions to resign will emerge from the intersection of different promises and from people's need to sort out their own priorities, especially in regard to their basic moral capacities and the legal requirements of the position.

Individuals can fail in the obligations of the office in any of several ways. First, an official might be the leader in a policy or program that fails to meet expected goals or loses its political support because of bad leadership. English parliamentary ministers associated with a failed policy or program often resign. Their resignations admit their responsibility but also protect colleagues, principals, and the administration by narrowing the responsibility to themselves.[24] In American democratic government, however, the lines of responsibility are far more diffuse. Public officials, whether elected, appointed, or career, face more complex accountability. Often they owe obligations to several principals as well as face scrutiny from oversight bodies and powerful stakeholders. Their institution may depend upon several sources of power and support, even if their line of reporting is to a direct superior. In this sense, officials may face plural and competitive lines of accountability. Without the clear lines of ideological and party accountability of a parliamentary system, policy or program failure does not always provide a clear warrant for resignation. Individual officials may hang on despite failure and even at great cost to their putative principal because of allies or links to other sources of accountability such as the legislature. Failure itself takes on a different dimension because plural sources of power create multiple perceptions of success or failure. They also make it possible for officials to recoup power or policy in ways that do not exist in a unitary parliamentary system.

Second, individuals might find that they do not possess the requisite competence. They may not have the basic skills to achieve the routine requirements of the position: schedules will not be met; technical execution is flawed; people who rely upon information or products find them too slow or unacceptable; internal procedures or accountability fall into disarray or unmanaged personnel conflicts disrupt performance. Their personal or agency actions may bring down a torrent of political or public attack that disrupts performance or spills over and tarnishes one's principal or one's administration. If these fall under official responsibility and the officials know they cannot perform the job to the expectations required, they should resign. In many positions, the shape and demands of the job change over time, and officials who might once have been able to do the job find that new required skills elude them and their performance erodes.

Finally, their principal or political supporters might change the direction of a policy that they have helped build. The official may be morally unwilling to dismantle what they believe to be a good system and to break faith with those who fought and worked for them. As one public official facing massive cutbacks in social services at her agency put it in resigning, "We don't want to sit in the control room and cut people off from social services." Rather than take responsibility to destroy what they value or build what they believe is wrong, they correctly resign.[25]

Personal disgrace or dishonor may undercut the credibility of the individuals to uphold the symbolic and legitimacy dimensions of the office. In 1967 press reports revealed that John Fedders, the very successful and respected chief enforcement officer for the Securities Exchange Commission, had beaten his wife during his marriage. In face of the media exposure, Fedders, who had done an impeccable job in office, chose—rightfully—to resign because the revelations of his private actions had destroyed his credibility as an enforcement officer.[26]

Personal disgrace becomes public disgrace if an individual violates the basic norms of his or her office and uses it for personal gain. For example, Representative Wayne Hays, a powerful and effective committee chairperson in the House of Representatives, hired his mistress, Elizabeth Ray, for a position on his staff for which she had no skills.[27] Facing a firestorm of protest when his actions were revealed, Hays resisted efforts to oust him; he finally resigned rather than face censure from the House Ethics Committee. In this case, his actions demonstrated his failure to live up to the moral and legal obligations of his office and brought dishonor upon himself and his institution. His disgrace justified resignation.

Individuals, especially appointees and senior executives, also possess obligations of loyalty to their administration. Often the terms of appointment involve informal but real understandings of the correct range of responsibility for the job and responsibilities to their principal who appoints or sponsors them. These might be as basic as doing a professional and competent job and not creating a fiasco to overseeing a major change of policy direction. Too often this pattern of linked personal and political loyalties is seen as a form of pathology at odds with the democratic administrative obligations that becomes a source of keeping people silent and undermining other obligations.[28] Although it can have these tendencies, these patterns of loyalty and obligation are central to the effective accountability of elected officials, and they are the main method by which legal and legitimate revisions of mission and implementation occur in the United States. Very often these webs of committed loyalty and shared visions are necessary to engage bureaucratic inertia or vested interests working to prevent legal change.

This means people often owe institutional and personal obligations to protect their principal's position since the principal supports not only their positions and policies but those of many others as well. Persons may be morally required to resign if they can no longer share their principal's vision, lose the trust and confidence of their principal, or fail to persuade the principal on issues about which they deeply disagree. This moment unites the basic concerns of integrity and responsibility when an official decides that although the policy may be carried on by others, he or she can no longer be personally responsible for its execution defense and execution. Duff Cooper served as First Lord of the Admiralty for Prime Minister Neville Chamberlain during the period leading up to World War II when Chamberlain tried to appease Hitler. Cooper worked hard to change Chamberlain's mind on appeasement, but he failed. After Chamberlain agreed to the German takeover of Czechoslovakia, Cooper realized he could not change policy and could no longer support actions he believed to be fundamentally wrong. One morning, while dressing, all his doubts crystallized, and he decided "I must resign." In his speech to Parliament, he laid out his reasons to leave, pledged his loyalty to the government, and concluded with an essential point about keeping integrity and resigning: "I have ruined, perhaps, my political career. But that is of little value—I can still walk in the world with my head erect."[29]

Additionally, individuals may be morally obliged to resign to protect their principal or the broader administration, especially if they find themselves in a position where their staying in office is undermining the political capital or legitimacy of the principal or administration. This choice, however, depends as much on the principal as on the circumstances. Some principals can entertain and expect a wide range of disagreement or tension, others may not. Dean Rusk, President Lyndon Johnson's Secretary of State, announced to Secretary of Defense Robert McNamara, "I must resign." Rusk informed him that his daughter planned to marry a black classmate at Stanford University. Rusk feared that given the racial conflict in the country and as a Southerner serving a Southern president, this would bring criticism upon him and upon the president, disrupting their ability to do the job. He wanted to save the president this further burden. McNamara counseled him that resigning would burden the president far more and urged Rusk to talk to him. When Rusk did so, Johnson congratulated him on his daughter's engagement, and the wedding had no political effect on Rusk or on the presidency.[30] On the other hand, when Chief of Staff John Sununu found that the media attacks upon his misuse of government property for personal purposes had begun to hurt President's Bush's administration and prospects for reelection, he—correctly—resigned to protect his principal.[31] This example also demonstrates that it may protect the principal to resign voluntarily rather than force a principal to demand a resignation since it minimizes conflict with groups who might be supporting the official.

At the second moral level, inability to do the job may have more pernicious and subtle moral dimensions. Superiors or principals may pressure individuals to take or ignore illegal actions, shade analysis, conceal information, or grant unfair or illegal favors to friends or supporters. In such cases, principals push loyalty beyond moral bounds by asking individuals to violate the obligatory promises of the office. As I have emphasized, officials, especially career officials, can sometimes find ways to oppose or subvert such requests. If no such strategies exist, if they fail, if such opposition exacts too high a cost in collaboration, or if the action reflects an inbred pattern of illegality, incompetence, or deception, then it is time to resign.

This type of problem covers not just the legal and professional core of office but also other moral understandings that may inform the appointment. In a classic example, Elliot Richardson was appointed President Nixon's attorney general in May 1973 to restore credibility to a Justice Department that had been tarred by the Watergate scandal. Richardson's reputation for "unimpeachable integrity," as Nixon put it, made him a perfect choice. At his confirmation hearings before a skeptical Senate,

Richardson made a solemn promise to "appoint a special prosecutor and give him all the independence" needed to investigate the Watergate affair. Richardson also promised that he would dismiss the special prosecutor only in light of "overwhelming evidence" of serious misconduct. He stated that he would resign rather than follow a presidential order to dismiss the prosecutor.[32]

By October 1973, the special prosecutor, Archibald Cox, had subpoenaed selected tapes that President Nixon had recorded of his conversations. President Nixon opposed the subpoena on the grounds of confidentiality and believed Cox was pursuing a vendetta against him. The Arab-Israeli Seven-Day War heightened the tension, and the White House saw Cox as threatening national security. Under constant pressure to fire Cox, Attorney General Richardson worked hard to broker a compromise between the special prosecutor and President Nixon. Richardson knew he had no grounds to fire Cox; he was ready to resign to honor his own promise, but had no desire to do so. He believed in loyalty to the president and loved public service, and he also knew that public resignation would hurt his standing with many Republicans who viewed him as a potential presidential candidate. He worked for two weeks to develop a compromise acceptable to Nixon, Cox, and the courts.[33] His efforts failed, and Nixon ordered Cox to pursue no more subpoenas. Cox refused, and Nixon's Chief of Staff Alexander Haig ordered Richardson to fire Cox. Richardson replied, "Well, I can't do that." Haig then asked him to fire Cox and then resign. Richardson refused. Nixon beseeched Richardson not to resign, but Richardson did, believing he could not act as ordered without violating his integrity. He did not want to resign and fought as long as possible to broker a compromise. When no acceptable compromise arose, he resigned.[34]

Effectiveness

The last leg of the moral tripod that supports public integrity involves prudential dimensions beyond legal or professional obligations. Effectiveness overlaps with the responsibilities of office and covers the active political skills that transcend the technical, routine, and even managerial skills required to maintain an institution's core competence. One can exercise all these skills and still end up merely "going through the motions," "serving time," or simply "maintaining the position." To implement a new vision, protect an agency in a turbulent environment, fight off power plays, change priorities, or influence policy beyond the agency, a public official needs two other sets of skills: the ability to build political support and capital and the ability to gain access and credibility in order to influence decisions.

The problem of prudent effectiveness is well illustrated when a technically superb administrator is confronted by complex political demands. For example, Lawrence T. Frymire served as the executive director of New Jersey Public Television for ten years from 1969 to 1979. During that period he had overcome significant internal and budget problems to build an organization of high technical competence. In the late 1970s, the political environment changed, and the new governor, Brendan Byrne, sought to move the organization in a new direction. Frymire opposed these directions, believing the agency had built up significant accomplishments. He continued to focus upon internal technical issues and made little effort to persuade Byrne or other constituencies of his policy goals. Byrne continued to build public support for his position and influenced the Board of Commissioners of the network. Community groups also wanted more responsive programming, and a number of powerful state legislators supported these concerns. Frymire made no effective effort to respond with new ideas or to build support for his own positions. Over time, he lost the confidence of the commissioners, the governor, the media, and the legislature. In doing so he lost the ability to shape policy or implement his own agenda. He ultimately resigned because he could no longer run his organization.[35]

Effectiveness can involve more subtle personal and bureaucratic dimensions than Frymire's very public problems. The loss of access or credibility within an inner circle can also destroy effectiveness. For instance, in April 1980 Secretary of State Cyrus Vance resigned when President Jimmy Carter approved a military mission to attempt to rescue the hostages held by Iranian militants in Tehran. Vance agreed to continue in office until the mission ended but stated that he would resign whether it succeeded or not. In considerable "anguish," he put it this way: "I recognized the President was in political trouble, and I wished I could stand by him. . . . I knew I could not honorably remain as Secretary of State when I so strongly disagreed with a presidential decision that went against my judgment as to what was best for the country and for the hostages."[36]

Although this one policy decision precipitated Vance's resignation and made it appear to be one of principled dissent, the actual decision climaxed a more serious problem of effectiveness. For three years, Vance had struggled with National Security Advisor Zbigniew Brzezinski for dominant influence over American foreign policy. Over time, Brzezinski came to dominate significant policy areas. Vance's own influence became progressively marginalized. In his last year in office, he won very few policy battles and increasingly found himself implementing policies about which he had moral misgivings. In an important symbolic act, the decision to rescue the hostages had been made when he was out of the country. He no longer faced "losing some and winning some" but was forced to confront the fact that he was consistently unable to make a significant difference. He served with honor and competence, but he had lost effectiveness.[37]

People may also morally resign because they are committed to make a difference and believe they could be more effective in another position. Kweisi Mfume, the powerful and well-respected chair of the Congressional Black Caucus, resigned from Congress in 1996 to become head of the NAACP. His own commitments had not changed, but he felt increasing frustration and lack of success in Congress and believed that he could "exercise broader leadership than was possible in Congress."[38] Resigning for effectiveness, on the other hand, can have an ironic aspect. Gil Silver, a career official in the U.S. Forest Service, created an innovative lumber program. He accomplished this by breaking an old network of support between the agency and powerful local lumber companies. He was able to build a new coalition for a more equitable plan. In achieving the policy, however, he made a large number of enemies, and opposition to the new program was largely sustained by personal animosity towards him. Once the program had acquired political and budgetary solidity, he resigned the local position to minimize future opposition. His resignation protected his accomplishments.[39]

Finally, effectiveness can be destroyed by attacks from the political environment. Personal disgrace, policy failure, misuse of office, even perceived ineffectiveness can all become focal points for media frenzies and political attacks. These require individuals to devote time and effort to meeting them rather than carrying on the job. One public official described her decision to resign after her agency experienced a media frenzy over an alleged scandal in the agency: "I had become a liability and it was time to move on to protect my agency and my boss." The attacks divert institutional resources and may tarnish the legitimacy of the institution or hurt the official's principal or administration. Just as they can break moral capacities or undermine symbolic obligations, this combination can undermine official effectiveness and justify resigning to protect the institution.

Resignation as Offer, Threat, and Lever

Resignation is costly not only to the person leaving but also to the people and the organization left behind. When a valued and skilled colleague leaves, implementation or deliberation may be degraded because an important source of skill or insight has been lost. A resignation can be felt as a public repudiation of a policy, and the media may use it as evidence of discord or failure in an office. Consequently, the option to resign creates potential leverage.

The leverage becomes important in a world of contingent power and moral ambiguity. Many people who consider resigning are struggling to change or resist actions, and they feel beleaguered. When the reasons flow from a disagreement over policy or involve loss of influence, then people can sometimes recoup losses with an artful exercise of power. If individuals could regain influence or effect an actual change, they could stay. In these cases, the threat or offer to resign can free individuals and sometimes restore their public integrity.

In essence, the threat to resign draws a boundary and defends integrity. During World War II, President Franklin Roosevelt once sought to have a magazine article critical of him deleted from the edition sent to soldiers. General George Marshall, the U.S. Army Chief of Staff, warned the presidential aide who conveyed Roosevelt's desire that if he should receive such an order in writing, he would immediately resign. Marshall set a clear precedent and drew a clear line; no such request ever came again.[40] In November 1985 the Reagan administration, seeking to stem leaks, announced a plan to give lie detector tests to all government employees who had access to classified documents. Secretary of State George Shultz believed that such tests were unreliable, insulting, and unnecessary except in cases of due cause, and he opposed the policy internally. However, Shultz was in Europe when the policy was approved and became public. At a press conference on his return Shultz attacked the policy. When asked if he would take the polygraph test, he replied, "Once. . . . The minute in this government I am told that I'm not trusted is the day I leave."[41] He met privately with President Reagan to inform him of his opposition and argue his case. President Reagan modified the order to focus on using lie detectors when due cause existed. Shultz's threat helped change a policy that violated his basic moral tenets. But such threats are not without their costs. Shultz's threat incurred the enmity of the CIA and the White House staff, who distrusted his integrity, doubted his team loyalty, and redoubled their efforts to get around his opposition to the Iran hostage initiatives.

Threats can sometimes be an assertion of power and increase one's effectiveness. For years, Robert Moses, the president of the Triborough Bridge Authority, exercised immense power over the city of New York. His legendary capacity to deliver services as well as brick and mortar garnered him immunity from effective political accountability. At several points in his career, new mayors or reforming governors tried to rein in his power. Each time he threatened to resign, and each time the public executive backed off because he needed Moses's help to accomplish the executive's own goals. Moses's successful threats accomplished several things. First, they identified his own power. Second, they exposed the other person's need for Moses. Third, they signaled to others that this particular official could not "get" Moses. The successful threats consolidated his power. However, as the case of George Shultz made clear two decades later, it is a good rule never to offer to resign unless you are willing to have your resignation accepted. In 1963 Moses tried his time-honored technique upon new Republican Governor Nelson Rockefeller, and Rockefeller accepted his resignation. Although Moses continued to hold other municipal posts, his power was never again as strong.[42]

The threat of resignation can help end a situation in office that makes it impossible to continue one's job. In 1994 Secretary of State Warren Christopher believed that his capacity to run his department and represent the United States was undermined by President Clinton's rumored disappointment in him. The media aggravated this situation with their own stories about Christopher's stature. He offered to resign and forced Clinton to decide. President Clinton declined to accept the offer and in doing so reaffirmed Christopher's position both internally and internationally. This enabled Christopher to regain status and strengthen his position in policy making.[43]

The honest decision to risk resignation is a defining moment for public integrity. It can also help regain the conditions under which they committed to take office. Resignation threats, however, work best when (1) they are believable, (2) the official is respected and needed, (3) the public costs to the principal of the resignation would be high, and (4) the threat focuses upon clear issues. Threats over wider and more vague issues of access and power often accomplish less. In the cases of both Christopher and Shultz, their president's refusals of their resignations did not guarantee full stature but rather became a warrant for them to fight to regain control over policy.

A Good Resignation

I have argued that resigning is a basic moral resource for individuals in office. It buttresses integrity, seals responsibility, gains leverage, and defines boundaries. I have also suggested that the moral terrain surrounding resignation is more complicated than the dramatic resigning over principle that looms so large in standard accounts. I believe case studies, biographies, memoirs, and interviews illuminate a moral theory of resignation in which the strong moral reasons to resign range from exhaustion to protecting a principal to resigning over principle. This analysis builds on an understanding that the moral relation between the individual and the office is mediated by promises supported by the domains of the tripod of public integrity. People's promises assume that they keep intact their personal moral capacities and commitments, live up to the obligations of office, and are effective.

Each domain and leg of the tripod is needed to support public integrity. Any one leg of the tripod, if it collapses, can deeply wound public integrity and provide strong, often definitive, moral reasons to resign. If more than one leg collapses, people are always obliged to resign. I believe the analysis in this chapter strongly suggests more people should resign than do because institutional and personal pressures discourage it. The case of George Ball, Undersecretary of State for Economic Affairs in the Kennedy and Johnson administrations, illuminates all these moral issues as well as how the tripod is interconnected. During the Johnson administration, Ball became the leading dissenter from the Vietnam War policy in the upper levels of the administration.[44] Ball maintained regular access to President Johnson and for three years continued to fight the policy and oppose escalation both privately and in staff meetings. Ball's own role emerged somewhat accidentally since most of his work centered in Europe, and Ball believed he served the country effectively in those areas, even as he continued as a "devil's advocate" against escalations of the war. Ball finally decided to resign in September 1966 after yet another Vietnam escalation.

His reasons bear repeating because they present a classic statement of how each leg of the tripod influences resigning:

> I found it practically impossible to interest the distracted President in any major new initiative. . . .
>
> My job had lost its savor, and, as our involvement in the Vietnam nightmare had passed the point where I could significantly influence policy, it was time to resign. . . . After six intense years in the diplomatic pressure cooker, I was depleted—physically, mentally, morally, and financially . . . and I was tired. . . .
>
> Flagging spirits produced a diminishing exuberance. A year or so before, when confronted with a challenging problem I would have felt the adrenalin surge and urgently set about mobilizing the State Department's resources in search of a solution. Now I was inclined to greet new problems warily and wearily, indulging the squalid hope that if left alone, they might cure themselves. Nor did I have the same confidence in my judgment. I was too tired always to seek the tough-minded, difficult answer, and to struggle for the support of preoccupied colleagues.[45]

Ball's explanation captures the responsibilities and interrelated obligations involved in being a moral public official. His story illustrates how the three domains of public integrity interrelate: he moved from energetic mastery of his own area and clear access to his principal to a situation in which his failure to influence affected his moral capacity and access, which in turn hurt his job performance and further lessened his influence. The three domains react back on each other in reinforcing patterns. This interrelation can be a source to recoup power but too often undermines the moral justifications to stay. The stories of Ball, Shultz, and others make clear that good public officials live with moral imperfection and that they can use other morally defensible avenues to influence policy. In the end, however, resigning remains the essential moral option and resource for public integrity: it should not be forgotten.

7

The Political Morality of Sleaze and Honor

I seen my opportunities, and took 'em.

George Washington Plunkitt, *Plunkitt of Tammany Hall*

S LEAZE has a long tradition in politics. The word, which originally
refers to cheapness or shoddiness of materials, now evokes a sense
of cheapness of character, flimsiness, or lack of firmness that makes things
or people less than they seem or could be. It alludes to hypocrisy and failure to live up to expectations. Politics, because of its mixed character,
invites sleaze. Political action can invoke people's highest moral aspirations for communal action. Political rhetoric emphasizes the possibilities
of cooperation, communal solidarity and care, sacrifice, and altruistic
actions to support others. Yet human self-interest, ambition, desire, greed,
and fallibility mingle with these ideals. Every political action is entangled
with possible gain or loss for people. The shimmering ideals are shadowed
by the frailty of the mortals seeking to live up to them. The aspirations
of ideals and common good conflict with the pull of self-interest and
parochial commitments to friends, family, supporters, and religious, ethnic, or other affiliations. Every political act implicates both poles of this
tension.

Individuals of integrity learn to hold these tensions in a productive if
uneasy balance aligning personal moral commitments, self-interest, and
broader moral and political goals. *Sleazeballs*, on the other hand, are people who pursue their own goals or interests in violation of the public good
while pretending to serve the public interest. Sleaze captures the traditional understanding of political corruption as the use of public office for
personal gain: "The essence of corruption in this conception is the pollu-
tion of the public by the private."[1] Yet there is nothing inherently wrong
with pursuing personal goals or even self-interest while in office. Personal

commitments to the public good, professional competence, self-esteem, and even decent wages to support oneself all energize and support performance in office.

The moral problems with sleazy actions lie in the person's failure to limit personal goals to the right context. The internal balances and self-discipline required by public integrity are upset. Sleaze occurs when individuals violate the obligations of office and standards required for holding a public trust, and it actually comprises several moral failures. First, individuals do not respect the obligations they take on in an office and ignore procedural and legal deliberation. Second, they use a position entrusted to their stewardship to pursue their own self-defined goals without reference to accountability. In the process they may convert public resources to their own personal use. Finally, they violate the normal rules of fair behavior and impartial and competent judgment required in office. The antithesis of sleaze is honor: the capacity of people to subordinate their interests in order to judge and act in accord with the requirements of a position. Honor signifies a willingness to sacrifice and risk one's interest in order to live up to promises and obligations of public office.[2]

Sleaze can manifest itself in a number of different and complex ways. Each pattern of sleaze indicates an imbalance among the relations of self to office and public trust that public integrity requires. This chapter examines three kinds of imbalanced relations, each with its own dangers that undercut public integrity. In the first, "honest" sleaze and patronage in particular, people see the pursuit of their own self-interest as a legitimate extension of public office. In the second, corrupted sleaze, people are initially committed to public office but become corrupted by their official power and lose the ability to keep personal interest separate from office. In the third and most dangerous kind, zealous sleaze, moral zealots cannot separate their desires from their moral commitments and believe their own commitments override the obligations of office; they treat public office as an extension of their own will and ideological commitments. I explore each variety of sleaze and how it affects public morality; I conclude by looking to a notion of public honor as an alternative to sleaze.

"Honest" Sleaze

In patronage politics, individuals understand that "to the victor go the spoils." "Honest" sleaze sees politics as providing lucrative rewards for successful practitioners. Participating in a successful coalition or machine earns a substantive reward from the public coffers. This reward might be a job for oneself or one's relatives or friends, a new street, better garbage collection, a local contract, or the simple use of government office for personal expenditures. Participants acknowledge that politics is self-interested, a quid pro quo activity in which self-interest is legitimately served. The indomitable George Washington Plunkitt, a successful maven of the New York City Tammany Hall machine, argued, "Yes, many of our men have grown rich in politics. I have myself . . . but I've not gone in for dishonest graft—blackmailin, gamblers. . . . There's an honest graft, and I'm an example of how it works. I might sum up the whole thing by sayin': I seen my opportunities and I took 'em." Plunkitt explains how he bought up land that he knew the city would want and sold it at a fine profit, and no one was hurt.[3]

Plunkitt's point can be generalized to a stronger claim. Self-interested patronage can be a form of accountability. Under patronage, many positions and contracts are awarded to the followers of a leader or party. Because the election returned the new leader or party, this replacement of individuals can be conceived of as a form of democratic accountability, as the original Jacksonians claimed. The newer officials, because their loyalty will in theory be more responsive to the initiatives and point of view of the new leaders, will work harder to overcome the intransigence or sclerosis of existing institutions and not be captured by entrenched interests.

Patronage provides strong incentives for people with fewer resources or the newly arrived to be socialized into the political system. Plunkitt points out that each citizen has "a marketable commodity—one vote." Entrepreneurs organize people with votes, deliver them, and begin the process of getting power and also benefit for themselves and those aligned with them.[4] All individuals possess the power to vote, but many choose not to use it. This results in skewed participation rates and a loss of power to the poor and less well educated, who vote at lower rates. The raw self-interest of a patronage machine can break the cycle of apathy and inefficacy that holds many back from voting or participation. It can become a source of mobilization for the poor and new immigrants. Rather than providing grand ideas to mobilize, politics is lived as an activity of clear and real benefits in the lives of people. The distribution of jobs and benefits to supporters can cement the ties of individuals to the political order. "Honest" sleaze connects politics to their lives in a very powerful way, with clear material incentive and reward to individuals. It can power grassroots mobilization by providing incentives for citizens to work for the party, get out the vote, and get involved, forcing politicians to attend to the concrete needs of people and neighborhoods.

Patronage politics and its sleaze can build coalitions that are cemented at the core by long-term self-interest. This politics builds on intense personal connections and is buttressed by strong bonds of loyalty and reciprocity over time. Such stability of support helps ensure continuous socialization of citizens, builds in incentives to recruit new and active citizens into the machine, and enables action. The stable coalitions can even extend their moral and political reach to grasp broader issues of justice or social integration among the various groups wedded by their mutual interest in continuing the flow of benefits.

Finally, self-interested sleaze is quite compatible with holding a strong concept of the obligations of the office. The honest, self-interested, patronage approach to sleaze can nestle in with the long tradition of geography-based representation. Many officials see themselves as patrons of their geographic areas or of their constituencies. Plunkitt proudly points out how hard such geographic patrons work to stay in contact with people, distribute benefits, and create and strengthen networks of reciprocity and support.[5] Elected representatives and officials who gain tax breaks, buildings, profits, jobs, or investments for their supporters and constituents are praised and rewarded as astute political players who respond to the needs of their people.

The success and the criminal conviction of Representative Daniel Rostenkowski of Chicago, the powerful and respected ex-chairperson of the House Ways and Means Committee, illuminate both the strengths and the limits of "honest" sleaze. Rostenkowski rose from the old Chicago Democratic patronage machine. Growing up through the machine, he learned to focus upon the "deal." He sought the practical and doable and learned the skill of weaving people's self-interests into durable political solutions.[6] He understood that accomplishing goals required both compromise and self-interest. He also knew that politics involves imperfect outcomes. At the same time, he possessed, as did many Democratic machine politicians, a commitment to the welfare of his constituents and a weaker but real commitment to the welfare of the "little guy." As he said at one point in his masterful leadership for the Tax Reform Act of 1986, "We have not written a perfect law. Perhaps a faculty of scholars could do a better job. A group of ideologues could have provided greater consistency. But politics is an imperfect process."[7]

Because of these honed skills, Rostenkowski demonstrated a deft touch as a legislator and influenced and spearheaded tax reform for both Presidents Clinton and Reagan. His work in getting the 1986 tax reform bill through a very reluctant Congress was superb. His seniority and success helped funnel resources and jobs back to his district in Chicago, making him a local icon. His style of building congressional coalitions stemmed from his experience as a ward and machine politician from Chicago. He looked after the personal interests of his committee members and those whose votes he needed. He could offer perks, access, and gifts, or he could ensure that important supporters affected by legislation were protected, and he could punish those who broke with him. He built up sufficient loyalty to himself as a leader that at critical moments he could call upon that loyalty, even against other interests, to get a vote through. As one of his allies said in a classic defense of "honest" sleaze, "When I'm bought, I stay bought."[8] Rostenkowski practiced politics as the weaving together of broader policy goals with the needs and interests of representatives.

This attention to the self-interested needs of politicians grew naturally from the personalized politics of Chicago machines. In the personalized machine politics of Chicago, there is a long tradition of politicians who reward friends, hurt enemies, and make a nice living for themselves, their family, and their friends.[9] Yet this politics invites a level of raw self-interest, greed, and pettiness. Rostenkowski was notorious for his long memory over slights and his willingness to "hurt" people who crossed him.[10] He also used his office to accumulate small amounts of personal money. For more than twenty-one years, he obtained kickbacks on the government stamp allowance, padded his payroll by hiring phantom workers, paid individuals with government funds to perform personal services such as hiring his children or remodeling his house or rental properties, and used government funds to buy expensive gifts for his friends.[11] All these rather minor offenses have a long tradition in a world in which politics is a means to personal ends of aggrandizement for oneself and one's associates. Rostenkowski's father, himself a powerful member of the Chicago machine, had been accused of similar actions forty years earlier. Commenting upon Rostenkowski's indictment, ex-Speaker of the House Thomas O'Neill pointed out that "fixing" the Civil Service rolls or helping people pay off tickets with your funds was part of the normal game of helping constituents.

Rostenkowski, a man of great pride and rough integrity, never dabbled in massive greed or bribery or influence peddling that might affect major government funds. Additionally, he possessed pride in the House of Representatives. At one point in the battle over the Tax Reform Act of 1986 he even shamed his colleagues for the dishonor they were bringing upon the institution by giving in to interest groups.[12] Instead, in classic honest-sleaze style, he squeezed a little here, a little there, for himself, family, and friends over a long period of time. The level and consistency of his behavior exemplifies the normal, petty, picayune attempt to make ends meet, get a little extra on the job, and deal with the unending crush of expense of being a political leader in Washington.

As Rostenkowski's case demonstrates, patronage-based sleaze can serve large and successful political purposes. Machine politicians are grounded in a strong sense of reality, of attending to effectiveness and stability, and of connectedness to the needs and desires of the people whom they serve. Yet this ethic can contribute to political stagnation and systematic theft—the use of politics solely for personal gain and greed, or kleptocracy. It can alienate and denigrate those outside a patron's sway and exclude them from representation as well as diminish the legitimacy of government. Rewarding friends over those who possess greater merit or competence generates incompetence, excessive cost, and a moral squalor that undermines respect for and legitimacy of government. Ignoring Rostenkowski's defiant claim that he had been made an "example" for doing "what everyone else did," Judge Norma Holloway Johnson at his plea-bargained sentencing correctly called his action a "reprehensible breach of trust in the House. . . . In your important position, you capriciously pursued a course of personal gain for you, your family, and your friends. You have stained them, as well as yourself, and the high position you held."[13] Great greed—or cumulative acts of small greed—violates public trust and undermines respect for the government.

Corrupted Sleaze

Judge William Sessions was appointed to head the Federal Bureau of Investigation in order to reform it in the wake of Iran-Contra. He was appointed because of his reputation for rectitude. Six years after his appointment, President Clinton, with bipartisan support, dismissed him from office in disgrace. He had blatantly used FBI resources for his own personal purposes. Marion Barry had championed the civil rights of black Americans for years and been a heroic leader. He had been elected mayor of Washington, D.C., on the basis of that record. Many controversy-filled years later, he resigned, convicted of drug use and abuse of office.[14] In more than one tragic case, political officials succumb to the temptations of power and demonstrate the second form of sleaze, in which individuals enter public life to do good but succumb to the classic temptation of power: they confuse their own welfare with that of their office.

Such individuals enter public life to live up to obligations of office and respect its procedures and responsibilities but over time lose sight of the higher goals or confuse them with their own desires. They grow comfortable with the deference and perks of an office, with the automatic respect accorded someone with power and influence. Those around them defer to their judgments and refrain from real criticism, so their world becomes a world of mirrors, reflecting their own images and ideas.

The Sessions case provides a clear illustration. After early successes in trying to reassert the integrity and independence of the agency, Sessions began to think of government property as his own. He commandeered aircraft for personal trips to visit friends and relatives. He often took his wife along on personal visits or shopping trips in other cities while passing the trips off as official business. He treated government resources not as a trusteeship for public purposes but as an extension of his own needs and whims.[15]

John Sununu, an effective ex-governor of New Hampshire and later President Bush's chief of staff, went to Washington committed to Bush's welfare and agenda. Yet very quickly against the advice of his aides he began to push the limits of his office. He flew in government aircraft to ski vacations in Colorado, dental appointments in New Hampshire, and meetings with old friends. He used government limousines to drive from Washington to New York to attend auctions. At other times, he borrowed corporate jets for his journeys.[16] All the actions violated ethical standards of office and created perceptions of conflict of interest or abuse of public resources. He compounded these actions with his exercise of power. He enjoyed his power and access to the president and insisted upon people respecting his status. His own personal style with subordinates verged on humiliation. He was effective but arrogant, hard, and demeaning. After awhile he had alienated many of Bush's supporters and totally confused his own personal needs with the requirements of his office.

When confronted with the charges, both Sessions and Sununu evoked a time-honored defense of such sleaze. They claimed that they needed the perquisites in order to do their jobs, to accommodate their "indispensability." Sununu argued that he had to be in constant touch with the president, so he needed government transportation wherever he went. Sessions argued that using government transportation made his own life more efficient and overlapped with official responsibilities.

Government officials with significant power are fawned over by those who desire access and favor. If their style is imperious, individuals around them fear to challenge their actions or call attention to the costs of their impropriety. Sessions and Sununu both ignored warnings from their staff about personal use of government property. Succumbing to classic temptations of power, officials lose perspective on what constitutes a legitimate personal action. Their personal convenience and needs become public necessities as their sense of their own importance inflates. They start to believe that every action of their personal life, from diet to travel to shopping, becomes vital to public performance.[17]

Like "honest" sleaze, corrupted sleaze is not confined to the top levels of government. Any official, overworked, beleaguered, and underpaid, can develop a sense of aggrieved worth abetted by wounded idealism. The use of government stationery, equipment, transportation, or time for personal reasons happens naturally. It becomes something owed to people to compensate for low salaries or lack of respect. It becomes necessary for maintaining morale in high-stress environments or enabling people to do the job efficiently. The excuses are endless, and some are even plausible, but the slow erosion of the boundary between obligations of office and personal convenience undercuts personal and public integrity. Individuals lose the capacity to distinguish self from office.

The most dangerous consequence of this form of sleaze occurs when individuals in office begin to use the office to protect or further their own power—they identify goals of the office with themselves. J. Edgar Hoover's long tenure as head of the FBI exemplifies these dangers. Early in his career Hoover performed admirable service in building the organization and in increasing the stature of the bureau. He ended patronage and overcame corruption, lack of control, and incompetence. He professionalized the agency, gave it a strong sense of mission and ethos, and honed its competence in many areas, giving special emphasis to the use of science in detection. Through adroit use of media and storytelling, he built a strong myth to sustain the agency and gathered great public support for it. Over time, however, he began to identify himself more and more with the agency and especially with the media image of the "G-man"; all the credit for victories went to him, and other agents were regularly overlooked. Although he never practiced graft or "honest" sleaze and never became wealthy from government service, the agency provided vacations and personal services for him that were covered as agency trips. Any agents who challenged his methods found themselves exiled or shunted from the agency. And, in the most profound abuse of power, he collected personal files on public officials, which he used to intimidate them and neutralize their oversight of the bureau. At the same time, he agreed to perform personal intelligence-gathering functions for presidents in order to curry their favor, even as he collected information on the presidents to keep them cowed. Hoover reached a point of unaccountable and unassailable power in the government at which senators and presidents feared him; he effectively could not be fired.[18]

In such cases, individuals can still pursue noble purposes, perform competently, and respect the public dignity and requirements of the office. But in other ways, they use public office as an extension of personal needs and no longer can differentiate between their personal desires and the needs of the office. They lose the ability even to understand the public perception of abuse of power and develop the capacity to rationalize their own preservation in power as indispensable to the welfare of the institution. Those around them reflect their own points of view and mute any criticism or honest appraisal. All those who oppose them become "enemies" of the public purposes that they now conflate with their continuation in office.

Zealous Sleaze

The word *sleaze* spread through the popular political vocabulary during the presidency of Ronald Reagan; it conjured up the legal and moral laxity that afflicted so much of the administration, ranging from the HUD scandals to the Iran-Contra affair.[19] The accusations of sleaze covered a wide range of corrupt practices, but the most serious of the administration's problems emerged from individuals ignoring or violating laws and procedures in the name of higher moral or ideological purposes. These incidents demonstrated a troubling and important truth: that sleaze can flow from an ideological self-righteousness that subverts public integrity.

The libertarian populism that infused the Reagan administration articulated a disdain for public service and most responsibilities of government. The values also inspired fervid commitment among many of Reagan's followers. The values permeated the administration because under the lead of top political advisor Lyn Nofziger appointees were tightly screened to ensure their commitment to the president's positions. Edwin Meese as presidential counselor and later as attorney general kept alive this political agenda in the inner circle of the administration. He and Nofziger created and rallied a wide network of ideologically committed protégés throughout the administration. Both men, along with William Casey, director of the Central Intelligence Agency, deeply influenced the ideological tone of the administration and the quality of appointments.

The ideologues of the Reagan administration collapsed the distinction between public and private. In doing so they destroyed the balance between public obligations and private commitments that public integrity requires. Many of the officials acknowledged no distinct set of public obligations and saw little difference between the methods and interests of the private sector and the responsibilities of public office. For instance, Meese and many other Reagan officials refused to set up blind trusts for their investments when they entered office. In effect they viewed government service with casual or overt contempt. An official investigation into Meese's behavior captured a widespread problem when it charged that Meese's behavior consistently demonstrated a "lack of seriousness" about government ethics.[20]

Because of this attitude, the Reagan administration and its ideological cadres could not generate a serious ethos of public service based on obligations of public office. They confused their private and public identities. This was not the corruption of noble purposes by power nor the self-conscious use of office for personal gain. Rather, it reflected a more profound confusion of the self, in which internal boundaries necessary to public integrity collapse. In the end, because many of the appointed officials had no strong commitment to public service and yet were committed ideologues, they were willing to override or ignore the requirements of law or procedure to attain their goals. The case of Emanuel Savas illustrates a widespread problem well: he left the Department of Housing and Urban Development after it was discovered that he had ordered his government staff to help rewrite his book on privatizing the public sector.

Herein lies the key to understanding this form of sleaze. Committed ideologues believe that their own moral commitments are grounded in moral certainty. This self-certitude and self-righteousness grows to encompass all their beliefs and desires, until all their actions and desires are justified by the truth and purity of their commitment. They do not experience articulated divisions and tensions within their integrity. The level of personal corruption in a totalitarian systems such as the former Soviet Union or China suggests that this collapse of internal boundaries and the resulting corruption is not unique to the United States. But it takes a particular turn with ideologues who have no respect for the independent obligations of office.

For the ideologue, the rightness of their moral and political commitments usually grows to encompass all their personal commitments and desires. They lose the ability to separate personal desire from ideological imperative. For an official, this means that the imperatives of their personal moral and ideological commitments merge into their own desires. They all then supersede the obligations of office. Yet public integrity requires fine distinctions between what office demands and what one wishes to achieve. Self-righteous people lose the ability to submit themselves to the discipline of responsibility, accountability, and deliberation. They can just as easily ignore law or procedure for personal as for political purposes. William Casey, the mentor of Oliver North, symbolizes this with his willingness to ignore governmental accountability as he set up independent networks outside the government to pursue his policy goals. At the same time, he refused to place his personal investments in a blind trust and give up the privilege of making money from stocks even when he invested in firms with which his CIA did business or when the CIA gave him privileged information about them.[21]

No one epitomizes this form of sleaze more than Lt. Col. Oliver North. At first glance, North seems the very antithesis of sleaze. He served as a person of exceptional self-discipline, hard work, intelligence, and commitment. He led well, commanded great loyalty from his soldiers, and excelled in getting the job done in face of great obstacles. His actions demonstrated physical courage, exceptional stamina, fearless optimism, initiative under stress, and devotion to the causes to which he was committed. For his efforts on behalf of the Contra guerrillas in Nicaragua and in seeking to free hostages held in Lebanon, President Ronald Reagan called North a hero.[22]

Lt. Col. North served as Deputy Assistant for Political and Military Affairs of the National Security Council during the middle part of the Reagan administration. After several years on the council, he had amassed considerable influence as the lead expert on terrorism. He became the main coordinator for the campaign to help Contra guerrillas overthrow the Sandinista regime in Nicaragua. He served through three nominal superiors: William Clark, Robert McFarlane, and Vice Admiral John Poindexter.

Under each superior, he gained more autonomy and discretion to pursue broad goals with progressively less managerial oversight. He spearheaded the NSC's move from advisory to operational actions and ended up managing two covert operations, both of which violated stated American policy and law. First, he initiated and managed the delivery of American weapons to the Iranians in exchange for Iranian help in releasing American hostages held in Lebanon. This violated the stated U.S. policy not to pay ransom for the release of hostages and occurred over the opposition of Secretary of State George Shultz and Secretary of Defense Caspar Weinberger. The operation ended with the public humiliation of the administration and the release of only three hostages while three more were captured. Second, North oversaw the efforts to keep the Contra guerrillas together "body and soul" during the periods when Congress refused to allocate funds for their support. He did this both by raising private funds and by transferring profits from the Iran weapons exchanges. Congress had also prohibited all U.S. government agencies from endeavoring to aid the Contras "directly or indirectly." In violation of these prohibitions and the neutrality laws, North, with Casey's support, created and led a large "off-line" covert operation funded by private citizens and foreign governments, largely solicited by North, to fund the Contras.

In these operations North bypassed the professional and institutional agencies of the government. He used a similar off-line operation to escape bureaucratic and legal accountability during the attempt to free American hostages. During this time and later during investigations into his activities of the Iran-Contra affair, North, with great regularity and without remorse, misrepresented his activities and lied about them to his superiors—especially McFarlane—congressional committees and investigators, the FBI and the CIA, and the U.S. Customs Service. He also cooperated in the falsification of records as well as ordered and oversaw the systematic destruction of incriminating records. At other times he bypassed the chain of command to report directly to Casey.[23]

North argued that he pursued a policy sanctioned by his superiors—in particular, the president—and that he kept his superiors informed at all times.[24] He believed his policies to be sanctioned by "the greater good," and by a "higher power," as well as by their own intrinsic rightness. North considered those members of Congress and other official leaders and agencies to whom he lied to be "timid naysayers," "enemies," and "Sandinista/KGB dupes" who threatened the ability of the United States to function in a brutal world beset by widespread conspiracies. He considered the laws as barriers to be overcome, not guides for action.[25] He argued the need for secrecy and lying to avoid leaks, even when most of the serious leaks came directly from him.[26]

The crux of this ideological sleaze lies in being morally certain of the righteousness of one's cause and in extending it to cover all judgments. North became so certain and committed to his own cause that the structure of law and accountability of government no longer mattered to him. When prevented from pursuing a course of action, he emulated the Watergate affair in which the Nixon administration had created a privately financed network to undermine and spy on its political opponents when government agencies refused to do the president's bidding.[27]

North, with Casey's sponsorship, developed a nongovernmental network—the "enterprise"—to pursue executive missions without any legal or accountable constraints. The enterprise involved a network of donors, arms acquisitions and shipments, and guerrillas.[28] This enabled North and his sponsors to pursue armed action or policy in any place they chose without congressional or bureaucratic oversight or control. As had been done in Watergate, he created a private "government" to do the executive's bidding. In many cases North ignored his own chain of command and took his direction from Casey. He subverted the chain of command and then diluted it with his own "misinformation" campaigns to influence Congress and public opinion about his operations while heading off internal efforts to trace his actions.

North demonstrated great imagination, endurance, initiative, and devotion. His actions, however, were neither honorable nor heroic. He systematically undercut the structure of accountability in American politics in act and in principle. Further, he had reached the point where he could influence his own superiors and lie with great regularity about his orders and access to President Reagan to reinforce his position.[29] This capacity for manipulation and subversion of the government reflected both his ideological certainty and contempt for the process of accountability and democratic deliberation.

So complete was his moral certainty that, like many of the Reagan ideologues, he confused his own personal desires with moral imperatives. He could not be bothered with regular process to apply for home safety protection and accepted a home safety protection system from one of his private entrepreneurs, Richard Secord. Later, when this was revealed, North backdated the letters to hide the transaction. Additionally, he accepted the assurances of another associate of the enterprise, Albert

Hakim, that Hakim would take care of North's family if he died by setting aside a $200,000 death fund from his profits on the arms deals.[30] Considerable controversy erupted over allegations, some probably true, that North had used some of the Contra money for personal expenditures on groceries, tires, and other personal items. North, like some of the other figures discussed here, had reached the state where he could not disengage his own interests from those of the causes he served. He believed that the purity of his own intention could both justify his actions and redeem him from any of the illegality or other dishonorable actions in which he engaged. Although North touted his honor, Senator Daniel Inouye at congressional hearings on Iran-Contra pointed out that the Naval Academy demanded total honesty and accountability and required that naval officers refuse to obey illegal laws. North had moved far beyond such mundane notions of public honor in his quest to save the world and himself.[31]

Public Life and Public Honor

All the variations of sleaze blur the distinction between the public and private realms. In "honest" sleaze, office and public life are treated as sinecures for personal and collective gain, and the individuals remain quite self-conscious of the distinction between self and government. Corrupted sleaze possesses a tragic and searing element different from the unapologetic self-interest of honest sleaze. The corrupted figure enters public office believing in ideals and purpose and not seeking personal gain but over time he or she conflates the two. As in zealous sleaze, the figure loses the conscious separation of self and office. Zealous sleaze is sleaze in its most dangerous form. The moral certainty of the individuals suffuses all their judgments and warrants their own disdain for law, due process, and accountability. Their moral purity and self-righteousness encompass not only their ideals but also their desires and interests. In all three types of sleaze, however, the fall of public figures betrays the public trust and contributes to mounting public cynicism that sees politics as corrupt.[32]

One powerful way to buttress the moral distinctions required by public integrity is to restore the ideal of public honor to office as both a moral and an institutional goal. Honor presupposes moral obligations embedded in a community and a web of legitimate expectations. Honor resides in serving an office that is warranted by the community for its contribution to the public good. Living up to the obligations of office becomes a source of personal satisfaction and good reputation for officials. The obligations of the office become references of their identity and a source of honor: committed standards that are supported by colleagues and public. A failure to live up to the obligations of office brings shame and dishonor upon them and upon the office. Officials take on both a personal and a social and communal obligation not only to meet the responsibilities of office but also to protect the honor and integrity of the institution.[33] The possession of honor means that a person's ethics and integrity are connected to the norms and perceptions of membership in an institution and to the public's expectations in regard to the moral stature of the institution.

Public honor also presumes a separate public realm with its own ideals, institutions, and practices. The public realm is bound by values, institutions, and the symbols and rituals. Public action realizes shared public aspirations through discussion, election, and politics and gives them reality through law and policy. This conception of public life and politics does not simply reduce to aggregated private interests.

Liberal democracies achieved something of great value when they enshrined the moral ideal that those who possess public power should exercise it in a disinterested manner according to public rules and accountability rather than for personal or tribal gain. This ideal legitimizes government for all groups. It also supplements accountability by making it a point of honor that individuals internalize fidelity to public values and the law. It warrants officials to serve as trustees of a broader public view and to provide a point of view not heard in the welter of private interests. Public honor requires individuals to restrain their desire for private gain and their private or tribal loyalties. Honor requires public officials to discipline their personal prejudices, impulses, interests, beliefs, and even personal and family relations as well as their deep affiliations such as religion and ethnicity. They strive to act from loyalty to institutional and legal processes of government and to be true to the values and practices that ground governmental legitimacy. This becomes a form of civic virtue.[34]

This notion of a public realm generates an ideal of service. It becomes a focus of managerial strategy in which individuals are linked to each other through honor-bound expectations by a mission nurtured by leadership, education, and management. An "ethos" within an institution supports the honor of individuals, and creating such an ethos becomes central to the managerial task. The military, at its best, exemplifies this ideal. People enter "the service" or "service academies." To "serve" here means to provide for the vital services that others need to flourish as human beings. Public service provides the necessary social and political conditions of a flourishing society. Real service entails a melding of power, duty, character, commitment, and even sacrifice. It is suffused with commitment to live up to standards and to care for the welfare of others. Service and honor require that a person in office not let others down. This ideal of public service presumes competency to perform an assigned responsibility, but it possesses deeper dimensions. The honor is embedded in conscientiousness and impartiality. The source of government funds places a special burden upon public servants to spend the government's money wisely and carefully. Taxes are not voluntarily given in a market transaction but taken by coercive power. Public funds should not be spent for personal purposes or spent on illegal actions or actions that violate the contract of government.

Public service is not just a job. It comes closer to a vocation—a calling to take responsibility on behalf of an enterprise larger than oneself. Here honor becomes even more important as an internalized and communally reinforced support for values and judgment. For public service can involve special powers and privileges not given to private citizens. Public officials also endure unending scrutiny, mistrust, and resentment from many individuals. A commitment to mission, sustained by the support of leaders and colleagues, provides the moral and social resources needed to survive in this environment without cynicism or despair.

The responsibilities and trials of public service require that public officials of integrity establish psychological and moral distance between their private and public worlds. They are obligated to seek some disinterested perspective, not passionless or impersonal, but one that distances themselves from their immediate private interests and frames their judgments by other standards. Public officials have special obligations to act in ways that defer to the existing laws, respect existing institutions, account for the voices of citizens and stakeholders, and earn the legitimacy and trust of the people. This is not easy; it requires moral and psychological courage as well as communal support. Being a member of a group committed by honor to this ethos is a powerful affiliation, and it can offset other affiliations that may threaten to subvert public judgment.

At various times officials need to obey laws with which they disagree, attend to citizens with whom they differ, and work towards solutions that build consensus and legitimacy even if these solutions are not the ones they prefer. Public officials need a capacity for moral self-discipline to resist the temptations of zealous sleaze. They should possess sufficient moral restraint to honor the outcomes of legitimate processes of government as well as the conscientiousness to ensure that they are fair and open. Finding support in the ethos of their colleagues and the mission of the institution supports these capacities and commitments. Public officials of honor can disagree, but they pledge to live the great moral compromise of liberal democratic life: to obey and serve the law while working to change the policies within the institutions of accountable politics.[35]

Every public action either strengthens or undermines the legitimacy of the public order. For this reason, public service in liberal democratic life needs public honor. This honor should not be that of noblesse oblige—superior and dismissive. Rather, public honor in a democracy should be grounded in humility: a capacity to listen, learn, subordinate one's interests or righteousness, and act according to the requirements of one's position. Honor depends upon the subordination of the self, not its inflation.

Lt. Col. North justified his action in two different ways. First, he claimed to be obeying orders. Second, he claimed to be honorably serving a higher cause that justified disobeying laws or ignoring normal constitutional constraints. Both justifications represent perversions of the public honor. Public honor does not submerge one's entire personality into an office and abandon critical reflection or moral responsibility by giving complete deference to authority. Nor does public honor inflate the self so that it imposes its own will and desires upon a role and redefine office in the name of personal commitments. Public honor depends upon balancing the complex but important tensions among the domains of public integrity. With public honor, individuals can humanize a role, can make a responsibility their own by suffusing a job with care, virtue, imagination, energy, and initiative. But making the job one's own should take place in dialogue with law, accountability, and deliberation.

Public honor does not ask that public officials forgo moral commitments, initiative, or self-interest. Honor in public life requires that people respect the moral foundations of their power and understand and act with the psychological and moral self-discipline required by official power to resist the allure of sleaze in all its varieties. Public officials agree to defer to law and process, to resolve disputes within a political order, to respect and foster civil deliberation on public goals, to spend resources upon legitimate public purposes, and to attend to the integrity of the institutions for those who come after them. In this world, public honor is the first casualty of sleaze.

8

Building the Common amid Differences

And mine is its heritage. Its dreams and broken promises, its lies
and its defeats. Each fulfillment is mine and every achievement.
Every failing likewise belongs to me. And with each failure and
broken promise I die a little.

    E. L. Harris, *The South of Haunted Dreams*

A city is composed of different kinds of persons; similar people
cannot bring a city into existence.

    Aristotle, *Politics*

DIFFERENCES DRIVE POLITICS. Contrary to James Madison's argument, the fact that humans are not angels is not what makes politics necessary. Politics arises from the reality that people differ with one another. Even the angels differed among themselves, and some revolted against their God. Human differences run deep, built into the genetic and evolutionary strategies of life. They can range from the shape and density of brains to temperaments to the pigment of skin, from the gender of a body to the God one worships. How different people can live and share a common life becomes the never-ending challenge of politics. In building this common life, public officials possess a special set of obligations.

Liberal democracy poses a unique answer to this question of the common and the different. The solution emerged from a struggle against a world in which differences in religion, birth, class, descent, or geography could permanently determine one's social and political fate.[1] These differences defined people and their possibilities and chiseled certain forms of identity as the foundation of permanent power and status. Liberal and democratic values shifted the focus from inherited identities to the integrity and freedom of an individual human. A person's relation to his or her identity became active rather than passive. Individuals could reflect upon and act upon their born status or enforced place in life.[2] The state sought to ensure social and political opportunities for such reflection and self-creation as well as provide legal and formal possibilities of new social, geographic, religious, or economic lives different from the one into which a person was born. At the moral and political core of liberal democratic theory, identity was no longer a born fate, nor was that fate sponsored or enforced by the government.[3]

In democratic political life, this settlement is being debated once again in the name of differences. Differences such as gender, skin pigmentation, physiology, religion, language, or ethnic background have erupted into political life as sources of demands for recognition and action. The debate is occurring not only in the United States. The collapse of the Soviet empire and the emergence of unbuffered ethnic conflict and violence amid its ruins as well as the weakening of the state structure throughout the world amplify the import of these differences. They signal the difficulties of discovering political solutions that enable difference and commonality to exist in a productive tension.[4] Identity politics and multiculturalism embody these challenges. Their intellectual underpinnings come from several sources. Postmodern critics argue that the dominant narratives of liberal democratic life offer no room for individuals and groups who are "different" to flourish or find recognition.[5] Communitarians claim that the desiccated formal identity of citizenship does not capture the full richness of humanity and fails to respond to the real needs and lives of situated and physical humans.[6] Some feminists have argued that demands for universal citizenship, equal respect, and procedural justice devalue and disenfranchise women and their ways of being.[7] Their political impetus arises from the demands of marginalized groups to achieve recognition in the political order.[8]

These claims pose special challenges for public officials in a liberal and democratic order. Within the constraints of the law and position, public officials possess considerable discretion in addressing them. Public integrity and honor in exercising this discretion are grounded in claims of competence and fair, impartial treatment under law, supplemented by an obligation to ensure effective action, equity, and participation. Public integrity and honor depend in a profound way upon a personal capacity to subordinate certain differences to the complex judgments required by office. The difference-inspired critiques challenge this moral conception of public integrity, often arguing for differential treatment of citizens or implying that only like can serve like. I believe public integrity should expand its concerns to address issues of difference without losing its core commitment to equal human dignity. Public officials should inform their discretion with a commitment to ensure peace and tolerance, foster common political interests and identities, inculcate human solidarity across differences, and build an inclusive political community. In doing this, they are obliged to nurture a common citizenship and counteract difference-based statuses that undercut equal dignity. As a counterpoint, they should not act in ways that morally insult individuals, create differentiated treatment of groups, narrow a person's identity to group membership, encourage a fragmented and discontinuous political culture, or undercut human solidarity.

The Importance of Differences

Differences matter morally. They constitute the components of individual personality and identity and open social possibilities that give reality to human freedom. Human differences also become the ways that people use to organize groups, communities, and cultures. These differences then react back and deeply influence the identity, status, and possibilities of people in a group. This matters because personhood and autonomy grow from the obligations, identifications, affiliations, and roles that people inherit or assume and hold together in a robust web of meaning under the rubric of personal integrity. Differences can also be a source of conflict and injustice within society.

The existence of difference requires a relational setting. If no other humans existed, then the only differences that would matter would be differences from nonhumans or gods. The experience of difference presumes a social context and the existence of others from whom one differs. Societies socialize individuals into social identities, in which certain aspects of selfhood are defined as legitimate and desirable and others are demeaned or punished. These become the common references of affiliation that enable humans to recognize social solidarity and affiliation.

The differences among humans such as families, communities, religions, or physical attributes become the matrix from which identity and freedom can be created. They are the tool kits from which humans have the capacity to shape their style and identity.[9] Personal identity, however, is not reducible to the sum of affiliations and backgrounds. Personal integrity and identity emerge through decisions, actions, and narratives that people create or revise to make sense of the diverse aspects of a lived life. To the extent that individuals constitute their selfhood by references to a particular aspect of self, the expression of their integrity and freedom hinges upon that aspect. It might be religious commitment, ethnic identification, professional skill, family, or any of the myriad other aspects of selfhood. Each dimension creates potential differences from other people. Each dimension also engages baselines of desirability or acceptability within a culture. Ultimately personal identity is a creation, not simply a sum of affiliations. Human identity becomes rich and nuanced as it is enriched, challenged, questioned, or supported by the opportunities of a complex world in which no one dimension closes and defines all other aspects. Often personal identity gets forged in conflict with the expectations of a culture. Differences across and within human beings become the building blocks of human relationships. Love and friendship depend upon difference to provide a context for the discovery and creation of the common bond; enmity, too, grows from perceptions of difference.

The existence of differences makes autonomy possible and gives substance to freedom. A world of infinite sameness would provide no field of reflection or choice. Differences give individuals the chance to reflect upon, judge, embrace, or reject the values and identities that they inherit. Differences backlight one's own beliefs and selfhood, making them more self-conscious. One can make individual values and affiliations "one's own" by embracing, rejecting, or redefining them in light of other ways of living and thinking. Living with difference creates new possibilities against the backgrounds of inherited identities or values. Against these possibilities, social norms can press upon identity: challenging and forcing one to reflect and act in a way that affirms or modifies identity. This process does not involve a form of hyper-individualism emphasizing total self-creation but reflects a form of realistic moral individualism.[10] Human differences are linked to the development of autonomy and integrity.

Differences can become sources of new knowledge and wisdom for a society. The discovery or invention of new insight can expand social discussion and cultural or personal development. Individuals and groups can introduce new ways of doing things that might be more efficient, more just, or more beautiful than the dominant practices. Such innovations can invigorate social, economic, and political life. In a similar manner, new syntheses can emerge when people combine the insights of different ways of doing things. These can be as simple as new ways of eating or greeting or as complex as different ways of thinking about love or organizing productive life. In this way differences meet in the borderlands of existing social practices; through intermarriage, work, social intercourse, or conflict they reshape identities and possibilities.

Differences gain immense political importance when groups organize around them. These communities can come in all varieties, but any such community has a sense of affiliation and membership determined by whatever differences its members hold in common. Any differences will do: blood, descent, gender, geography, language, or religion, for example. Differences may also be chosen, for example, adopted religion, profession, hobbies, married family, or adopted geographic region. Sometimes such communities are created from the outside rather than organized from the inside as, for example, when a society inflicts a stigmatizing identity upon individuals who share a particular lineage. Their political import arises because communal differences become sources of power and mobilization; they can set groups apart or against others or can justify the provision or denial of justice.

Communities based upon common differences can serve many useful roles. They can be both the constituents and anchors of integrity as they socialize people. They can provide a "home."[11] This feeling of being at home provides a place where individuals know connectedness and warmth in a cold and harsh world. Membership can overcome personal vulnerability and enable intimacy and creativity. Connectedness to a community can provide strong supports for personal development and security and may have deep evolutionary advantages.[12] Such groups give reality to human choice by providing opportunities to choose socially supported life patterns. At the same time, a diversity of groups in a society provides diverse solutions to problems and makes a society less vulnerable to disruption from hazards.[13] Communal differences can also produce constructive conflict in a political order. Individuals from different groups can experience different dimensions of a social order. They see where normal politics or social practices hide injustice or do moral harm to others similarly situated. Members of the group can bring this hidden pain or social disfigurement to the attention of the society.

On the other hand, human differences produce great moral problems. At the most fundamental level, differences provoke conflict. Humans may be evolutionarily disposed to react with suspicion and even hostility to relatively minor differences in appearance or affiliation. This conflict is aggravated by a common psychological tendency of groups: to define and intensify their affiliation by comparing themselves to "other" groups and to raise their own worth by denigrating others. What Reinhold Niebuhr called the temptations of "collective egotism" can generate deep passions of affiliation and equally deep antipathies.[14] These identifications and enmities are taught and handed down over generations. In such an encapsulated, simmering coexistence, the latent possibility of mobilization against other groups is strong.

Dostoevsky, in "The Grand Inquisitor," pointed out that in human history one of the keys to domination has been people's willingness to surrender their individual responsibility to a communal identity. At the same time, group membership enables individuals to claim illicit moral credit for the actions of other group members and link their own sense of self-worth not to their own integrity but to the achievements and demands of others who lead or embody their "group."[15] Political entrepreneurs and demagogues will encourage and exploit these tendencies to solidify their power. Leaders will fan intergroup conflict to justify overcoming outside threats or to dominate dangerous "others."[16] Human differences remain the most enduring source of serious conflict and violence within political society.

Differences pose more moral problems because being different can either uplift people or make them the object of discrimination or suffering. The moral wrong done in discrimination involves a fundamental insult to people. People categorize and judge a person's moral worth on the basis of a morally irrelevant attribute—a difference such as race, gender, religion, or descent. The insult arises because people do not acknowledge the full moral personality of a human being whose achievements, skills, and character are ignored or dismissed on the basis of one perceived difference. Further, people are denied the possibilities of change and growth when they are confined to one way of being that is socially determined by this difference. This injustice can lead to their group's being denied resources and opportunities. The group itself then becomes an enduring source of enforced identity and injustice internalized over time. In a mirror-image injustice, members of a group possessing a desired difference cumulatively accrue undeserved power and status.

Political orders organize themselves and membership around a strong narrative of legitimacy and commonality. When these stories and myths build in exclusions and denigrations of people who are seen as "different," it denies them the possibility to flourish and often denies them voice and action to change the definition of membership. In these cases, difference becomes the foundation of injustice. One set of individuals accrues advantages, while other individuals are denied moral goods on the basis of their differences. The political order imposes costs based upon natural or externally imposed differences. Even when they are not excluded or denied access, the cost of attaining social ends becomes higher for those who do not possess the accumulated social capital of people in the mainstream.[17]

Responsibilities of Facing Differences

At the end of Aeschylus's *Oresteia*, Orestes throws himself at the feet of Athena, begging for help. The Furies have hounded him and ravaged his kingdom to punish him for his murder of his stepfather and his mother, Clytemnestra, to avenge their murder of his father, King Agamemnon. Agamemnon had earlier sacrificed his and Clytemnestra's daughter Iphigenia to the gods in order to pursue the Trojan War and avenge his brother's dishonor. Beneath the story lies the tale of the relentless demands of group loyalty unhinged in a cycle of never-ending violence and vengeance and the decimation of the social order—a not-unusual tale. Athena ends the cycle by creating a new order and set of institutions—the polis—in which all families and citizens possess an overarching loyalty to each other and to common institutions.[18] The new political institutions end the cycle of group vengeance. The polis becomes the new "home" for citizens—the new source of justice and protection. Athena's creation of a political community with loyalties transcending group differences symbolizes the integrity and responsibilities of modern public officials. Like Athena, they are responsible for creating a home for myriad individuals and groups—a place where people live and belong, where they find security and can flourish according to their talents. The state provides a civic hearth for the citizens, and the hearth is tended by the public officials.

Public officials exercise considerable discretion and leadership. This discretion is bounded by law and delegated authority, informed by the obligations of office, and driven by a demand for effectiveness. It makes public officials the tenders of the common good and calls on them to both model and encourage active citizenship. In general terms, this means attending to the competence and legitimacy of their institutions. Democratic office requires ensuring accountability and truth telling and attending to the interests and aspirations of fellow citizens. It adds a special obligation to focus upon issues of equity, ensuring that both the long-term interests of society and the interests of those lacking voice and power are protected.

Claims of difference, however, introduce special issues for public office. They seem to undermine this model of public integrity by demanding differential treatment according to group identities and suggesting that only members of one's own group can understand and serve each other with justice and fairness. Unlike the claim that only like can serve like, I believe that differences can be accommodated by an enriched conception of public integrity and responsibility. To address the issues raised by difference, government and public officials have several strong obligations to inform their discretion. First, they must provide security and become peacemakers. Second, they must model and promote tolerance. Third, they must promote inclusion, welcoming all citizens within the civic culture and public institutions. Fourth, they must promote a common political culture and solidarity across differing individuals and groups. Fifth, they must protect and encourage human agency and keep open the possibilities for individual free choice. Sixth, coursing through all these obligations lies the obligation to address injustice caused by differences. These responsibilities essentially require public officials to model the behavior necessary to sustain political order as a common home for many different people.[19]

First, the government's basic obligation in the face of differences is to ensure order and peace. As Thomas Hobbes reminds us, differences are the major locus of conflict and civil war. Too often "race" and other differences become the justification to fight and dominate.[20] To enable a civil, economic, and political society to emerge, government must provide physical security and rein in the tendency of disagreement to flare into violence. Public officials should limit cruelty first and pursue the conditions of "common decency" in everyday interactions.[21] Peace as limiting violence and coercion, however, is only a minimal obligation of government. Public officials serve as peacemakers and should seek not just to limit violence but to reconcile factions and move beyond a society of simmering segregation and distrust. For different people not only can argue, fight, and hate, but they can also love, befriend, and cooperate with each other. Public officials should work to provide the civil processes, language, safe places, rituals, and symbols that make civil engagement possible among different people.

Second, creating a culture of tolerance supplements peace making.

Tolerance of those who differ is crucial to building a peace that does not require costly government force as a constant referee. Tolerance signals the willingness to live with and not persecute people who differ. It involves the self-discipline not to work to disenfranchise individuals, even if one dislikes their differences. To many tolerance seems too limited or too negative. To tolerate someone does not mean accepting or respecting people or their differences. Morally speaking and given the limits of government, however, to demand tolerance becomes the first obligation of public officials, and to achieve it requires far more effort than is commonly thought.[22] Enforced tolerance is the social prerequisite of acceptance and respect. Acceptance can grow over time only after people have the possibility of interacting with each other in safety. As models of citizenship, public officials have the severe duty to accept and respect individual citizens and to model this behavior for others. Tolerance creates the social space where individuals who differ can earn respect or, over time, grow into acceptance.

Third, as tenders of the common hearth and home, public officials have an active duty to include people within the civic order. Public authority is built and restored by pulling in and engaging the interests of all citizens.[23] This outreach begins with ensuring that public service is accessible to all individuals. It involves acknowledging the stories and wisdoms of all descent and physical groups and seeking out and highlighting the contributions of groups previously ignored. Public officials have special obligations to ensure that all groups are enshrined within the ritual and symbolic spaces that memorialize the common home.[24] This means that public officials are obliged to work to acknowledge and welcome all individuals into the public conversation. Government becomes the sponsor of possibilities as it fosters new voices in the life of society; public officials have special obligations to listen and learn.[25]

The duty of inclusion means that public officials should act to open possibilities for individuals with different identities. The provision of service, respect, or acknowledgment makes it possible for individuals to have different identities compatible with citizenship. Public officials should minimize the salience of identities such as ethnicity, race, gender, and religion as sources of tension with citizenship. Public inclusion should make it possible for individuals to hold multiple affiliations within themselves rather than having to set one identity against citizenship or solidarity.[26] Service and recognition can create loyalty and affiliation to the regime within different groups or individuals.[27]

Fourth, public officials have a responsibility to work to create a common political culture. Given the dangers and dynamics of difference, public officials have special responsibilities to attend to the social solidarity of the citizens who differ among themselves. Too often the dynamics and rhetoric of democratic coalition building can polarize and alienate, as political leaders mobilize support by setting groups against each other. In another vein, differences can encourage communities to devalue the common humanity of "other" citizens. Groups can raise themselves to a privileged position that denies the rights or status of others. Within a minority group, conflict can occur over who should represent the group's interests.[28] Entrepreneurs have strong incentives to claim and control group identity. Against all these tendencies, public officials serve as the bulwark of social solidarity; they are the stewards of a common humanity, a common vulnerability, a common environment, and a common fate within the country. They should serve as public healers of the fissures growing from politics and group dynamics.

Aristotle suggested that public officials have a responsibility to remind and persuade citizens that "what they have in common is more important than what divides them."[29] In a diverse world common references and common understandings or a common civic language and mutual respect do not happen naturally. Government and public officials must devote thought and effort to creating social alternatives to polarized conflict. At one level this means encouraging an "affirming pluralism" through which individuals appreciate the unique qualities of others rather than see them as threats.[30] It means sponsoring and defending a robust civility in which differences and conflict can play out without intimidation and violence.[31] But the possibility of affirmation, respect, and civil contention depends upon a shared political solidarity that citizens take for granted. Discussion, learning, and persuasion depend upon rhetorical resources that can connect to group understandings and link them to common debate.

Even a shared concept of justice is not enough for a political community.[32] Public officials need to tend to the affective dimension of public affiliation. They should sponsor communal experiences and symbols; these can be common reference points that distill shared experiences or commitments, making cultural and social integration possible and grounding persuasive communication.[33] Such experiences and rituals enable individuals to link their personal emotions and identities to the larger political order. They become the positive dimension of civic and political peace. They allow differing individuals to meet, experience each other, and forge new more inclusive understandings. The common symbols, processes, and experiences create social references through which people can understand themselves and others as members of a common political culture embarked upon a joint project of not only surviving but flourishing. The experience of common symbols activates emotional responses in people to contribute to the welfare of others by the recognition of a shared history and solidarity.[34]

Community depends upon communication. Public officials have a special responsibility to engender a common language that will enable both older and newer inhabitants to enter into a common political life. Maintaining and furthering a language entails some loss for new immigrants, but a vast and vital gain for the society at large. In an immigrant-based culture such as that of the United States, it is a perfectly just requirement to demand that newcomers acquire the common language, even with the costs this entails. The common language makes the shared political culture viable and undercuts the long-term isolation of groups.[35] However, tending to the common language means working to ensure that the language itself be open to transformation—that is, to help rid of it demeaning or stereotypical terms of common usage.

Public officials should work to evoke internal motives in citizens that arise from public symbols and rituals and connect all members of the community. These internal emotions and affiliations should help transcend parochial identities.[36] Officials can do this through their language, respectful service, engagement, welcoming, and maintenance of a civil public language. Each point of personal contact with citizens either builds or undercuts their emotional connections to the public order. Public officials should act to identify people as citizens, not victims. In this sense every point of contact, celebration, open process, and ritual becomes a stepping stone on the ongoing governmental task. To forge a sense of social solidarity that flows through different people takes constant efforts.

Fifth, in liberal and democratic life, the focus of protection and responsibility for public officials should remain the integrity and autonomy of individuals. Public officials have a special responsibility to protect the psychological and social space that permits free self-development of human beings possessing their own integrity. This entails the obligation to provide social and civic opportunities through which individuals can step back and find the moral room to reflect upon themselves and make decisions about their future and identity. Difference and freedom are intimately linked, since a life without different possibilities means that freedom becomes a formal lie. Unless it can be demonstrated that such differing expressions of selfhood cause serious harm to others, they should in general be tolerated and protected. It is extraordinarily important, however, given the pervasive power of government and the self-interest of groups, that the actions of public officials do not foreclose integrity; they must be wary of consigning individuals to a group identity that confines their individuality to one set of terms sanctioned by government policy.

Democratic public officials committed to serious freedom have a crucial obligation to preserve the quality of reflection for individuals in their relations to their differences and communities. Autonomy becomes a sham if there are no social and political places where individuals are not bound and trammeled by the authority of the groups that claim to define people's identity. Only such protected opportunities will give people the possibility of free reflection and choice or permit them to find new interactions with others who differ from themselves.[37] People should be free to affirm and accept affiliations as well as live through them, but at the same time the possibility of choice, change, or exit must be preserved.

At its core the liberal and democratic political community has a non-blood-based and nonphysically determined notion of citizenship that exists beyond any ascribed or asserted ancestral affiliation. This means that public officials must work to prevent harm, insult, ostracism, or disabling that occurs because of descent or physical attributes. The purpose of public action, hiring, modeling, and ritual should be to break down the barriers and stereotypes that limit the possibilities of individuals based upon their born identities.[38]

Human dignity and human agency are related in intimate ways. To be a human with an unquestioned identity that comes from a group has some admirable dimensions. Such an unquestioned identity, however, does not respect the unique human capacity for self-development and for reflective judgment about one's own beliefs and commitments.[39] Identity is not just given by others but forged by reflection and choice. To the extent to which people possess a defined identity because they know no better, are denied a chance to question or change, or have uncritically internalized the images of others, their own integrity is undercut.

Any group or community can subvert this personal capacity for self-reflection by encouraging the isolation of its members and willfully refusing to listen to or engage other points of view or refusing to permit other ways of life to be lived under the banner of difference identities. Any community can enforce a form of social lobotomy because it fears that individuals who question given identities can develop individual consciences and might question or leave their own community. Freedom and reflection can be the enemies of tradition, power, and socialization within a group.[40]

Public officials have special obligations to respect and protect people's capacity for agency and autonomy in order to make possible real personal integrity through which people can change, or affirm an identity rather than just live an inherited or socially enforced similarity. Government protects the vibrancy of community by protecting voice and exit for individuals relative to communities of difference. All individuals have the protected rights to exercise their voice about their community, to exit a community or identity, or to shape a new one—perhaps by joining a new community or perhaps by simply holding many different communal affiliations within the strands of their integrity.[41] Public life and participation enable people to discover that they are more different than they thought and at the same time share more in common than they believed possible.[42]

Sixth, just as public officials can acknowledge voluntary affiliations and ways of life, they should approach unchosen or "born" identities—that is, those over which individuals have no control—with great care. Morally all these features are undeserved and unearned by individuals.[43] To the extent that any of these differences become the basis on which options might be permanently foreclosed, they need to be addressed, and sometimes compensated for, by public officials. The point of a polity dedicated to respecting the freedom and integrity of individuals is to protect them from being excluded by attributes that have no moral relevance. Public officials have an active role in eliminating such disabling limitations.

In summary, liberal and democratic public officials have a set of special responsibilities within public integrity in engaging differences. They become the guarantors of peace and tolerance, the creators of the conditions of social and political discourse, and the sponsors of inclusion by eliminating disabilities and acknowledging worth. All these obligations permit voluntary communities based upon differences to flourish within the political community and focus upon enabling individuals to discover whatever level of civic, political, and economic affiliation or participation they choose to pursue and can attain.

This liberal and democratic conception of public responsibilities complements the classic conception of public service. It has, however, been challenged by theorists of identity politics and multiculturalism. These aligned positions argue that government should recognize and treat individuals as members of different groups. In particular, they suggest that the systematic oppression of individuals based upon differences may generate a permanent form of oppression, disabling, and vulnerability; this history of oppression, they argue, then creates a permanent identity in which all members of the groups are stigmatized and enmeshed.[44] This argument is often augmented by the independent claim that the differences are so deep and profound that people from outside groups cannot successfully understand or relate to a group's understandings of the world and its values.

The critique goes on to posit that public officials cannot address these oppressions and fundamental differences merely by working to protect and promote individual freedom and integrity. Rather, it requires that public officials recognize a form of differential citizenship. Individuals from oppressed groups would be granted significant protection, support, and recognition based exclusively upon their membership within the oppressed class. This approach demands positive and preferential treatment in order to compensate for past oppression and deal with continuing oppression. Further, it intimates that because of the profound divisions involved, people in oppressed groups cannot be well served by members outside the group. In some cases this might mean that members of the groups should be served only by members of their own group. At a deeper level, it demands delegating of control to the groups, which could form their own publicly sponsored and financed endeavors and have veto power over policies that might affect them.

Under this approach, public officials should not deal with individuals per se, but rather with the "collective concrete other," a social entity in which relations are informed and guided by individuals' group identification.[45] Such government-mandated identification and support of groups and enclaves as independent units displaces public citizenship as the major civic identity.[46] In a form of syndicalism, difference-based groups would possess considerable autonomy and self-direction. Representation and policy making would be by group affiliation, and the groups might choose to avoid requirements of a common public culture. Only individuals like themselves would be allowed to provide basic government services; any officials "different" from them would be excluded because such different people could not understand or appreciate the unique needs and understandings of the group. This would call for a fundamental reordering of the classic conception of public integrity and responsibility.

The Limits of Difference

A little difference goes a long way in politics. Conflict, discrimination, and violence have flared over something as minor as an accent or as major as arguments over differing concepts of God. No sense of common identity, whether based on race, gender, ethnicity, language, or even family, has been strong enough to ward off violent conflict over even minor differences. Consequently, the task of government and public officials to balance the common with the different becomes delicate and complex. I believe that this task is better served by the liberal democratic conception of public response and integrity than by the differentiated-citizenship response of identity politics and multiculturalism.

Identity politics and multiculturalism can proceed at one of two levels. Level one argues that marginalized individuals and groups should be acknowledged and incorporated into public life. This involves attacking stereotypes and discrimination, opening the public culture to a richer and more robust view of life and membership, and opening up possibilities for individuals who have been marginalized by past practices. This approach might be called "liberating" identity politics or multiculturalism, and it is quite compatible with the liberal democratic conception of public integrity. Level two involves encapsulated identity politics or multiculturalism.[47] This approach shifts the focus away from freeing individuals and turns to groups. It envisions each individual's identity as anchored within a group. In this vision, government and public officials relate to citizens by virtue of membership in a sponsored group. Public officials do not relate to people, but to beings mediated by the mandated category.

For public officials committed to liberal and democratic values, this approach has numerous deficiencies as a guide to public discretion; I will discuss only three. First, it is based upon a moral insult. Second, it fails to recognize that identity groupings can narrow the life possibilities of people confined by mandated identities. Finally, it creates political incentives that encourage fragmentation and undercut the social solidarity of the democratic order while disenfranchising large numbers of individuals.

First, this form of public action insults and dehumanizes. This occurs when people are not acknowledged or responded to in the fullness of their humanity—their character, spirit, skills, or achievement. Often it means that instead of being judged by character or skill, people insult them by judging them on the basis of only one dimension of their self-hood. It denies their humanity, integrity, and freedom.

Human personhood is a rich and complex endeavor. Personhood and integrity emerge in a dialogue of the inherited and socially imposed with the reflective and chosen. Each person experiences many alternative influences and aspects that can be affirmed, denied, or changed: in a sense every person is multicultural and multi-identity.[48] The different aspects within each person create the possibility of freedom as well as change and contribution. New social identities can also grow from this personal struggle. This notion of personhood means that someone's significant affiliations should be freely chosen, not forced upon them.

To demand by law that public officials relate to people in service provision, acknowledgment, or action on the basis of only one aspect of their identity insults people. It forces public officials into immoral actions and limits human potential. Instead of acknowledging or encouraging the emergence of new identities and social possibilities, officials are asked to constrict and narrow people's identity. In one of its many ironies, encapsulating identity politics reinforces the very either/or identities that have sustained the unjust cleavages in American society. Individuals are not permitted to mediate their own relation to these identities. Rather than respecting a particular person's own separate peace with race, ethnicity, gender, or any other aspects within a complex personality, public officials are asked to address only one aspect of that identity and often using only one politically correct understanding of what a person's relation to race, ethnicity, sexual orientation, or gender must be. Public officials become corroborators and enforcers of narrowing possibilities and identities.

This approach also insults the public officials in two ways. First, it assumes that they are not capable of acting with fairness, impartiality, and care towards others who are different from them. It assumes that they cannot act with self-discipline to overcome possible prejudices, but also that they cannot by acts of education, imagination, and empathy learn to respond with effective concern to different people. Second, by asking public officials to relate to other human beings mainly on the basis of these differences, it forces public officials to narrow their own moral and professional imaginations. This form of treatment inculcates in public officials a civic identity at odds with the norms of democratic respect and inclusion. It asks them to limit their capability to respond to people as individuals and rather than expand the range of their moral imagination to contract it into a narrowed self that only mirrors prejudged understandings of people in the groups.

Second, this approach requires that public officials ignore an important reality: that groups are sustained by power. This power replicates the social features of the group community and is exercised by individuals within that community who, by tradition or self-election, influence group identity. Because a group or a culture incarnates structures of power that shape identity, these can profoundly affect the quality of an individual's life. The range of available possibilities, the patterns of acceptance and deference, the attachment of significance, the willingness to consider other people as fully human or equals—all of these arise from socialization within groups and cultures and are handed on by the existing power structure. Rhetoric, peer pressure, ostracism, and other techniques of coercion enable activists or traditional authorities to dominate others and enforce a definition of what it means to be a "good" member of the group.

The claims of identity activists and theorists to differentiated citizenship romanticize such groups and grant them immunity from moral and political accountability.[49] They leave untouched the potentially narrowed and parochial identities forged by the power structure. They also miss the point that groups and cultures are not static entities. Many strands and subgroupings exist within a "culture," and many identities are linked in different ways. No culture exists in isolation, and they are profoundly influenced by their interactions with other groups. Ethnic groups and other new immigrant groups not only profoundly change their own culture when they settle in a democratic culture but change the culture into which they immigrate as well.[50] If such ethnic enclaves are granted exclusion from the requirements of liberal democratic political culture, it means that their own class and power structures are now untouchable by public power. The advocates of differentiated citizenship assume that these groups exist in a sort of isolation, with a clearly defined set of essential norms and practices. They end up freezing the culture by handing it over to the tyranny of the activists or traditional leaders and granting the power and class structure legal status.[51] This in turn enables the activists to ostracize or undercut people who do not meet their own standards of what a member of the group should be, standards that are now enforced and accepted by the government.

This whole approach, so sensitive to the power of the "dominant culture," ignores the reality that any group, even minority groups, that helps shape identity exercises concealed power and authority. Any constituted identity is by definition in place before people arrive at self-consciousness and full reflective power. The inculcating of the children is done by other human beings—family, church, neighborhood, elders, peers or leaders, activists, peers. A group or culture does not exist as an independent rigid entity independent of the mortal humans who make it up. These multiple influences all work to induce or force children to internalize cultural expectations and norms. Once inculcated, affiliation, guilt, or shame continues to impress these norms upon people, independently of reflection and choice. The more widespread, continuous, and closed the socialization by a group, the more people growing up are denied the chance to reflect upon, discuss, and judge these internalized norms.

Every community creates the possibility of sophisticated automatons carrying on in an unreflective manner bound by loyalty, guilt, shame, or enjoyment of the community over which they had no control. This array of unaccountable power exists within any community, and the claim of any community, minority or otherwise, to escape accountable judgment means that its own structures of power and class will remain intact. Many communities often severely limit the possibilities available to women as well as to those who are considered inferior. They use their power to narrow the human possibilities of many members, especially females, yet the encapsulated approach requires that public officials refrain from intervening against these cultural practices that subvert the freedom and independence of women and inferiors.[52]

Third, this approach creates incentives for political leaders to undercut the social and human solidarity with which public officials are charged. As the modern world makes all too clear, the most common result of significant differences is horrible conflict and violence. Public officials must work hard to create and sustain a political world in which individuals can create and enjoy complex identities that do justice to their lives. They must work to maintain a political and social order in which people can hold group affiliations that remain compatible with citizenship. The demand for government sponsorship of group identities changes the dynamic upon personal identities in profound ways.

Once government sponsors differentiated rewards, service, and status on the basis of identity differences, cultural and political entrepreneurs have incentives to solidify group boundaries and identities to strengthen their own power. The leaders have incentives to narrow the political and moral options of individuals who may fit within the sponsored group in order to keep them beholden and limit the possibility of their group power breaking down. So, for example, keeping members of an immigrant group tied to their native tongue rather than learning the common language becomes a way to sustain both isolation and power. Enforcing an orthodoxy about how to be an authentic member of the community eliminates opponents and the possibility that members might defect from the group to form other affiliations. People in the group who brave the broader society and forge new and more complex identity for themselves threaten the power bloc. The moral world of state-sponsored multiculturalism has little room for complex individuality.

The political incentives of encapsulated identity politics encourage political difference and separateness. In order to maximize short-term power over long-term social integration, activists use media and peer pressure to impose identities upon individuals and ostracize or attack those who might differ for moral or spiritual reasons. Such "different" people are accused of being "inauthentic" or "selling out." The incentives of state-sponsored identities also discourage and penalize activity upon the boundaries of different groups. Mixed marriages, mixed churches, working relations, professional affiliations, friendships, or political alliances beyond the defined orthodox community all become suspect. These cases threaten the political leaders and activists because real, living individuals—for personal reasons of love, passion, spirit, knowledge, or self-interest—choose to link with others different from themselves and embark on the arduous and exciting journey of creating new identifies and new forms of life. Such pioneers are shunned as threats by the cultural and political entrepreneurs of the sanctioned groups. They may be harassed or discouraged from such interaction. Government recognition and emphasis upon difference encourage leaders who draw ever-narrower boundaries of identity, and this makes public officials collaborators in the limitation of identity.[53]

The state of mixed-race people in America reflects the ironies and limits of encapsulation. Many white Americans of European descent have multiple descent traditions and are free to choose among these traditions—affiliating closely with one dimension or ignoring them all. On the other hand, black Americans have been denied such choices. Many have both African and European descent, but American society has forced them to be black, denying them any complexity or choice among their affiliations. A child of mixed-race parents has been defined socially and by law as a black child. These people were denied the freedom others had to choose whether to identify or not with a descent group and recognize its traditions and affiliations as their own.

In a liberal and democratic model, government officials should be working to open up possibilities so that individuals with complex descents that mix perhaps Asian, African, European, or Latin American ancestors may choose to affiliate or not and to claim what riches they wish from such descent lineages.[54] Once the government sponsors a group identity based on existing models of race or affiliation, such mixed-background children have their own choices narrowed. The children are now forced by government to choose to identify with one parent rather than both and to accept one defined identity rather than forging their own. In the case of children of African descent mixed with other lineages, the children end up defined as black in officially sponsored enclaves in schools and work-places, and they face peer pressure, testing, and harassment to conform to the identity norms within the enclaves. Political entrepreneurs also seek to capture their numbers. In controversies over census counting, many civil rights leaders oppose changes on the census form that would either permit individuals to check multiple boxes or create a new mixed-race category because either change would dilute their power base.[55] Under the encapsulation rubric, public officials sanction one narrowed identity rather than work to broaden the social possibilities or the borderlands where new identities are lived and created.

All this results in a narrowing or denial of the human moral imagination. Although humans cannot remake themselves by acts of existential will or become Lockean clean slates, they can, nonetheless, use imagination, empathy, study, conversation, listening, friendship, art, and science to experience and explore different worlds and understandings. They can question many aspects of their own worlds and the worlds of others while discovering and affirming solidarity with common human capacities and vulnerabilities.[56] Most important, humans have the capacity to stand back and reflect and to transcend their immediate positions and parochial interests. With empathy and even rigor, they can reach across the barriers of descent, class, and blood. Attempts at understanding and serious impartiality do not guarantee truth, but they do contribute to richer, more complete, more accurate, and more defensible understandings. In contrast, the opposite model presents a picture of isolated islands within a closed society, coexisting in a sea of incomprehensibility.

The demands upon government and public officials of the identity and multicultural encapsulation strategy rest upon fundamental moral flaws. In the end, not all differences deserve respect or celebration. Groups who hold slaves, practice casual racial superiority, or victimize women or other vulnerable members, to name a few moral issues, deserve serious political scrutiny and restraint. An approach that grants immunity to moral scrutiny to any difference-based or "oppressed" group misses the complex role that difference plays in engendering both freedom and personhood, but it also minimizes or ignores the problems of conflict, identity narrowing, and discrimination. Instead, it privileges difference and insulates "difference" groups and individuals from moral and political accountability. This approach asks that government officials cramp their own moral views and collaborate in narrowing and limiting the humanity of individuals within the group as defined by the self-appointed leaders and the cultural police of that group. The different treatment model that emerges from identity politics warrants a form of unaccountable cultural imperialism on the part of the government-sponsored activists who control the officially sanctioned identity within groups. Claims of difference per se do not entitle anyone to immunity from either moral judgment or political scrutiny. The obligations of public officials to support individual dignity and freedom encompass claims of difference; they do not end at claims of difference.

Building an Inclusive Public Life

The existence of differences among humans gives dynamism, opportunity, and danger to politics. The realities of freedom, integrity, and community deeply depend upon a government's engagement with human differences. Yet these same differences all too often become the loci of injustice, conflict, and violence. Any government faces the challenge of holding difference and commonality in a tense and productive relation that permits individuals and groups to flourish yet also constructs a political community with shared human and civic solidarity.

Government and officials are the major trustees of the solidarity of all citizens. The centrifugal forces of difference obscure the realties of a common fate, economy, environment, and vulnerability, as well as shared responsibilities for the land, the future, and each other. In such a political world, public officials have special obligations in attending to difference. They must be mindful of the common and tend it. These obligations enrich and extend the concept of public integrity in liberal and democratic life.

Václav Havel has suggested that a country must be a "home" for all its citizens—a place of belonging. Public officials tend this hearth at which all people are welcomed and included: "To establish a state on any other basis . . . means making a single stratum of our home superior to the others, and thus detracting from us as people. . . . The outcome is almost always bad. . . . A state based on citizenship, one that respects people and all levels of their natural world, will be basically a peaceable and humane state."[57] To sustain the common hearth, public officials need to work always to sustain the solidarity through the myriad differences that constitute individuality and communities. They should work to provide security and become peacemakers, demand and promote tolerance and model mutual acceptance, demand and promote inclusion and welcome all citizens within the public institutions, promote and build a common political culture and solidarity, protect and encourage reflective human agency and the potential for individual to flourish, and address injustices meted out in the name of differences.

Amid the clamor and incentives of identity politics, such principles are easier enunciated than carried out. Yet the politics of encapsulation demands that individuals be engaged on the basis of one aspect of themselves—a difference, often one linked to oppression. This insults and dehumanizes both public officials and other human beings. In addition, it demands that they refrain from evaluating and judging injustice to other humans within groups and that they collaborate in the narrowing of identities or in the fragmenting and limiting of new possibilities of social cooperation. Identity and multicultural encapsulation demand immoral acts of public officials.

This is not a call to ignore differences or one to support public policies of exclusion and denial. Issues of inclusion, recognition, and injustice can and should be addressed without resort to encapsulation. Public officials should pursue strategies to include, affirm, acknowledge, respect, and protect—where warranted—differences in individuals and groups. This does not mean, however, that government officials must refrain from engaging injustice or the denial of human integrity within groups or under the name of differences. Facing difference does not mean suspending judgment, but rather attending well, understanding, and then deciding. Further, public officials have special obligations to ensure the possibility of exit for people within groups and to attend to the border-lands and boundaries where new identities and new possibilities of civic life can be forged. A mixed middle born of new insights and synthesis should become a goal to honor, not undercut. On the other hand, public officials should not take actions that provide government sponsorship for group-controlled identities or that distribute government resources upon a mandated group identity.

Public officials tend the common hearth not just to rectify past injustice, but to heal and reconcile. They should be working to nurture and protect the new possibilities of relations that arise on the boundaries, not working to solidify past categories of affiliation or injustice. In these boundary lands, difference enables freedom and the growth of a new civic culture. The point should not be, as Milton warned of Satan, to make humans smaller by narrowing their identity but to help them become larger and greater in their possibilities.

9

Saints, Sinners, and Politicians

How Private Lives Matter

> What infinite heartsease
> Must kings neglect that private men enjoy!
>
> *Henry V* 4.1.236–37

> I have really been pulled kicking and screaming to the conclusion that if
> you choose to run for public office you give up any zone of privacy at all.
>
> Hillary Rodham Clinton

S CANDALS IN THEIR PRIVATE LIVES have destroyed the careers of
many prominent American public officials. In recent years a vice
president of the United States, a Speaker of the House, eight governors,
two chairpersons of the House Ways and Means Committee, a House
whip, five senators, over thirty members of the House, and a director of
the FBI have resigned under pressure because of private scandal. Four
presidential campaigns have been ruined and three Supreme Court nom-
inations withdrawn because of scrutiny of the candidates' private lives.
In the last decade more than thirty people have been convicted of treason,
and in all but one case private reasons involving money, sex, or substance
abuse motivated the treason. Discussions over private matters of friendship, economics, family, religion, or sexual relations have intruded into
campaigns, nomination hearings, and even consideration of career officials at all levels of government. The private lives of public officials have
become public with serious consequences for the quality of political life
and discourse. When President Clinton's White House lawyer, Vincent
Foster, committed suicide, he left a despairing note complaining that in
American politics "ruining people is considered sport."[1]

Attacks upon the private lives of public figures are as old as politics. But the intensity of the modern focus upon private lives has come about for several reasons. First, the tacit agreement of the press to avert their eyes from officials' private lives has ended, while legal developments have limited the scope of libel claims that public officials can bring against malicious accusation. Second, the decline of the political parties has given the media more prominence as gatekeepers to office and has made politics more person-focused. Third, candidates and interest groups exploited the new media standards and used private scandals to discredit competitors and their positions. Finally, groups ranging from religious conservatives to some feminists have questioned the validity of the traditional separation between public and private life, thereby weakening the claims of privacy that public officials might assert.[2]

Because of these cumulative changes, many public officials find themselves all but stripped of a private life, and this situation will remain. Faced with this breakdown of privacy, many people have advocated a return to a strong "relevance" standard both to limit the flow of information about officials and to judge the information when it comes out.[3] I believe that such a strong defense is warranted but ultimately naive and that it will not protect private lives. This situation arises not only from the dynamics of politics and media but also because of an irony of public integrity. Public officials need strong private lives to sustain their integrity. Private lives provide the social and emotional support for moral commitments as well as a place for reflection upon the dilemmas of public life. Because the strength of public integrity often depends upon aspects of private life, private lives often do matter. The private and public lineaments of personality and relations entwine sometimes reinforcing and sometimes pulling against each other. This means it is impossible in advance to have a clear line demarcating public and private in a life. Additionally, the lack of definitive information in official life can sometimes justify legitimate scrutiny of aspects of an official's private life.

I do believe, however, that citizens—and public officials in particular—have strong claims to privacy. Maintaining public integrity requires a protected private life, and here I explore the arguments for such privacy. At the same time, I think that even using traditional relevance criteria to screen private information will not provide strong and clear defenses of that privacy. The dynamics of media and press as well as weaknesses of the relevance standards will continue to erode the privacy of public officials. In addition, citizens often have legitimate reasons to look at private lives. To respond to the continuing cascade of information about private lives, I propose a set of guidelines by which officials can analyze their own lives and that others can use to judge the private lives of public officials. These standards seek to balance a respect for privacy with legitimate scrutiny of private conduct.[4]

Privacy Claims of Public Officials

The rights to privacy involve the capacity to protect realms of one's life from scrutiny or control by others. Privacy usually preserves a range of realms: one's body, thoughts, emotions, and religion; relations of intimacy and friendship; and property rights and personal associations. Privacy rights also extend to strong moral expectations about how private information will be weighed or used when it is obtained. For instance, individuals may not be able to control public knowledge about their religion or intimate life, but they have the right to ask that this knowledge not be considered in certain judgments about them, much as a jury might be instructed to disregard certain information in reaching its verdict. The actual scope of privacy rights is determined within a society and can change over time. Privacy is achieved through internalized social practices that demonstrate respect for others' privacy such as refusing to eavesdrop on a conversation or averting one's eyes when passing an open window.[5]

At its foundation, the moral worth of privacy flows from its intimate connection to personal autonomy and integrity. Privacy underlies the capacity to take possession of one's own life. Individuals need the ability to stand back from the welter of demands of public life, peer pressure, or authority. They can reflect in solitude or with others to make sense of, reshape, or accept the multiple internalized dimensions of selfhood. This enables them to make sense of their life and claim it as their own.[6] Claims to protect one's body from unwanted intrusions form the foundation, but these protective claims move quickly to encompass attributes of mind and spirit such as thoughts, emotions, religious beliefs, and intimacy. Privacy provides an antidote to the incursions of socialized power into one's psychological and physical world and becomes a crucial support for reflective integrity.

Privacy gains greater moral worth from its central enabling role in human relationships. Relations of intimacy and friendship need privacy to flourish. These become the anchors of personal commitment that are fundamental to public integrity and reflective judgment. The exclusionary and protective nature of the private realm can encourage the risk taking and revelations through which intimacy and trust grow. It abets the growth of common and shared experiences that become foundations for reference and trust between human beings. In private relations, individuals can legitimately, with no moral harm, prefer some people such as family members, friends, colleagues, or co-religionists.[7] Privacy encourages cooperation and trust within many different types and levels of relationships ranging from personal and family affiliations to clubs, economic partnerships, or religion. This enables individuals to withhold self from or reveal self to people in different ways and helps sustain a rich personal life in which people develop unique types of relations with other individuals. Private relations allow a communal sense to grow and nourish diverse forms of social practice and association.[8]

Privacy sustains integrity by contributing to critical judgment and encouraging free reflection. The constant scrutiny of others who possess authority, power, and influence over individuals makes it very difficult to think and judge with honest clarity. Judgment will be distorted by such scrutiny.[9] In private individuals can give and receive advice with honesty and care without worrying about how it will be distorted or misperceived by others. Privacy becomes a crucial adjunct to maintaining integrity under public pressure, for others can provide the candid feedback an individual needs in order to avoid self-deception and assess the consistency of his or her conduct. Privacy also contributes to creativity and innovation in life. Withdrawal or escape from conventional demands and scrutiny can provide the psychological, physical, or social space from which to challenge accepted wisdom or find unique insight or interpretation of the world. All these aspects counterpoise the world of Winston Smith in George Orwell's novel, *1984*, in which "Big Brother" monitors every action.[10] At the other end of the continuum from privacy lies slavery, a state in which people cannot initiate a private life or relations of intimacy or have control over body or creations.[11]

The right to privacy plays out as a social practice, morally grounded and socially sustained. It should not, however, be elevated to an irrefutable right. Claims of privacy can be abused and can hide harm or oppression. For instance, the "privacy" of family can protect the "rights" of a spouse to abuse, or the "private" suffering of a cancer patient hides the fact that the cancer was caused by the dumping of toxic wastes by a "private" company. Any claim of privacy can be challenged by other moral claims and renegotiated on those bases.

The moral realm of privacy has particular cogency for public officials. The boundaries of public and private enable officials to construct a public persona or role that presents and reinforces the best of their character and aspirations. Privacy provides space for individuals to reflect upon their actions and practices and recover from the physical and psychological demands of public office. Private lives enable people to keep alive intimate relations with family, friends, and partners that can otherwise wilt from neglect under the stress of official life. Energy, courage, and independent judgment flow from the resilience and richness of private life. Private life can also provide additional sources of reference beyond interest groups that can be crucial in maintaining the balance of public integrity. Finally, privacy carves out a realm for intimacy, reflection, grace, or prayer to restore people and anchor their moral life against the pressures of public opinion and media pressure.[12]

Contrary to some feminist commentary, privacy in public life has particular moral urgency for women and minorities,[13] who often enter the public realm as "outsiders." Social mores place stricter limits upon their acceptable behavior than upon the behavior of men in general and white males in particular. Social myths that have sustained their outsider status and limited their access to power have often stressed their "private" place in society or private "insufficiencies." For women, in particular, because of their traditional association with the "private" realm, entering public life entails a number of risks. They can be accused, in the way men seldom are, of abandoning their private obligations for public ones. Additionally, the sexual and economic mores and limits regarding acceptable behavior for women are drawn more rigidly and narrowly. Violations of these strict codes can be, and have been, used to subvert women's credibility in public life. Women cannot normally rely upon patterns of acceptance or rituals of public excuse or forgiveness to escape public censure and delegitimation in the way men might to handle accusations of private impropriety. Even as mores change and public presence is created, female and minority public officials need the protections of privacy to limit assaults upon their legitimacy through exploitation of their traditional roles, images, and limitations.[14]

The Erosion of Privacy

Politicians have always attacked the private lives of others as a way to destroy them. As the range of private actions subject to scrutiny widens, the incentive for politicians to use private attack in lieu of political debate increases. Any peccadillo, real or unproved, becomes a target. Appointed, elected, and even career officials can be attacked for past improprieties.[15] In a classic example, Speaker of the House Newt Gingrich, when he was a minority Republican member of the House of Representatives, intentionally undertook a systematic campaign of alleging and uncovering relatively minor private economic deals in order to destroy Speaker of the House Jim Wright. Earlier congressional Democrats had used allegations about Senator John Tower's drinking and womanizing to discredit his nomination as Secretary of Defense.[16]

The culture wars in American politics provide a perfect framework for attacks upon private lives. Individuals and voters tend to identify certain private issues such as sexual practices, religious beliefs, or marital fidelity with broader political and economic issues. Political leaders have a strong incentive to paint others as embodiments of cultural corruption. Issues related to the character of officials are often debated around private issues, rather than public performance. This displaces political consideration away from the moral complexity and compromise associated with concrete legislation and implementation.[17]

At the same time many citizens legitimately seek to know and understand the character of public officials, especially candidates, in more personal ways. The breakdown of the party system in the United States means that no real political screening or disciplining mechanisms exist for candidates or high-level executive officials.[18] Candidates use party labels to advance their own power, and politics is built around a swirl of personal coteries vying for power. Citizens get little reliable information about a candidate from party labels, and party loyalty provides little buffer against personal accusations. In the absence of institutional structures to screen and control candidates, the quality of the person becomes much more important.

Public officials often present themselves as individuals with impeccable private lives, adducing their marital status or their religious beliefs as "proof" of their integrity. Candidates rely upon consultants who craft careful images and use campaigns that structure the presentation of candidates. The electronic media are particularly well suited to create an illusion of intimacy that persuades citizens that they know a person well. The power of the projected image enables a public official like Ronald Reagan to inspire widespread confidence despite the fact that many individuals disagreed with him on most issues.[19] In this world, citizens legitimately look to private lives to reveal the quality of the person hidden by images.

Public officials will use private lives as vehicles of attack or as warrants of their worth. Citizens will look to private lives to provide clues about the integrity of individuals. The incentives of the media and press amplify both trends. Ironically, many editors and reporters cite the standards of relevance discussed here as their justifications for exploring every aspect of a person's private life. The standards of relevance, however, are meaningless when the press engages in "feeding frenzies" that indiscriminately dig up any aspects of personal lives and throw them to the public to judge.[20] The "character issue" has become "an excuse to cover anything we want."[21]

In the mid–twentieth century, most elements of the press adhered to a system of informal rules that protected the private lives of public officials from serious scrutiny. Such informal rules buttressed the public integrity of officials such as President Franklin Roosevelt by both underplaying his own physical infirmities and concealing the family discord and unconventional marital arrangements with Eleanor Roosevelt.[22] Such rules also covered up serious abuses such as the alcoholism that afflicted Wilbur Mills, chairperson of the House Ways and Means Committee, or the physical infirmities that debilitated President John Kennedy.[23] The emergence of private scandals that had clearly influenced public performance, the investigative-reporting successes of the 1970s, and the demise of reporting as an all-male bastion have all transformed the culture of the press, making it far more skeptical of the private lives of public officials and far less tolerant of private abuses of public trust. Given the media's power and resources, the capacity of public officials to exclude or protect domains of privacy has been severely weakened. The dynamics of competition, moreover, drives media coverage to the lowest common denominator. Even a newspaper or network that refuses to break a story about a private problem will report the same story after it has been broken by another paper or network. Consequently, tabloids and other journalistic entities with little editorial screening based on relevance often drive mainstream reporting.[24]

The media's obsession with private lives encourages public voyeurism, which itself rebounds to drive the media itself because such privacy-invading stories garner readers, viewers, and profits. The production of scandal has become a profitable staple of media entertainment. Any attempts to edit information on the basis of relevance within the media are often neutralized and ineffective because of the dynamics of competition.[25]

Most disturbing for any privacy claims, the media coverage can create a circular and self-fulfilling dynamic that permits any personal issue to destroy a public official. To have a legitimate claim to a position, any public official must be effective, but effectiveness can be undermined by the accusation or revelation about private actions even when the actions have no bearing on judgment. Actions irrelevant to governing can dominate a public official's life even if they are unsubstantiated. Officials will spend inordinate amounts of time answering questions and worrying about the issue. Their families, friends, and work life will be invaded and affected by the inquiries. The turmoil distracts from their ability to do the job, and the attacks can tarnish their office and hurt their principals. Ironically a media frenzy can ultimately render them ineffective, creating "good" reasons to resign. The ineffectiveness had nothing to do with their actions and everything to do with the pattern of the media coverage.

The consequence of this erosion of privacy is that public life in the United States presents a case study in what happens when the effective claims of privacy are destroyed by the politicization of all aspects of personal life. The practical elimination of all distinction between public and private lives leads to a moral free-fire zone. Many innocent human beings are hurt as they are pulled into public scrutiny over private lives and relations of public officials.[26] The emergence of a network of special prosecutors and ethics investigative units has further eroded private protections. The structure and discretion of these offices and vagueness of the standards open the lives of public officials up to indiscriminate public investigations that often end up in the press.[27] The quality of life permitted public officials has declined, and this discourages others from entering public service. Political conflict vacillates between personal exposure and image. Little political or rhetorical space remains in which conflict can take place without resort to personal attacks. When individuals are opposed or attacked, the assaults are not limited to claims about their beliefs, competence, or performance. Political and ethical claims mingle in a politics that aims at the demonization of foes, not indictment of their competence or disagreement over their policies. This undercutting of civility reflects a noninstitutional politics in which people, not parties or institutions, become the focus of judgment and action.

The social geography of public and private makes excessive scrutiny of private lives especially perilous to women entering public office. The past rituals and rhetoric of public life excluded or questioned women's ability to act in public responsibilities. Often their very entrance into the public domain defined them as "public women" and thus neglectful of their private obligations. The scrutiny of their private lives can endanger their credibility in many more areas than men face. For instance, no one would think to attack an absent father for devoting time to public office rather than to child-rearing, but a woman can be labeled an "absent mother" for devoting too much time to public obligations.[28] The collapse of private boundaries poses particular vulnerabilities for women in public office.

Office and Relevance

To respect private lives means reestablishing the social practices and norms of judgment that give strength to privacy claims. All individuals start with a strong prima facie claim to privacy that limits the ability of others to pry into their lives. The dilemma arises from the legitimate moral rights of principals—and citizens acting as principals—to evaluate the people to whom they delegate power and authority. Principals have a moral responsibility as citizens, legislators, or superiors to ensure that the people to whom they give career, appointed, or elected office have the skills and competencies necessary to do the job. As individuals who will depend on the officials, principals have an additional moral interest in ensuring that officials will not abuse their power. The actual range of areas that principals have a right to know about, and how they should weigh information, depend upon the structure of the office. Public office involves what Michael Walzer calls "separation" in that the public realm has its own moral logic and demands that are not necessarily extensions of, although they may be grounded in, the rest of one's moral life.[29] The realms of private life cover the areas of life outside of competencies needed for the office. They generally encompass most events prior to taking office such as private economic relations, religious affiliations, friendships, familial and intimate relations, recreation, sexual life, gift giving, personal pleasures and hobbies, thoughts, secrets, and even personal prejudices and beliefs.

In this tension between two moral claims, the rights of privacy suggest that people should be judged only on the basis of what is relevant to their performance. Any legitimate scrutiny of private lives should be linked to whether the private considerations are relevant to the competent performance of official duties.[30] This means that pieces of information such as "scandals" in private life in which personal conduct violates accepted mores but does not affect the official's ability to perform in office should be ignored or discounted. The power of the relevance standard to exclude or discount private information depends, however, upon a notion of integrity, the idea that humans are not seamless creatures, and the clarity of boundaries.

Institutional responsibility depends upon personal integrity that enables a responsible individual to demarcate private and public lives and hold both in tension within himself or herself. The very idea of role or office depends upon this capacity. Public office is bound by law, standards, and expectations of impartial, fair, and competent action. To live up to such a role requires public integrity, which presumes that people can live up to promises they make and yet be consistent in their commitment to different roles that often entail discontinuity and tensions within a self.

Citizens rely upon public officials to provide careful and competent judgment and service, and they reasonably expect public officials to limit private considerations in fulfilling their official responsibilities. For instance, citizens expect officials to put aside personal hardships such as marital problems, family pain, or just plain "bad days" when performing their jobs. Officials are also expected to overcome personal prejudice or dislikes in their judgments about other citizens. It can be a mark of character and public honor when people overcome personal travail or prejudice to fulfill their responsibilities. Public integrity sustains this capacity for separation; it helps constrain political conflict within an institutional framework and prevents it from being reduced to vendetta, while permitting civil conflict.[31]

This capacity for internal separation is regularly confirmed by the factual paradox that private rectitude does not guarantee public honor or effectiveness, nor does private "moral stumbling" indicate public moral insufficiency. Henry Adams remarked ruefully that when his father, Charles Frances Adams, the American ambassador to England, fought to keep England from aiding the Confederacy during the Civil War, all the men whom the elder Adams most respected as private individuals, such as Gladstone and Lord Russell, lied and supported the Confederacy despite their opposition to slavery. However, the individuals whom Adams did not respect as private individuals, such as Palmerston, proved to be reliable allies in keeping England from direct support for the Confederacy. When he was Secretary of the Treasury, Alexander Hamilton paid extortion money to the husband of a woman with whom he was carrying on an affair. Yet when the husband asked for a government position, Hamilton refused because the man was not competent to serve. Hamilton revealed the entire sordid affair and risked public humiliation over his private actions rather than sacrifice his public honor.[32]

The problems arise, however, because there are not clear and absolute demarcations of private lives and public offices. The structure of public office points to several legitimate concerns for citizens: accountability to public authority, delegation, honesty and promise keeping, exercise of coercion, use of public resources, power over others, and symbolic and ritual responsibilities. Morally public officials derive their authority, power, and privilege from the claim that they are acting on behalf of citizens. Citizens' consent and obedience authorize the actions of public officials and ground their legitimacy. Citizens finance their offices and rely upon their principals to oversee and ensure accountable action. Public officials act on behalf of laws, which carry the full coercive control of the state behind them. In theory, public officials are accountable to all citizens, and all citizens have the right to acquire relevant knowledge about the officials' public performance, most clearly in election campaigns in which all citizens judge candidates.

The rights of citizens to acquire relevant information about public officials, however, are limited by delegation. Legal and moral delegation removes the right to scrutinize lives from the general citizenry and places it in hands of the individuals who oversee them.[33] This delegation respects privacy because it limits the number of people who have a moral warrant to intrude into the privacy of officials. However, the higher the level of responsibility, the more power and discretion an official has, the more legitimate broad public scrutiny will be. Usually this implies that career officials have the most protections, appointed officials fewer, and elected legislators and executives the fewest privacy claims.

Office is defined by a web of obligations held together by promises. When individuals take on public responsibility, they promise to abide by the standards, laws, rules, and procedures that constitute their positions. They pledge a good-faith effort to perform conscientiously and to act with competence. They control public resources, which should be used with efficiency and care, but they often face temptations to use government power and resources for personal gain. Some officials exercise considerable coercive power over the lives of citizens and may abuse it. In addition, the exercise of power, itself, can be enjoyable.[34] Office also entails discretion. As power and responsibility increase, discretion also increases. This discretion involves constant pressure from the morally complex and troubling decisions that face officials. Often they must make tragic choices and live with dirty hands and morally problematic outcomes; over time these psychological tensions can erode the moral commitments of officials.[35] In addition, the exercise of coercive power puts a real strain on the moral capacities and character of individuals, which can erode their integrity.[36]

Finally, many positions carry with them a symbolic and ritual dimension. Officials may perform public rituals that help legitimize and provide access to citizens. Often they invoke ritual and rhetoric and represent the aspirations of a people or a program. Their ability to act well in these ceremonial capacities can increase the public's favorable perception of government as much as their actual effectiveness in office can. Moral leadership and persuasion can move citizens in new directions and unite them in common beliefs and aspirations.

In sum, public responsibilities demand individuals who are willing to be honest and accountable, are competent in the skills of the office, possess the integrity and self-discipline to keep promises and resist temptations to abuse their power, are able to exercise judgment under complex and difficult circumstances, and have the imagination and skill to exercise the symbolic dimensions of the office. Each of these characteristics is notoriously difficult to assess, but all place the quality of the person at the center of legitimate scrutiny.

Furthermore, the principals who must elect, appoint, and oversee these officials must often judge prospectively before individuals take office. In these cases, public integrity and judgment as well as competence are embodied in and revealed through habits of decision and learning formed over time and tested and revised in light of experience and deliberation. They reside in the person in a unique and essential way and cannot be reduced to formula.[37] That judgment, integrity, and competence cannot be rationalized and are tied to contexts means that principals should focus upon people's performance in office. Their public record of performance presents the best testing ground in which the judgments and quality of character reveal themselves, and it should be the focus of assessments of suitability for office.

The reality, however, is that private life can influence public office in many ways. The complexity of public office suggests that, beyond ministerial jobs and very tightly controlled technical positions, there will be no clear ways to set absolute and clear boundaries around private areas. For instance, two areas that are clearly private immediately become subject to legitimate scrutiny within a performance focus. First, personal health can be legitimately examined to ensure competence, safety, and balanced judgment. The state of an individual's physical and mental health, his or her strength and stamina, and any predispositions or weaknesses influence all realms of life. Physical or mental impairment can affect judgment and performance, and both are legitimate grounds for inquiry. Alcohol or drug use can debilitate judgment and performance or lead to abuse of office. Inspectors, safety officers, and any officials who have substantial responsibility for vulnerable citizens warrant particular scrutiny to ensure against these problems.

Personal health can also affect performance at the highest level of power and visibility. Wilbur Mills, one of the most powerful and effective chairpersons of the House Ways and Means Committee, drank so excessively that he often did not remember his actions on the House floor, yet he served for years. Senator Edward Kennedy suffered from a drinking problem yet served as an effective and powerful senator. But the costs of substance abuse creep up over time. Representative Mills eventually ruined his career when he ended up drunk in a fountain with a stripper named Fanny Fox. Senator Kennedy drove off a bridge on Chappaquiddick Island, and a young aide, Mary Jo Kopechne, drowned in the drinking-related accident. Kennedy's own effectiveness and stature were later further diminished by his alcohol-related entanglement in rape charges that were brought against his nephew.[38]

The second area that can legitimately be examined are personal economic assets. Most conflict-of-interest laws and disclosure requirements build upon three related issues that undermine this "private" area. First, economic self-interest in one's area of authority can corrupt judgment; second, these interests can tempt individuals, and people with heavy responsibilities should avoid undue temptations; third, economic conflict of interest can undermine the appearance of fairness and impartiality and hurt the legitimacy of government. Additionally, the overlapping economic interests of family and friends can be an area of legitimate inquiry. The actual nature of the information a principal may need in these areas may be negotiated, but they clearly fall within the legitimate concerns of principals, especially at levels of greater responsibility and discretion.

Finally, past performance and public records can have serious limits as predictors of future actions. Relevance tied to public record depends upon consistency of people over time and comparability of the positions. People, however, change—sometimes slowly, sometimes quickly. They can reach breaking points as the multiple stresses of life press upon them. Divorces, new marriages, illnesses, and other events can change them. Many job pressures corrode personal integrity and skill over time. Individuals can also move from one level to another—staff to line, legislature to executive, local to state or state to national office, private to public sector—where proven skills and success may not transfer. Each change, especially changes in which people take on more responsibilities and higher stakes, involves confronting new challenges and pressures that past experience may not capture. For instance, many officials who move from the private to the public sector are frustrated by the slow pace and politics. They can also become enmeshed in conflict-of-interest problems when they carry private-sector practice into public office. In these cases, aspects of a person's private life may provide valid information that past office failed to reveal. The most careful study of this issue concluded that "it is often not possible to tell in advance what private activities may be relevant to our assessments of official performance." Private actions may "raise reasonable doubts about future performance on the job even if an official's past performance has been faultless."[39]

The rights of principals to have adequate information on people they delegate, hire, appoint or elect to public office are strong and legitimate. These rights, however, are limited by strong privacy claims. The need to resolve issues of integrity and competence related to the complex structure of public office does warrant looking into some private areas. But areas of belief, intimacy, religion, and many associations still should have strong boundaries around them because of a prima facie lack of relationship to performance in office.

Guidelines for Judgment

In seeking information about officials or in responding to the welter of information thrown by the media and by political opponents, citizens and principals, and even public officials themselves, need a clear approach with good guidelines. Any guidelines for assessing the private lives of public officials should attend to the claims of privacy, account for the structure of public office and legitimate needs of assessing officeholders, and provide some basis for screening and weighing information about private lives. These guidelines derive from the strong presumption that knowledge from private realms of life is not generally relevant to decisions about office unless other strong reasons intervene. These standards resemble older standards that were formerly used by the legitimate press to screen information but are often ignored by the modern media.[40] These judgments involve a two-step process. First, ask whether the information is relevant to assessing performance in office. If not, it should not be sought or should be dismissed or ignored. Second, if it is relevant, then ask how it should be weighed in judging a public official's worthiness.

This approach has eight guidelines, which frame a set of priorities in which, if the prior guideline is insufficient, one can go to the next:

1. Focus on public performance.

2. Examine personal health and patterns of economic interest and advice.

3. Distinguish between legitimate private actions and abuses of power.

4. Keep the circle of scrutiny to the lowest possible number.

5. When the record is weak or inappropriate, look to areas that can illuminate the person's integrity, honesty, and promise-keeping ability.

6. Examine a public persona for consistency.

7. Examine actions relevant to the symbolic dimensions of office.

8. Place the private action in the context of a person's character over time and the alternative choices for the position.[41]

These guidelines are commonsensical. Because private lives can matter for public performance, they will not provide clear and definitive assessments. They will, however, provide an initial set of standards by which to screen and judge most information. I address each in turn.

Attend to the relevant public record and past performance in office. Public actions over time reveal if individuals are hardworking, caring, promise-keeping, honest, honorable, and competent. The relevance guideline generates questions such as Does the information relate to the skills needed for the office? Does it demonstrate the judgments needed for the office? Were the skills in the past tied to similar areas? If not, can the experience be analogized to the type of judgments that will have to be made in the new office? Are the pressures, scope of authority, and stakes in the new office similar to those in the previous arenas? To the extent that past performance reflects plausibly similar pressures and stakes, performance in office should be the overriding determinant of suitability for office.

The concentration upon competence and public record should create a high threshold for the use of private information. In order for private information to be considered, it must pass two primary tests: insufficient information exists from public performance to judge the person, and the private information is clearly relevant to the capacity to carry out the obligations of office. These relatively strict standards provide a plausible way to direct and judge examinations of the lives of public officials, while excluding a wide number of realms from scrutiny.

Unfortunately, a private life can leak into and influence public life in many ways and, to the extent that it does, can be scrutinized. Turmoil, such as a difficult divorce or a family tragedy, can preoccupy officials, making them unable to exercise the effort and skill demanded by their position. Other forms of disruption in private life can also undermine capacity. In 1885, after ten years of consistent service in the U.S. Senate, Florida Senator Charles W. Jones missed two years of Senate meetings because he had been smitten with a wealthy woman and spent all his time in Michigan wooing her.[42] Sometimes a spiral occurs in that the pressures of office erode the quality of one's private life and undermine a marriage and friendships. These losses in private life then rebound to cause changes in behavior in office. In the end, an official can lose the ability to separate the two realms, and they can intermingle, with serious consequences.

Principals have the right to know about any health condition and economic interests that affect an individual's ability to live up to responsibilities. Health and substance-abuse problems can disqualify individuals from office and are legitimate objects of inquiry. Opening these areas up to scrutiny is legitimate but can be costly for individuals. The revelation that his vice presidential candidate, Senator Thomas Eagleton of Missouri, had once been treated for depression threw Senator George McGovern's 1972 presidential campaign into disarray and forced Eagleton from the ticket. On the other hand, the overcoming of physical disabilities or of addiction can be a source of strength and pride, as when Governor Ann Richards of Texas was attacked about her past alcohol-abuse problems and she readily admitted them and revealed how she had conquered them. Mayor Marion Barry of Washington, D.C., also turned a physical issue into a political asset when he argued that overcoming his own drug problems and serving jail time provided a metaphor of redemption for the city of Washington.[43]

Similarly, private economic interests and patterns of advice and friendship that may influence judgment are legitimate subjects for public scrutiny. Economic connections with friends and family fall under a legitimate rubric. There is no rule against public officials making private gains.[44] Scrutiny of the private economic lives of public officials is warranted, however, because most public corruption involves issues of economic interest. Economic interests can also undermine the credibility of an official's judgment, the appearance of fairness, and the legitimacy of an institution when an official must act on an issue affecting his or her private interests. This happens most often when one's economic interests overlap with the areas one has responsibility for in office, such as when Attorney General Edwin Meese held stock in Bell companies during the period when he supervised the AT&T divestiture case. Likewise, members of Congress accepted below-value stock in the Credit Mobilier company while voting on investigations into it.[45] Debt, business interests, and new desires or obligations can all make people vulnerable to temptations for self-serving. Economic interests can also be used as a condition of special access, such as when Speaker of the House Jim Wright sold thousands of copies of a book he had written to interest groups, which bought the book in bulk in order to gain access to him.[46]

Public officials' patterns of association can provide information about the quality of their judgment. For instance, a police officer's association with organized crime or the Ku Klux Klan would be a subject of legitimate inquiry. Family and friends matter when they can influence the exercise of power or profit from decisions. The need to make decisions that affect one's friends or relatives not only unduly strains independent judgment but also casts doubt on the very appearance of fair judgment. Things have improved considerably since the days when senators such as Daniel Webster received retainers from companies for their services.[47] But "friends" who give gifts or preference to relatives—such as the company that gave a job to the ex-wife of Senator Robert Packwood just as he was scheduled to vote on an issue important to the company—illustrate how privacy claims break down. Similarly the wife of Senator Mark Hatfield, a senator noted for his integrity, received a $55,000 fee for dubious services from a Greek financier whose billion-dollar scheme for an African pipeline had come before Hatfield's committee.

The increasing number of two-career professional couples in public life aggravates the issue. Often one spouse will suffer as he or she must make career adjustments to avoid conflict of interest.[48] This area, like all the others, possesses ambiguity because the connections are unpredictable but real. Suppose, as in the case of President Ronald Reagan and his wife, Nancy, that a public official values and respects the advice of a spouse and consults with him or her on all issues. Suppose that this spouse goes to an astrologer for information that influences the advice handed on to the executive. This very personal pattern of relations could have significant bearing on public decisions and would be a legitimate focus of scrutiny.

The use of office to satisfy private desires or to effect private gain is not a private action but a public crime. Any claims of privacy depend upon the assurance that private actions do not violate other moral claims. Yet individuals in office deceive themselves into believing that their actions are merely "private." The use of office for financial gain or to extract favors, however, violates the trust of office and the conditions upon which people are granted power. Public integrity depends upon a capacity for honest self-reflection and self-discipline. The abuse of public office can be most notorious when individuals use official power to gratify their own personal desires and lose the capacity to separate their private desires from their public actions. Sexual relations that because of their intimacy enjoy a basic privacy protection can nonetheless provide vivid examples of abuse of public trust. Representative Daniel B. Crane was correctly censured for having sexual relations with a teenage House page, as was Representative Gary E. Studds. Wayne Hays, a powerful committee chairperson in the House of Representatives, correctly resigned after it was discovered that he had placed Elizabeth Ray on the payroll as a typist in exchange for sexual favors, despite the fact that she could not type or even answer the phones competently.[49] As these cases demonstrate, individuals demonstrate a moral blindness that cannot distinguish private desires and commitments from the obligations of a public official. The corruption of power often twists office to favor one's personal goals over loyalty to public institutions.[50]

To the extent that it is legitimate to inquire into private lives, the information should be limited to the smallest possible circle of people who oversee and evaluate individuals. This limitation of scrutiny tied to delegation is the most important qualifier of the permeability of private and public lives. Whatever inquiry does exist should be kept within the minimum circle, while information that comes out beyond that circle should be discounted as "none of our business." For instance, when the Clinton administration entered office in 1993, it permitted up to forty individuals who had previously used drugs to work in the White House. This information, which came up in the normal course of Secret Service investigations, revealed past, not current, behavior. After internal debate, the administration initiated a voluntary drug-testing program to monitor the officials in the future to avoid lapses in judgment and threats to security. Yet the entire program remained administered and handled in-house.[51]

Where the public record is limited or insufficient, one can look to other areas to discover the quality of promise-keeping, caring, integrity, competence, and judgment. As we have discussed, the focus upon past office has serious limits as a guide to evaluation; its relevance depends upon the consistency of the person's actions over time and the comparability of the positions. Given the importance of democratic accountability, a person's integrity and ability to keep promises matters profoundly. A strong past record of public trust should seal off inquiries into private life. However, if significant doubts exist in this area, it can sometimes open the controversial area of sexual relations and fidelity. In other countries and cultures, marital infidelity is an accepted fact of life, and there seems to be little evidence in general that marital fidelity correlates with public honor and effectiveness. Yet an individual's fidelity to his or her spouse can reflect a basic capacity for keeping promises or for disciplining one's own desires for a broader communal purpose. Infidelity, especially if it is of long duration and consistent, suggests a capacity for extended deceit to intimates and friends.

Moreover, frequent womanizing (since males are usually the issue) can manifest as a problem not just with commitment but with women—a disrespect or obsession with them as objects of desire and satisfaction. It suggests a tendency to discount the pain inflicted upon spouse and family by betrayal and deceit. People committed to a political order that accords women equal respect and opportunity may be alerted to disturbing attitudes towards more than half of humanity. Repeated marital infidelity can cause citizens to ponder whether a politician is driven more by the needs for power and adulation than by the desire to serve, since the womanizing and ambition may spring from the same character source.[52]

Yet even infidelity provides no clear litmus test. Marriages can wither or become hollowed out within public life just as they can elsewhere. The death of a marriage is no clear measure of the quality of a person. In some cases, commitment to a dead marriage for the sake of the children can manifest a strong moral commitment, and spouses may develop their own uneasy sexual agreements to keep the marriage afloat. A marriage can remain intact based upon affection, respect, and partnership yet lack

a strong sexual dimension between the partners, and affairs can compensate for this lack. A marriage can even die because public commitment
and devotion to office have denied the married couple time for intimacy
and communication. These complexities suggest that infidelity is seldom
a clear or helpful indicator of public integrity.

*If people make their personal lives an issue in the public presentation of their
personae, then they open their private life to judgment in those areas, especially
if they have claimed their private life as a proof of their integrity.* When individuals attack others for transgressions or propose regulating the private
lives of citizens, their own adherence or lack of adherence to equally high
standards is open to legitimate scrutiny. Citizens can then judge the public hypocrisy or authentic capacity for truth telling and moral consistency
of individuals.

This is one area in which issues of infidelity can become relevant. Public officials often present themselves as committed family members and
use these images to "prove" their commitment to certain values. If the
official is found to be living with someone or having an affair, this may be
legitimate—if uncomfortable—information if he or she projected a different image. In the 1890s W.C.P. Breckenridge, a member of Congress
from Kentucky, thrilled the nation with his impassioned defenses of
"chastity as the foundation, the cornerstone, of human society." "A pure
home makes pure government," he argued. These positions created a
national constituency. In 1894 Madeline Pollard proved that he had
seduced her at age seventeen and fathered two children by her. The scandal rightly destroyed Breckenridge's career. In 1980 Robert Bauman, a
leading Republican ultraconservative in the House of Representatives,
was charged with soliciting sex from a sixteen-year-old nude male dancer
in a gay bar. Bauman, married for twenty years and a father of four, had
cosponsored legislation to bar gay men and women from housing and
jobs. With suitable justice, Bauman lost his family, job, and career.[53]

Officials can also choose to make their private lives a public issue.
When President Clinton appointed Roberta Achtenberg as an assistant
secretary of Housing and Urban Development, the fact that she was
openly lesbian made her intimate private life a public issue. Given the
political climate, Achtenberg and President Clinton chose to air the issue
for the very purpose of breaking the barrier to public service imposed by
prejudice against lesbians and gays who are open about their sexual orientation. They sought to confirm in a public forum that a homosexual

could be a competent and effective professional and that the private issue of sexual orientation should not be central to the decision of whether to hire, elect, or appoint.

In his first presidential campaign, Bill Clinton made his marriage a central issue by claiming that he and his wife Hillary constituted a team. He argued as part of his appeal that he respected and listened to her advice and gave great weight to it. In making this a direct point of the campaign and granting her significant influence in the formation of his administration, he made his wife and their relationship an issue of scrutiny.[54]

Some private actions can subvert an individual's ability to live up to the symbolic dimensions of an office. Some public offices require officials to exercise "moral leadership."[55] However, this demand can be carried too far, especially if it is generalized to the claim that any public official must represent in some way a set of idealized "values" that are ideologically infused. Officials, however, should act in a manner that inspires respect for their position and the laws and policies that they represent or espouse. During the Reagan administration, Appeals Court Justice Douglas Ginsberg's name was withdrawn from nomination to the Supreme Court when it was revealed that he had broken the law and smoked marijuana in his office with students while a law professor at Harvard. Other public officials escaped condemnation by revealing that they too had smoked marijuana earlier in their lives, but they argued that an event in their youth should not be grounds to judge their present character. What gave the charges cogency was Ginsberg's very limited history as a judge, combined with the habitual and recent nature of his actions as well as the fact that they had taken place in a workplace setting with students whom he should have been teaching to respect the law. Furthermore, he had been nominated by a president who had mounted a national campaign against drug abuse, and he would have had to make judgments about the laws dealing with drug use. None of these charges against Ginsberg addressed the issue of competence, but they focused—quite rightly—on the cost to the legitimacy of the office.[56]

When private and unneeded information comes to the attention of principals, they have special obligations to dismiss or discount the information if possible. In assessing information, they should focus upon the integrity and character of the official over time. This means that they should analyze whether the information indicates an isolated mistake, an experiment, a tragedy, or a character flaw. Singular events and tragedies matter far less than patterns of actions over time that reveal basic lineaments of character. In judging these actions, individuals should fit patterns together and try to discover whether public and private actions reinforce each other or reveal discontinuities. In *The Laws* Plato advocates exposing would-be rulers to vices so that the experience will deepen their knowledge of the stakes. Living a "boring" life does not necessarily make one a mature, wise, or fine human being. Overcoming failure, personal wreckage, or addiction or rebuilding a marriage or a life can demonstrate dimensions of character and strength as well as extend a person's moral imagination. It makes sense to exercise a "statute of limitations" on incidents that occurred years earlier, even those germane to public performance, if they are offset by a long and honorable life lived after the incident. The past should not be a prison for anyone.

Additionally, in any judgment of a public official, citizens need to ask, What are the alternatives? All humans are imperfect, and in politics citizens may face a choice between a flawed but skilled human with desirable positions on issues and one whose private life is less flawed but who is less competent or holds less solid policy positions. Even if private scandal is judged harshly, the realities of power and the ironies and complexity of human beings can lead to imperfect but defensible judgments.

Three stories involving the troubling area of sexuality and fidelity demonstrate how these standards can be applied. In 1995 Senator Robert Packwood was accused of sexually importuning female lobbyists and members of his staff. These unwanted overtures occurred over a fifteen-year period. Packwood had served for two decades as a senator with a strong public record, including consistent support for women's rights. After a year of hearings that proved the allegations, Packwood chose to resign from the Senate rather than face certain expulsion. Regardless of his public record, he had clearly and continually abused his power and office. In the 1884 presidential campaign, the Republicans revealed that the Democratic presidential candidate, New York Governor Grover Cleveland, had fathered a child out of wedlock. The uproar over the revelation hurt Cleveland, but ultimately his long and impeccable record as a public executive of the country's most powerful state, coupled with the fact that the affair had occurred in the distant past and that he acknowledged the child and had provided for her support, overrode misgivings about the private scandal. Additionally, the Republican candidate, James Blaine, had serious problems of his own with conflict-of-interest charges.

A century later, front-running presidential candidate Senator Gary Hart challenged reporters to follow him after charges of infidelity had been raised against him. Having made the challenge, he continued his affair with Donna Rice. When the affair was exposed, he denied the charges and acted petulantly and erratically. The revelations ended Hart's campaign and destroyed his support, because people were already concerned about his very thin legislative record and his uneven performance in official roles. In moving from the legislative to the executive branch, Hart would also have considerably more power, responsibilities, and pressures upon him. His weak record and the higher stakes involved led the public to examine other areas of his personal life—a process that raised enough questions about his strength of character, honesty, and judgment as to cause considerable unease even among his supporters. The affair and his handling of it, rather than being overridden by the quality of his public service, reinforced the concerns about its weaknesses.[57] Cleveland's conduct, on the other hand, revealed honor even towards his own private failure while his impeccable public record towered over Blaine's tarnished one. Private scandal can signify great import with someone like Hart or reveal little about suitability for office with someone like Cleveland.

In summary, public officials have a very strong right to protect their privacy. However, private lives can matter in the evaluation of public officials. A number of legitimate reasons to inquire into private lives of public officials do exist, and these expand as the level of responsibility increases. Even then, most information should be treated as irrelevant in light of the standards I have suggested. Morally questionable or "scandalous" actions from private life should always be considered in context. Each private action may or may not illuminate public integrity, and the same action may indicate different things for different individuals. The standards suggested here provide guidance about how to frame judgments but not a definitive set of determinations.

Finally, when people confront the moral flaws of public officials exposed in their private lives, they should beware of their own self-righteousness. Saints and prophets make notoriously bad rulers. We should judge as mortals judging other mortals. The possibility of redemption should exist in political life as well as private life. We should judge with mercy.

10

Political Prudence

Between the idea
And the reality
Between the motion
And the act

T. S. Eliot, *The Hollow Men*

Ruling others has one advantage: You can do more
good than anyone else.

Baltasar Gracián, *The Art of Worldly Wisdom*

IN A FAMOUS PASSAGE Machiavelli wrote, "The man who wants to act
virtuously in every way necessarily comes to grief among so many
who are not virtuous. Therefore if a prince wants to maintain his rule he
must learn how not to be virtuous."[1] This paradox haunts any arguments
about the role of ethics in public life. It echoes the claim the Athenians
make towards the city of Melos in Thucydides' history two thousand
years earlier that "right, as the world goes, is only in question between
equals in power, while the strong do what they can and the weak suffer
what they must."[2] Both writers suggest that the effectiveness domain of
the public integrity triad overrides the obligations of office and the personal moral commitments and capacities. The realist school of politics
formalizes this claim with the argument that public officials and leaders
cannot afford ethics in a world of serious responsibilities, powerful institutions, and committed adversaries.[3] The realist view has contended over
the centuries with an alternative moral concept of leadership in the natural-law and the Kantian traditions, which argues that political action
should follow the requirements of ethics.[4]

Writings on public leadership reflect this split between the Scylla of
expediency and the Charybdis of moralism. Classic studies in the Machi-
avellian tradition focus upon the tactical and personality dimensions of

leadership.[5] A number of writers, however, call for an explicit recognition of the moral nature of leadership.[6] These studies succeed in identifying the moral responsibilities of public officials and leaders, but they seldom can provide consistent guidelines about what leadership ethics should focus on. For an approach focused upon the judgment of individuals, an ethics that emphasizes virtues and moral dispositions provides considerable moral resources to sustain public integrity.[7] From the time of Aristotle, prudence has been regarded as the linchpin of political judgment, and prudence is the third domain of public integrity. Any explanation of the ethics of leadership and public office needs an account of political prudence.[8]

The claims of political prudence will not supersede or replace moral norms or principles. In a world of vague and often conflicting norms and immense constraints upon action, however, political prudence defines a domain of obligations that complement moral and legal obligations. Prudence provides concrete shape for the obligations of office and personal moral commitments. The requirements of prudence arise when officials must find concrete outcomes to give reality to their commitments. Political prudence expands the moral resources of judgment for public officials by enabling them to engage political limits rather than assuming that those limits override moral and legal concerns. Although it does not abolish the tension between realists and moralists, a focus upon political prudence avoids the overdrawn division between naked power and moral commitment.

Building upon the tradition that sees person-centered virtue as central to judgment and integrity, I argue that political prudence completes public integrity and provides a basic moral resource of public officials and leaders. This chapter presents a concise and usable analysis of political prudence to which individuals can refer for guidance. In it I focus upon the operational requirements of a prudence to guide and evaluate actions. I believe that the obligations of prudence flow from the nature of political achievement and generate strong responsibilities to which officials of integrity must attend.

Virtue and Leadership

Public office demands leadership. Leadership requires ethics because public officials and leaders possess responsibilities. People in positions of leadership can make a difference; they can bring about changes in behavior that would not occur without their actions. Leadership opportunities exist throughout political and organizational life, even informally in positions that are not linked to formal authority. Fellow citizens, colleagues, and subordinates depend upon officials and leaders and are vulnerable to the consequences of their actions. They rely upon officials' competence and promises. Citizens depend upon official leaders to act in ways that will protect their security, welfare, and basic interests. Colleagues and other officials depend upon leaders to enable them to perform their offices. The integrity of leaders who hold public office is grounded in a promise to respect that reliance, vulnerability, and dependence within the constraints of law.

The ethics of responsibility requires leaders to attend to the consequences of their actions.[9] Given the stakes of public office, the first responsibility of leadership and integrity resides in what Adam Smith called "self-command" or "self-mastery." All public virtues—all capacity to live up to promises, to obey the law, and to follow directives—depend upon this primary moral capacity.[10] People in positions of responsibility have an obligation to control their passions and overcome the temptations of power. Without this self-discipline, they could abuse their power or fail in their responsibilities. In a complicated and often hostile world, leaders need to have the capacity to engage obstacles and to direct their talents and energies to the resolute achievement of goals. When internal or external stimuli affect them, they should have the self-control to think through the situation rather than to react instantly. Without self-command, integrity remains impossible.[11] Self-mastery, however, only lays the foundation for ethical leadership.

Thinking about ethics as building upon virtues extends self-mastery to the way humans should develop their patterns of reaction and engagement with life. It attempts to identify the characteristics required by people who possess roles and responsibilities.[12] A virtue embodies a pattern of habitual perception and behavior. Such patterns and habits arise not only from how people are raised but also from their own training and self-development. To possess a virtue such as prudence is to have one's emotions and perceptions trained and aligned with broader moral purposes so that they support, not subvert, responsible judgment. Personal character embodies a habitual way of engaging and responding to life. These habits play out over time as choices that reinforce the habits and build internalized patterns of behavior that recognize and respond to the morally important aspects of a situation.[13] Personal virtues are not immutable;

people can train themselves over time to approach problems in different ways, to judge according to different standards, and to choose in new ways.[14]

Thinking of prudence as a virtue reinforces public integrity because it focuses upon the responsibility of the person. Without this focus upon responsibility, the exercise of power can reduce to what Václav Havel calls the "innocent power" of the individual who becomes an "innocent tool of an 'innocent' anonymous power, legitimized by science, cybernetics, ideology, law, abstraction, and objectivity—that is, by everything except personal responsibility to human beings as persons and neighbors."[15] Instead of being responsible agents, individuals become vessels carrying the intent and justification of other people and ideas.

To unite moral and practical concerns in a world of conflict among people, responsible political leaders and officials need to exercise judgment constantly.[16] Personal virtues define the stable cognitive and emotional responses to that world that guide, inform, and energize judgment. They become the underlying bones and sinews of public integrity. This process involves not just emotions but also a trained perception through which individuals can identify the morally relevant aspects of a situation and frame judgments around them.[17] Virtues do not replace laws, norms, or duties in political life, but they give life to these moral dimensions, helping people humanize obligations as their own. As situations grow complicated, difficult, and lengthy, virtues provide the stability of judgment and the emotional endurance that make it possible for individuals to pursue moral commitments over time and across obstacles.

Virtue alone cannot sustain public integrity or a full political ethics. Many virtues such as courage, temperance, generosity, and mercy should inform political action. But virtues understood as simple emotional dispositions to action without reflective judgment can be blind or can fall prey to Aristotle's reminder that any aspect of life carried to an extreme can become a vice.[18] For instance, if a generous person wants to act, he or she must still figure out when to be generous, to whom, and by how much. Similarly in real life, multiple virtues, moral principles, and laws will often conflict in a situation, and a person will still have to figure out what concrete action is required of these moral commitments. Finally, virtues can be subsumed by other, less-desirable ends. Courageous soldiers can serve an evil cause; evil dictators can act with mercy; greedy individuals can show generosity to friends. Virtues alone cannot provide the moral foundations of all actions.[19] They exist in dialogue and tension with norms, principles, and conceptions of the good that bound them and give them direction. Consequently, classical discourse about politics and judgment cites prudence as the central virtue. Prudence involves synthesizing the complex moral and reality dimensions of an action and finding a concrete "shape" to moral aspirations, responsibilities, and obligations.[20]

Unfortunately modern accounts of prudence have done little to bolster its classic role. The first modern analysis builds on Hobbes and postulates prudence as a form of extended rational self-interest.[21] Prudence is reduced to almost algorithmic formulas of how to maximize one's goals within constraints and over time, or it becomes the engine for garnering consent among self-interested agents. It suffers from a very high level of abstraction and offers little help in the actual formation of the goals themselves.[22] Adam Smith referred to such prudence as important but limited, a virtue recommended with "cold esteem," but incapable of sustaining a full moral life.[23]

The second modern analysis arises mainly in international affairs but extends to all of politics and statecraft. The realist tradition seeks to "maintain the autonomy of the political sphere," in Hans Morgenthau's phrase.[24] It accepts and builds upon a separation of morality and action and focuses upon power as the exclusive legitimate goal of political leadership. The realist views the moralist, or one who carries serious moral aspirations into political office, as either ineffectual or dangerous. Realists argue that responsible leaders should set aside their moral commitments and goals; they view political leaders as entering a world of the morally condemned who must risk their souls for the state or act with "dirty hands," hardened hearts, and rough consciences.[25] Any other moral goals, they claim, demonstrate naïveté and betray obligations to fellow citizens. The realist approach, however, offers an arid and limited view of political leadership and pays scant attention to the complex moral aspects of durable political achievement. Power exists as only a means to achieve goals. Both these analyses grant prudence little independent moral content but see it as only a tool for asserting one's will.

The theory of political prudence that I believe to be consistent with public integrity builds upon an older account of political prudence, which Alberto Coll identifies as the tradition of "normative prudence." This tradition focuses upon the character and judgment of the official or leader who must act in an imperfect and constrained world.[26] Normative prudence centers upon the obligations to achieve moral self-mastery, to attend to the context of the situation, and through deliberation and careful judgment to seek the ends of excellent political achievement.

Prudent Judgment

The traditional understanding of normative prudence sees it as contributing to the correct choice of moral action on two levels. First, it helps humans sort out and balance decisions when multiple norms conflict. Second, it comprehends efforts to give reality to moral commitments and responsibilities. Although conceptually distinct, the two may interact. For instance, if several principles or goods conflict, individuals may choose to act on the ones they believe are most feasible, will endure the longest, or involve the least amount of violence. The dimensions of prudence then legitimately affect the first level of judgment. I focus upon the second level of judgment and explore the prudential dimensions entailed in political achievement.

Prudence, in this sense, can be considered the architectonic virtue, the one that gives form and shape to actions—the virtue without which no moral aspiration would have a concrete reality. This understanding of normative prudence is broader than its modern narrow concept of extended self-interest, encompassing judgments that implement responsibilities and obligations and moving far beyond realist equation of prudence with power. Saint Thomas Aquinas calls it the virtue of "imperative decision." As a natural-law theorist, Aquinas grants great weight to independent moral justifications of principles but sees prudence as a necessary complement to moral ideals and commitments. Prudence pervades the "doing of human acts" and involves the "correct marshaling of means to end" in situations in which there is "no final way of reaching an agreement."[27]

The actual content of most virtues can be best understood as the normative practices entailed in seeking excellence in a realm of human conduct. The standards of excellence derive from the ends of the activity within the realm of conduct.[28] Discussions of virtue can be notoriously vague about the exact nature of virtuous actions. In general, virtues are referred to by citing examples of action, but the attempt to specify virtues is often very unclear. Too many analyses end up looking like little more than "virtue is as virtue does." To avoid this vagueness, I argue that political prudence encompasses the logic of excellence in political achievement. This account insists that a complex and rich understanding of political achievement extends the range of morally relevant concerns. Excellent political achievement consists of outcomes that (1) gain legitimacy, (2) endure over time, (3) strengthen the political community, (4) unleash minimum unforeseen consequences, (5) require reasonable use of power resources, and (6) do not require great violence or coercion to enforce the outcome.[29]

Political prudence consists of a family of justifications tied to excellent achievement in politics. Prudent judgment identifies the salient moral aspects of a political situation that a leader has a moral obligation to address in making a decision. This approach emphasizes achievement, not success, because the two are not the same. A leader can achieve a momentary success because of luck or sheer brutality rather than judgment and care. A success can be fleeting, or it can induce tremendous adverse consequences that overwhelm it; a success can be aimed at personal aggrandizement, not political order. This approach moves the understanding of prudence beyond the reciting of examples and extracts generalizations and reference points that give an intellectual content to prudent obligations. The failure to account for the prudential aspects of judgment means a leader is morally negligent.

Political prudence encompasses eight aspects of political achievement that fall into three related and overlapping areas. The first covers the capacities that a leader must cultivate to act with prudence: disciplined reason and openness to experience and knowledge and foresight and attention to the long term. The second covers the modalities of statecraft that leaders must master: the acquisition and deployment of power and resources; timing, momentum, and direction; and the proper alignment of means and ends. The third covers the attributes of political outcomes to which prudent statecraft must attend: the durability and legitimacy of outcomes; minimal violence and coercion; and build and sustain community. These dimensions generate concerns that prudent leaders have an obligation to address. They provide standards for leaders and for those who wish to advise, direct, or criticize the actions of leaders.[30]

Disciplined Reason and Openness

The word *prudence* derives from a Latin word meaning "to see ahead" and reinforces the emphasis upon self-mastery. Prudence requires disciplined reason: the ability to see and think clearly and not be overcome by passions or egocentricity. Talleyrand suggested that good political leaders must bear little malice and hold few grudges.[31] Emotion-driven decisions undisciplined by reflection can lead to irresponsible judgments or to great losses for little gains.

Prudent reason builds upon openness and attention to the complexity of reality. Good judgment requires good information and a willingness to learn. Prudent leaders seek out knowledge of the physical, social, and economic world around them in order to see it more clearly. Additionally, reason and openness lead to deliberation and learning. Cardinal Richelieu, like Machiavelli, constantly urged public officials not to listen to flatterers and friends in making official judgments. A clear sign of prudence is the willingness of a person to seek the advice and help of skilled experts in making and implementing decisions. Richelieu emphasized the need to build into institutions the capability for honest and expert advice and the tradition of encouraging individuals to speak the truth, not hide it.[32] The capacity to learn from and utilize others more capable than oneself highlights the centrality of reason, deliberation, and openness to prudent judgment. It also guards against the self-deception and arrogance that tempt many leaders.[33]

Attention to openness means that a prudent leader does not close off options needlessly or prematurely, nor overcommit to one solution that might generate unanticipated consequences and harms. Prudence requires that officials and leaders be willing to confront the limits as well as strengths of their actions and to rethink them if necessary. A consistent enemy of prudent judgment is ideological rigidity that interprets all information within one frame of reference and leads to one outcome regardless of costs. To be driven by ideological certainty, emotion, vengeance, anger, ambition, or pride violates the responsibilities of public integrity and the requirements of political prudence.

In political life much prudent knowledge is historical knowledge. Such knowledge involves discovering as much as possible about the history and context that influences political actors. Leaders have special obligations to know the constraints upon their allies and adversaries and build these into their own decisions. They need to learn and listen carefully in their interactions to comprehend the different practices of negotiation, truth telling, and promise keeping of friends and enemies to be able to work with them. In understanding others' constraints and practices, prudent leaders can anticipate actions and avoid being manipulated or making rash mistakes. They also have a much better chance at negotiating solutions that do justice to all sides. Officials have strong obligations to understand the degree of trustworthiness as well as the intentions and capacities of their adversaries. Most important, they need to develop the capacity to project themselves into the minds of others and know their cultural and historical background and constraints. A refusal to explore and understand all the historical aspects of a situation, given limits on time and knowledge, violates political prudence.[34]

Foresight and the Long Term

As its Latin derivation suggests, prudence involves foresight. Prudent leaders try to anticipate future issues as they scan the power and interests of the actors in their political world. For Machiavelli, the hallmark of a good leader was the capacity to foresee and address political problems early.[35] Foresight requires leaders to try to think through the consequences of action and avoid actions whose probable negative consequences would overwhelm their good effects. Similarly, they must be careful to prepare for reasonable contingencies and to anticipate the power and hostility of others. In real life, however, one cannot prepare for all possible contingencies, and the press of daily politics and demands for immediate results can powerfully erode such anticipatory preparation. Successful foresight, then, must be wedded to courage and skill.[36]

This mode of thinking pushes responsible individuals to take the long-term view of politics. Thinking of the long term disciplines a leader to think more clearly, to be less overwhelmed by the passions of the moment or the clamor of groups demanding an immediate solution. Although everyone is dead in the long run, this discipline of reflection focuses upon issues of durability and legitimacy and drives prudence beyond narrow self-interest. For instance, the moment of victory truly tests prudent statecraft. In 1805 when Napoleon won the victory of Ulm over Austria, Talleyrand could not persuade him to treat Austria well. Napoleon's short-term ambition sowed the seeds of the long-term alliances against him. Sixty years later, after the German victory at Sadowa, on the other hand, Bismarck persuaded the Kaiser to treat Austria leniently and thus sowed the seeds of a future alliance.[37] The long-term perspective will compete with and conflict with the short-term requirements of power and maintaining a coalition to attain a goal. At the Versailles peace conference the British Prime Minister Lloyd George constantly fought, usually allied with President Woodrow Wilson, to soften the harshest conditions that were imposed upon Germany. At several points, however, he acceded to such problematic issues as war reparations and the war-guilt clause either to hold France in the coalition or to satisfy his parliamentary supporters in London.[38]

Viewing from the long-term perspective enables individuals to discover more clearly what their moral commitments require in a constrained situation. When Dag Hammarskjöld became Secretary General of the United Nations, he worked with great care to build his office into a significant power in the international arena. The institution had no real resources and little stature. But with a constant attention to the long term, Hammarskjöld created an important role by building on the rhetorical and legal possibilities of the UN charter and incessantly practicing self-disciplined civility. When leaders were enmeshed in spirals of rhetoric and confrontation as in the 1958 Lebanon crisis, he filled a crucial role as an intermediary. Every action he took was predicated on the notion that "only partial results can be expected in each generation" and that humans and institutions must "grow into" solutions to problems.[39] Prudent leaders understand that preparation for windows of opportunity and building coalitions' acceptance of policies all depend on sustained efforts. Often they look to achieve results in the momentum or direction of policy, rather than a particular outcome.

Deploying Power

In political life, power determines the range of possibilities for achievement. Too often individuals of self-conscious integrity see power as corrupting to their rectitude. Too often people in positions of authority disdain the exercise of power as contaminating them or their office. They believe that their uprightness, technical competence, or official status should ensure their position. No one with responsibilities, however, can stand above the play of power. All official life is rife with politics, and official or unofficial leadership requires skillful mastery of the art of acquiring and deploying power. Political achievement depends upon the hard work of marshaling power and resources to the achievement of a goal, whether it involves augmenting one's own power, empowering others, or undermining the power of another.

A leader must also understand and appreciate the power of adversaries and allies. When Konrad Adenauer became president of a war-devastated and divided Germany after World War II, he presided over a desperately weakened and powerless country. Yet he developed his own power base by earning the trust and respect of his allies. He also played on their fears of Communism to obtain their aid in Germany's redevelopment as well as to gain support for Germany's rearmament and reintegration into the Western European community.[40] Good leaders understand power in all its manifestations, know how to create it from resources at hand, and appreciate its deployment. Power must also endure for achievements to endure, and the deployment of power must account for durability as well as initial success. When Nancy Hanks took over the fledgling National Endowment for the Arts in the late 1960s, the agency struggled with little support and much skepticism. Hanks built allies within the Executive Branch, Congress, and the arts community and worked to create a mission that connected arts funding with the aspirations of democratic life. Her nonpartisan institution building enabled the endowment to survive through several changes of administration and much controversy.[41]

Titian's painting *An Allegory of Prudence* embodies the Renaissance understanding of the prudent leader that highlights these concerns. A man's head has three aspects: youth, maturity, age. Each aspect of the face looks in a different direction and merges into an animal form. A dog looks to the rear, a lion looks across the plane toward the viewer, and a boar looks forward. The dog respects history and what came before; the lion looks to the present with strength and fortitude; the boar seeks to divine the future and anticipate the consequences of action. In more colloquial terms, prudent leaders cover their rear, flanks, and front.

Timing and Momentum

The ability to time one's actions to accord with the greatest strength of a position and the weakest position of an opponent is crucial. Sometimes this takes years of patient preparation in order to attain a particular alignment of power and produce the cultural and political conditions for acceptance of one's goal. Thurgood Marshall and the NAACP Legal Defense Fund crafted a twenty-year plan of numerous and difficult court challenges to set legal precedents that cumulatively undermined the legal edifice of segregation in the United States. They had to carefully choose cases in the face of many urgent issues, assessing their budgets, the status of the law, and the politics of a particular location and court.[42] It may mean working and waiting for a shift in the terms of debate or seizing on an incident that galvanizes support around an issue, as President Lyndon Johnson did when he used John Kennedy's assassination to make the civil rights bill a testimony to a martyred leader. Similarly President Harry Truman and Secretary of State George Marshall used the Communist threat in Eastern Europe to overcome domestic opposition and isolationism and push the Marshall Plan to reconstruct Europe after World War II.[43] Political leadership involves the ability to act with care and wait with patience, then move with quickness and surety when the opportunity arises. As Machiavelli suggests, the lion and the fox should dwell in the same person or leadership cadre.[44]

Prudent leadership does not mean cautious or cramped leadership. Although avoiding harm to one's citizens and society matter profoundly, prudence seeks, as Saint Thomas Aquinas argues, to accomplish good.[45] A prudent leader's intelligence seeks for the opportunities that permit action to be taken consonant with one's goals and power. In real-life situations, principles and ideals often do not dictate one clear action. Achievement often consists of maintaining a direction and unfolding of goals, of initiating and sustaining momentum towards greater achievement later. For ten years Congress would not revise the Clean Air Act because of the complex politics involved. Senator George Mitchell, who led the Democrats as both majority and minority leader during this period, was committed to a revision that would not destroy the law's intent. He liked to talk of his "patience muscle" and spent much of that decade weaving together the threads of a compromise one strand at a time by authorizing reports or keeping various issues alive in subcommittees. When President Bush signaled his willingness to work for a bill and break a decade of gridlock, Mitchell pulled together the various strands he had woven together over the years to make a compromise possible.[46] Patience and timing do not reduce to opportunism or quiescence, but represent a dialogue of possibilities with ideals.

Statecraft never achieves final or perfect solutions. Given the constraints of politics and the power of both allies and adversaries, most outcomes comport only partially with a leader's moral aspirations. They will be imperfect. In such a world, leaders need to think in terms such as direction and momentum. Sometimes even a defeat can signal progress: it may galvanize allies or bring an issue to the attention of others. An achievement may not be perfect, but when thinking of the long term and of the need to build legitimacy and durability, a leader may often settle for movement along a road through achieving an incremental gain or improvement. Timing also involves the capacity to keep in mind that, as Titian's painting symbolizes, the past, the present, and the future should always be seen as a continuum. Actions must account for the past, attend to the present and its constraints and opportunities, and aim with care and humility towards future consequences.

Means and Ends

The tradition of normative prudence emphasizes the importance of connecting means and ends. The pressures to reach the ends often override concerns about the means. Linking the two is crucial to acting with public integrity and prudence. The challenge has three dimensions. First, the right means must be found. The means of influence are many and varied, and the right combination of deliberation, persuasion, incentives, coercion, and authority is crucial. Mismatches between means and ends will ensure failure. Second, the means used, the resources expended, and the opportunities forgone should be proportional to the end sought, and the means must substantially contribute to the end, not be gratuitous, wasteful, or inefficient. Although the use of coercion is most often cited as the test case for the requirements of proportionality and contribution, these standards apply to all dimensions of political action. In 1986 the Reagan administration sought to deter leaks and spying by pushing a program to require lie detector tests of all government officials with access to classified material. In a case discussed earlier, Secretary of State George Shultz fought the program to the point of threatening to resign. He believed the proposed solution to be imprudent because it would have high costs of undercutting his leadership style, which was built on trust and respect, sabotaging the culture of the State Department, and putting innocent people at risk while failing to deter trained spies. The lie-detector proposal failed the proportionality test.[47]

Third, prudent leaders must recognize that means profoundly affect the end. Ends achieved with morally appalling means may be undermined by the illegitimacy, resentment, and anger that are moral residue of such methods. The means used can also rebound and affect the quality of humanity of the people pursuing the policy. The United States learned during the Vietnam War that the means used can undermine the legitimacy of the leaders and institutions pursuing the policy. Additionally, the means used, as in forming a coalition, can rebound forward to shape the outcome of the goals. Senator Mitchell's final clean air bill was shaped by the need to keep the coalition together, so its provisions ranged from tax breaks for ethanol to subsidies to end acid rain.[48]

Durability and Legitimacy

Real political achievement endures. Fleeting success, or actions that arouse backlashes that undercut the outcome, should not qualify as acts of real achievement. A prudent leader will work to ensure that his or her achievements will endure and gain legitimacy in the eyes of the individuals who must live with them. A real political achievement earns its legitimacy with people by the provision of benefits, respect for the people's interests and commitments, and links to their self-understandings of what is right. David Lilienthal served as a founding commissioner of the Tennessee Valley Authority. The public corporation was approved after a ten-year congressional battle and faced great opposition and skepticism. Lilienthal, much like Nancy Hanks at the National Endowment for the Arts, worked with other members of the board to develop a legitimizing rhetoric of "grassroots" democracy, coupled with strong consultation to anchor the TVA. The Authority focused its mission on the provision of basic needs that benefited the local constituencies and earned their loyalty. The rhetoric blunted the conservative opposition to public provision of such services, while the benefits cemented local and regional support. This combination stabilized the mission and support of the TVA for decades.[49] Additionally, prudent leaders should attend to their own and their government's legitimacy and credibility. These are essential social and political resources for society, and as trustees officials are responsible not to squander but to protect, restore, and augment them.

When Konrad Adenauer worked to establish democratic practices in the barren and infertile political soil of Germany after Word War II, he realized that providing economic welfare and prosperity would earn the government trust and legitimacy as nothing else could. Adenauer, allied with his brilliant finance minister Ludwig Erhard, devoted time and energy to forge a viable and vibrant economy.[50] Together they helped created a strong and viable democracy and the greatest European success of post–World War II politics.

Similarly, the means used affect the quality and durability of the outcome. When George Washington led the fight for independence in the American colonies, he instructed his soldiers not to steal or forcibly take supplies but wherever possible to buy them and respect the property rights of the landowners. At the same time, he treated the loyalists with leniency to avoid their long-term alienation from the new state. He believed that only such treatment could build loyalty and legitimacy for the beleaguered revolutionary government.[51] In perhaps his greatest act of prudence, he retired from the presidency after two terms. This set an indelible precedent, ensured a peaceful transition of power for a revolutionary regime, and ended all aspirations for a monarchical government.[52]

In all of these cases, durability depends upon connecting the achievement to the perceived interests of the parties and citizens involved and realizing the intimate connection of ends to means. Accomplishment or policy, however well intentioned or morally defensible, will not endure if it does not ground itself in the interests of those affected.[53] This requires attention to the actual needs and interests of allies and adversaries as well as a willingness to provide the trade-offs on the side and outcomes that others perceive as meeting their needs.[54] In doing this, prudent leaders address the durability of the outcome and the policy's ability to earn its own way. Without this focus, solutions will erode or dissipate or will require greater and greater amounts of coercion and violence to maintain them.

Limiting Coercion

Politics often takes on a Mephistophelian character because it so often seems to reduce to issues of coercion. But prudent political achievement should breed accomplishments that endure and gain legitimacy with an economical use of violence and coercion. The more sustained violence an achievement requires, the less likely it is to earn legitimacy or acceptance, or to endure.

Coercion, however, is often necessary to define the boundaries of acceptable behavior. The threat of coercion often gives others the incentive to comply with an outcome. At other times, government coercion can deter, defend, and set boundaries on individual and institutional behavior and protect individuals from exploitation. Without this power, the practice of daily rights and freedoms would become very difficult. Prudent leaders, however, recognize violence as a dangerous means that can entangle and poison the ends sought. It should be used with economy and care.[55] Gains wrought by coercion have their own dynamic and exact a never-ending cost from a society in terms of resources spent, investment deferred, and social strictures imposed.[56] Over time coercion can seem to silence opposition and induce grudging acceptance. Forced-compliance strategies can create a world of illusory agreement and brittle acceptance, but the unending application of coercion generates significant moral problems and is inconsistent with political prudence at its core.

Building Community

Just as the legitimacy of their institutions and offices must be attended to and guarded, so public officials and leaders have special obligations to maintain and strengthen community foundations. Václav Havel has argued that "those who find themselves in politics therefore bear a heightened responsibility for the moral state of society, and it is their responsibility to seek out the best in that society, and to develop and strengthen it."[57] Havel discusses the obligation of leaders to sustain a civil society in which diverse interests can engage in political conflict and cooperation. The conditions of social integration, and the capacity of members and groups within a society to feel solidarity and interact peacefully, to act with a modicum of civility and respect towards each other, can be influenced by the example and policy of leaders and officials. Regardless of its outcome on the field, the Vietnam War tore American society apart with consequences still lingering decades later, and such communal considerations should be central to any assessment of a course of action. President Nelson Mandela of South Africa responded to just such concerns about long-term community, when after years of imprisonment and with rising terrorism and tensions in his country he became its first black leader. He initiated a careful campaign of national reconciliation designed simultaneously to reassure the once-dominant white minority and to provide hope and rewards for the newly enfranchised black majority. His policies attempted the very difficult feat of creating a political community where civil war had raged and of establishing trust where little existed.[58]

This obligation to strengthen communal affiliations and bonds among members of a society is a substantive demand of political prudence. The possibility of political community depends upon trust. Trust of other citizens and trust in institutions are social resources and social capital that leaders and major institutions should work to create and sustain. Without mutual trust among citizens, institutions, and leaders, society's capacity to act for common purposes declines. The cost of common endeavors increases, as do the costs of all social interaction. Trust, like all social capital, is increased by interactions over time and solidified by the meaningful creation of social welfare. People in positions of political leadership have special obligations to develop this dimension of political community.[59]

Prudent Leadership

Prudence does not encompass all of public ethics, but it provides a different account of public ethics than does either a realist or a moralist account. It avoids the overdrawn distinctions between politics and morality. The morality of statecraft is neither demonic nor romantic but built upon the foundations and circumstances of human ethics as people live and act. To the extent all moral actions involve underdetermined norms and principles and take place in a world of limited resources and constraints—and with independent human beings—all morality is "imperfect." All relational morality strives for the best outcome "all things considered" or "given the circumstances." Politics does not differ fundamentally from the morality most humans live in their daily lives. Political leadership may be shaped by the obligations of responsibility to others, by lack of mutuality or by hostility and threats, but it differs in degree, not in kind.

This understanding of prudence as a shaping and active virtue connected to foresight and dynamic judgment means that prudence does not reduce to caution or conservatism. The British historian G. M. Trevelyan described Lord Grey's achievement in the great Reform Act of 1832 that abolished rotten boroughs in Britain and extended the suffrage as "one of the most prudent acts of daring in history." He added that "a more perfect Bill [judged by twentieth-century standards] would have failed to pass in 1832, and its rejection would sooner or later have been followed by a civil war."[60] Lord Grey, like many prudent leaders, saw the need to act boldly to avoid severe problems, and then he carefully set out to gain the greatest good permitted by the circumstances of the time. He needed to build a coalition and solution that would endure and earn its own legitimacy despite its imperfections. In a similar vein, when Secretary of State George Shultz recognized the fundamental shift that had occurred in the Soviet Union with the advent of Mikhail Gorbachev, he began the arduous task of changing President Reagan's hostile stance towards the Soviet Union. Shultz worked to persuade a recalcitrant administration to change forty years of unremitting hostility and resistance towards the Soviet Union to one of cautious and effective support of reform.[61] Political prudence as a moral virtue possesses extraordinary versatility, and it has been a modern mistake to narrow its meaning to either self-interest or caution.[62]

To understand prudence as the shaping of solutions within constraints means that "circumstances" or "necessity" are not always the strong moral justifications they appear to be. What often distinguishes great leaders from good leaders is their capacity to understand that circumstances themselves can be subject to prudent action and change. Many leaders try to justify or excuse their actions by claiming they acted from necessity. But this moral claim of necessity assumes (1) that the public purposes remain immutable and fixed, (2) that the action required is the only way to achieve the fixed purpose, and (3) that the circumstances and time constraints require one to do only this action at this time to achieve this goal.

The necessity excuse enables individuals to let themselves out of moral responsibility by claiming that they "had no choice" but to act one way to achieve a goal. The justification, however, proves too much by ignoring the real choices individuals make. According to the insights of political prudence, individuals choose that goal from among many; individuals choose to accept only one shape as the outcome of that goal and its trade-offs; individuals choose to accept the circumstances as determinative and do not choose to try and change those or the rules of the game.

Statecraft demonstrates that enemies can become friends with effort, imagination, and self-interest, that coalitions can be restructured, and that resources can be rearranged and redirected to meet goals. Richard Nixon's opening to China demonstrated his grasp that the rules of the Cold War were limitations on action, not immutable rules of history. Through careful preparation, he waited for the right opportunity and transformed the relations of the United States to the dominant partners of the Communist world. In forging the Marshall Plan, President Truman and Secretary of State Marshall helped change the political landscape. They co-opted the opposition by connecting exports to Europe to the Midwestern farmers and gaining conservative support—in much the same way as the later creation of a food-stamp program for the poor transformed political constraints by using vouchers, which helped swing the support of conservative Midwestern farm states towards the program. Political prudence understood in this way narrows tremendously the argument from necessity and rejects an unimaginative and passive acceptance of "circumstances" or "conditions" as permanent necessities.

Political prudence deeply informs public integrity and responsibility. Starting with the obligations for self-mastery, it generates a checklist of vital concerns that responsible leaders should account for in their judgments. Political prudence does not reduce to a disposition of character nor a list of exemplars. It is a virtue linked to the moral responsibilities of political leadership and office to discern the prudential aspects of a situation and respond to them. Political prudence's intellectual and normative content arises from the full dimensions of excellence in political achievement. The nature of achievement generates a family of concerns that carry moral weight and to which leaders have an obligation to attend.

They should direct and structure a person's perception of and reflection upon a situation. These provide guidance for leaders, but they also provide standards of judgment that others can use in assisting or criticizing their actions:

1. Disciplined reason and openness to experience and knowledge;
2. Foresight and attention to the long term;
3. Acquisition and deployment of power and resources;
4. Timing, momentum, and direction;
5. Proper alignment of means and ends;
6. Durability and legitimacy of outcomes;
7. Minimal violence and coercion;
8. Building and sustaining community and trust.

If leaders and public officials attend to these concerns, they have lived up to part of the ethical responsibilities of public integrity; if they fail, they are guilty of moral negligence and irresponsibility. Political prudence does not cover all morality, nor does it guarantee success. Negligent leaders can succeed by accident, by luck, or by the incompetence of others. Paradoxically, even prudent leaders can fail. Political prudence flows from the responsibilities of leadership and power. It provides a necessary—but not sufficient—ground for public ethics.

Epilogue

If I were a wise man, I would do my part.

  Christina G. Rossetti, "In the Deep Midwinter"

I think the king is but a man, as I am. The violet smells to him
as it doth to me; the element shows to him as it doth to me;
all his senses have but human conditions. His ceremonies
laid by, in his nakedness, he appears but a man.

  Henry V 4.1.98

PONTIUS PILATE, the Roman procurator of Judea, had a problem. He was a successful and ambitious Roman official, but he faced an angry and worried local elite and a touchy mob during a sacred festival. They demanded the death of a man, Jesus, who might have been a lunatic, a blasphemer, a rabble-rouser, a revolutionary, or God—it wasn't clear to Pilate which. Pilate could find no harm that Jesus had done, but the elite and the mob wanted action. Being a clever administrator, he found a jurisdictional issue. He sent Jesus to be judged by Herod Antipas, but his ploy failed, and Herod sent Jesus back.

Pilate could still find no crime Jesus had done, but he needed to act. His contempt for the elite of Judea had already gotten him into trouble, but he disliked the idea of showing weakness by giving in to their demands. A compromise, the flogging and humiliation of Jesus, failed. The crowd turned ugly and the elite insistent, accusing Pilate of coddling rebels. Searching for a way out, he gave the crowd a choice: in honor of the sacred festival, he would release either a notorious insurrectionist and murderer, Bar Abbas, or Jesus. The crowd, seeing in Bar Abbas a local hero and egged on by the hecklers, demanded freedom for Bar Abbas and death for Jesus.

Pilate saw the potential risk only too clearly: another riot in an already overwrought Judea on a sacred day. He had already quelled several riots with heavy loss of life. His superior, the legate in Syria, was watching his violent methods. In addition, he would need even more troops, and the slim chances of cooperation with the local elite would evaporate. Going along could gain some leverage with the elite. The necessities of the situation pushed in on him.

Pilate made his choice: he released Bar Abbas and handed Jesus over to be crucified. Pilate knew his action was wrong. His conscience warned him, the law warned him, his wife warned him, but the stakes were high. His career was on the line, and long-term policy seemed to require short-term sacrifice. When he made his decision, he took the kind of action that haunts this book. He "took water and washed his hands in the full view of the people, saying, 'My hands are clean of this man's blood; see to that yourselves.'"[1]

Every serious political decision tempts people to act on the basis of expediency or self-interest. All decisions entail imperfections and problems, and these tempt individuals to deny responsibility for the consequences. Individuals blame necessity, or policy, or orders. Pilate embodies the "innocent power" that Václav Havel so feared and that has wreaked so much harm through the ages. In denying responsibility, individuals violate their integrity, diminish their dignity, and erode the moral quality of their soul. Both as people and as officials, they abet a coarser institutional morality with less concern for the full moral consequences of actions. Their self-deceiving rationalization conceals both the wrong and the responsibility.

This book's theme is that individuals who hold public office should strive to act with integrity. The public integrity I recommend requires a balance among the three domains of personal moral commitments and capacities, obligations of office, and political prudence. It depends upon self-conscious reflection, honesty, and the self-disciplined ability to resist temptation and act upon beliefs and commitments. Possessing integrity obligates individuals to know and address the legal, moral, and practical dimensions of an issue in making their decisions. I believe that this concept of integrity grounds ethics, fosters higher-quality decisions, and supports the delegations of power central to liberal and democratic life. Without people of integrity in office, trust in government and the capacity for public action decline, and the costs of oversight and enforcement rise. Amid the cascade of media scandals, the quiet and complex integrity of most public officials remains unremarked upon but all-important. In this epilogue I want to recall the major variations upon the theme of integrity that run through the book and connect its stories into a moral whole.

The Primacy of Promises and Responsibility

Political morality is created by a promise. Officials cannot rely upon a clear natural—or supernatural—morality to define the scope of their obligations when they take on an office. Instead, they "take on" an office and in so doing make a promise, explicitly or implicitly, to live up to the obligations of that office. The presumption is that morally mature individuals exist prior to and separate from taking on the office; they make the promise. Often people are hired, elected, or appointed for the skill, commitment, and character they already possess. This separation of person and office is central to western political theory and governance but also highlights the issue of integrity and responsibility.

The agreement to serve in office presumes two levels of conditions. First, people commit in light of their own beliefs and capacities; second, they agree to act in accordance with the standards of office and defer to the authority structure within which they serve. The agreement, promise, or oath becomes a moral commitment and entails the person in responsibility for actions in the office. Taking office means that individuals agree to frame judgments and defer to, but not surrender to, authority. This nexus of responsibility also means that individuals are enmeshed, to a greater or lesser extent, in the moral consequences of their actions. The act of promising, however, does not collapse their moral personality into an office but creates a distance from which they are obligated to judge the moral quality of their actions. At times of significant moral disagreement, they may resign, or they may oppose and try to change actions through legitimate means.

The promise also highlights the interaction of the person with the office. Individuals utilize their own skills, character, energy, and physical and mental capacity in office. They infuse office with the style, energy, and unique insight derived from their personal character, skills, and commitments. As leaders they bring a vision to institutions, large or small, and influence the lives of others in office and those who depend upon them for competent performance. Public integrity, then, depends upon the balance between the personal and public, not on their total separation from each other. Individuals cannot escape responsibility because this connection does exist. The office continues after a person leaves, but each individual makes the office his or hers in a unique way. Even the shape of the office after they leave will be affected by their actions, the precedents they set, and the relations they build. This interpenetrating reinforces the claim that integrity requires the balance among the three domains. Further, the ironies of rectitude are such that the promise to act in office often puts intense strain on other obligations—to family, friends, ethnic group, religion, for example—and may even involve betrayal of some of them for the public good. These moral strains, like sleaze and other temptations of power, press officials to eliminate the tensions by either collapsing selfhood into the office or imposing selfhood on the office, or by using it for their own desires. Endless variations on this theme exist, but the strong lesson remains the need to design institutions and manage institutions in ways that protect the balance and monitor those temptations and powers.

This ideal of public integrity and promise-bound office encourages the tension and expects individuals to act with initiative, insight, and vision. It expects people in office to perform with competence, to constantly assess their own performance, and to change and adapt. Accepting this tension and its advantages as well as its dangers places great weight upon institutional accountability: personal initiatives, insights, and actions must not dominate or manipulate but should be subject to law, process, and the dialogue of accountability.

The Responsibilities of Trusteeship

The ideal of public integrity expands the range of responsibilities that go with office. Traditionally these basic responsibilities are competence, efficiency, and accountability. The other responsibilities lie latent in positions and become more self-conscious as the range of discretion and power becomes greater. Those in leadership positions possess even wider obligations. Public integrity conceives of the promise to take office as more than a performance-based contract. It obviously places great weight upon competence and effective implementation but adds the obligation to seek excellence in political achievement. It builds in a strong obligation to move beyond going through the motions, pushing people to make a difference, to lead with prudent action consistent with constitutional values and buttressed by personal commitment and character.

Public integrity builds on the ancient ideal that taking office makes people trustees. Trusteeship entails many dimensions. People rely upon public officials to perform with competence to protect the public good. Officials are entrusted with public resources and money taken by the coercive power of the state, so they have special obligations to act with conscientiousness and efficiency. Public integrity also involves a strong trust not to abuse the power given by those who have little power and who rely upon officials to protect and serve them despite their vulnerability. Taking office means inheriting institutional power and institutional purposes that depend upon public legitimacy and support. Officials have powerful obligations not only to build the capacity of their organizations but also to attend to the larger issues of earning legitimacy and support. The viability and capacity of their institutions stand as both their inheritance and their legacy.

Trust and legitimacy are at stake in every interaction with fellow citizens because each interaction earns or undercuts the legitimacy of public institutions and purposes. Every official act comprehends the opportunity for conscientiousness and efficient action. Every interaction includes the opportunity to respect and include fellow citizens in the polity or to alienate and insult. These opportunities play out in daily interactions and in cumulative decisions, not just in great moments of tortured conscience. Managing the quality of daily interactions and performance is central to the leadership agenda of public integrity because public integrity is lived in daily interactions.

Being a trustee supports the ideal of democratic responsibility, which builds upon conscientious, competent, and efficient performance and requires truthful accountability. This also entails accepting the outcomes of democratic process while being willing to engage the terms of policy in an accountable manner. It reminds us that officials have special obligations to attend to the unheard voices and the underrepresented groups so that the common good, not just the organized good, is addressed. In a similar vein, they should work for the long-term view against short-term demands of political life. This expanded ideal of integrity also demands that they never forget obligations to build peace. In a diverse and conflict-ridden society, officials should model respect, enforce tolerance, and provide the matrix for the new possibilities of human growth and identity.

Threats to Integrity

The temptations of power and sleaze, the ironies of office, the erosion of integrity under the stress of opposition, the moral incompleteness of success, the betrayals implicit in holding office—all of these are unceasing. Every day the demands of office nag at people. The source of pain might be the need to deny benefits to or to incarcerate a member of an affiliated group. It might be the suffering that individuals cannot address because of regulations. It might be wounded anger in response to unruly opposition or to activists who impugn integrity or undercut a good program. The dynamics of institutional life strain the balance as well as the self-conscious honesty and reflection required of public integrity. The daily grind insinuates itself with these temptations. In this book I have examined those that cluster mainly around the breakdown in the balance among the domains of integrity: the collapse of self into office, the assertion of self over office, the denial of the humanity of opponents, the costs of betrayal, the diminishing of emotions and moral discernment that comes from hard jobs done over the years. The problematic means of political power, coupled with high aspirations and stakes, generate these problems in all areas of public life. The paradoxes, ironies, and tensions of exercising power in the name of the public good by mortal humans invites cynicism as much as arrogance.

These threats also point to the need to make managing integrity a basic part of leadership, management, and institutional design. The integrity of individuals cannot be taken for granted, and widespread integrity of people in office is achieved only through significant effort. People of good will can convince themselves that anything they are doing is right. So training, modeling, active recruitment, aligning incentives with performance, supporting and framing discretion, monitoring abuse—all can sustain and support integrity-based judgment in office. Building an ethos of honor among colleagues mutually supporting these values buttresses the other strategies. In a similar fashion, a knowledge of the temptations highlights the need to oversee, monitor, and attend to conflict of interest in vital areas, especially where external stakes and pressures are high. It also warns how secrecy can exacerbate the worst tendencies of abusive power and subverted integrity.

Character Matters

An ethics of character cannot capture all of morality. It ignores the broader issue of the right and purposes that character serves. Some classical moral theory argues that good character serves only good ends, but such tautological definitions do not capture the complexity and ironies of life. Nonetheless, I believe that focusing upon integrity does illuminate many powerful obligations of officials. In addition, being mindful of character emphasizes individuals' capacity to live the balance and bear the burdens of integrity and action. Public office brings great satisfactions. It serves others, can make profound differences in the quality of people's lives, and can help those ignored or hurt. Officials can experience the honor of serving with others committed to a cause that matters. Yet, in daily official life, so much remains undone. Law, regulations, or accountability might limit the scope of officials' initiative and imagination. They may have to act in ways that harm others or use coercion and other methods that are morally dangerous, but justified. In regulatory and criminal areas, they too often see citizens at their worst. The fractious, angry, and rambunctious politics of democratic life often leaves them burned and unrespected even as they are the ones trying to pull solidarity and justice from the fray.

In a world in which no good action seems to go unpunished, individuals can turn sour and angry. They can lose their commitment, burn out, become negligent, or simply go through the motions, poison the atmosphere for colleagues, become game-players, or use power in ways that abuse others. The betrayals, costs, and temptations of power can lead to exactly the threats and mini-tyrannies so feared by opponents of government. So integrity depends strongly upon the capacity of humans to carry the slights, disappointments, attacks, and disagreements inherent in public life yet continue to act with respectful care and competence. It sounds too trite to be true, but the capacity to carry on despite the disappointments and sorrows matters profoundly to the moral quality of public life. Quiet courage and endurance, sustained by family, friends, and colleagues, enables people of integrity to continue to act despite the paralyzing temptations. The ability to forgive or to see possibilities in moral wreckage sustains moral sanity and endurance. Public integrity acknowledges personal limits and prejudices yet still challenges individuals to act and judge with good faith knowing that they need accountability to protect government as much from themselves as others.

More powerfully, their character and the stances they take deepen and enrich their leadership. This type of realistic integrity does not seek refuge in innocence; individuals can appreciate the difficulty others face in "soldiering on," because they know the type of support needed. This awareness can sharpen the nature of their judgments and help them act with sensitivity and discernment. Their integrity leads them to welcome power and responsibility, even knowing its costs and temptations. Too many individuals of rigid integrity see power as corrupted or as beneath them. Yet the skills of exercising power are crucial to doing good and making a lasting difference. Public integrity obliges individuals to risk the temptations of power. For them power does not corrupt, it enables.

Integrity Does Not Stand Alone

The movie *High Noon* captures the iconographic ideal of public integrity in America. In the movie Gary Cooper plays a sheriff of a small town who has just married a Quaker woman, played by Grace Kelly, and plans to retire from his office. After the wedding, he learns that a murderer whom he had sent to jail years before has been pardoned and is returning to town with his gang. The criminal has sworn vengeance and will arrive on noon train. After initially running, Cooper returns to the town and prepares to meet them and their threat to public order. In the process, his deputy deserts him, the judge leaves town, and his old mentor abandons him. The town's mayor persuades people not to help the sheriff because he believes a gunfight would be bad for the town's economic development. Even his new wife leaves him after begging him to escape and give up the violence he had promised to leave behind.

At high noon, his frame a little stooped and his worn face creased, Cooper faces the four gunmen. He stands abandoned by family, friends, colleagues, and all the institutions he had done so much to support. Much like George Smiley facing Karla, he is alone. This is the image everyone who sees the movie remembers; it captures the sense that integrity is earned alone, unsupported, facing evil. In the gunfight that unfolds, Cooper battles by himself while the townspeople watch from behind locked doors. At the very end, he is caught in a crossfire, but his wife has returned. She risks herself and her own soul by shooting one of the gunmen. Together she and Cooper leave the town, bowed but unbroken.

The image of Cooper standing alone reminds us that we earn integrity with our individual decisions, but the return of his wife also reminds us that we cannot sustain integrity alone. The real world of ethics and integrity depends upon the help and support of other humans. Integrity requires careful education and growth. It needs honest self-reflection and a capacity to learn and adjust to situations. Its enemies are self-deception and denial of responsibility, or falling into the traps of groupthink, or collapsing one's selfhood into the office. To achieve integrity, we need the support of others. We grow ethically with the help of family, religion, teachers, and mentors. We arrive at good decisions with the help of others who know more about issues or whose advice and judgment we trust. We sustain ourselves against the erosion of integrity through solidarity with the honor of our colleagues and commitment to common goals and standards.

A web of relations strengthens the web of our integrity. We can avoid self-deception by relying upon honest advisors who are not afraid to tell us the truth. Friends and family outside of office can help us see more clearly, to avoid the traps of groupthink and even of too closely held honor. Such relations can provide an emotional refuge and a distance from which to see what presses upon one. They anchor beliefs or challenge actions and force us to rethink decisions and actions. Because private life and commitments do matter to sustaining public integrity, individuals need these webs of relations. A sure sign of fragile integrity is the collapse of personal life under the pressures of public office.

Integrity also plays out in how we view others. The pressures of office and conflict lure us to devalue opponents and enemies. Differences invite anger and exclusion. Conflicts aggravated by deep differences appeal to our worst instincts to dehumanize individuals. Even our own sense of being different can be a source of aggravation, self-denigration, and conflict within ourselves and against others. Public integrity reminds us of the disciplined obligation to attend to human differences with care while building peace. Officials bear special obligation to build solidarity and community and not act in ways that polarize and destroy political community.

Public integrity also needs strong institutional support. The *High Noon* myth belies the need. But most of us are not Gary Cooper, and, as we have seen, even heroes need allies. The greatest of Greek heroes, Odysseus, could not have made it back to Ithaca, however strong he was, without his knowledge of Penelope's love and the help of his loyal sailors, his mentor Athena, his son, and his loyal swineherd. Those of us who have human-scale integrity need the sustained support of people and institutions in order for it to flourish. The fate of many whistle-blowers reminds us that individuals trying to keep their integrity intact in pathological institutions can be hurt deeply. They can be marginalized as troublemakers. Their mental and physical health and their families can be broken by the relentless pressure of ostracism and attack by a threatened institution. In this century, of all centuries, decent humans have demonstrated the capacity to perform the most horrendous institutional evil sustained by denial and self-deception.

If individuals should act with integrity and public office needs integrity, then managerial leadership and institutional design should aim to sustain it. Policy and management should focus upon creating cultures that support strong commitment, professional judgment, and real accountability. Leadership at all levels must model integrity and prove that success in an institution should not demand self-deception or mindless acquiescence. Public integrity needs the support of personal and institutional leadership and management. No easy cost-benefit analysis justifies this central role of integrity. But I believe integrity anchors personal moral life, is true to the role of office in democracy, and results in better governance and higher quality of judgment and political life.

Integrity is often linked with the injunction "know thyself." This is a good place to start, but public integrity needs more than self-knowledge. It requires the knowledge of issues that bear upon an impending decision. This knowledge leads to responsible action, but it also leads us to reweave integrity in response to growth and learning. Public actions take place in an arena in which ideals, self-interest, and expediency are in constant conflict. Nor is this situation unique to public life; the life of all mortals entails just such a mixture of imperfections. Individuals of integrity connect the tensions and limitations into a life of moral worth. Those who act without responsibility lessen their dignity and the quality of their soul and contribute to a diminished political order. Under the constant stress of hostility and hope, officials striving for integrity are responsible for weaving the strands of gain and loss together into the fabrics of institutions, policies, and communities. They do so in a way that sustains their dignity, respects their humanity, and contributes to a flourishing political order.

Notes

Chapter 1. Integrity in Office

1. Legislators possess considerably wider discretion when it come to making laws because they are often elected because of their personal moral commitments and the interests of their constituents. They, nonetheless, possess serious obligations to respect law, due process, institutional legitimacy, and effectiveness as they pursue their own professed goals. See Dennis F. Thompson, *Ethics in Congress: From Individual to Institutional Corruption* (Washington, D.C.: Brookings Institution, 1995), for an insightful and nuanced account of legislative ethics consistent with this account of integrity.

2. Max Weber, "Politics as a Vocation," in *From Max Weber,* ed. and trans. H. H. Gerth and C. W. Mills (New York: Oxford University Press, 1958), 77–128; Woodrow Wilson, "The Study of Administration," *Political Science Quarterly* 2 (1887): 197–222; Herman Finer, "Administrative Responsibility in Democratic Government," *Public Administration Review* 1 (1941): 335–50.

3. These insights are implicit in the classic work of Stephen Bailey, "Ethics and the Public Service," in *Public Administration and Democracy,* ed. R. C. Martin (Syracuse, N.Y.: Syracuse University Press, 1965), 283–98. Dennis F. Thompson is the most articulate defender of personal responsibility; see *Political Ethics and Public Office* (Cambridge: Harvard University Press, 1987). Terry Cooper, *The Responsible Administrator* (New York: Kennikat Press, 1982), integrates public obligations and personal responsibility. Kathryn G. Denhardt, *The Ethics of Public Service: Resolving Moral Dilemmas in Public Organizations* (New York: Greenwood Press, 1988), defends the most far-ranging version of the thesis. Also see Michael Harmon, *Action Theory for Public Administration* (New York: Longmans, 1979).

4. Norton Long, "Power and Administration," in *Public Administration Concepts and Cases,* ed. Richard J. Stillman, 6th ed. (Boston: Houghton Mifflin, 1996), 105–10; Eugene Bardach, *The Implementation Game: What Happens after a Bill Becomes a Law* (Cambridge: MIT Press, 1977); Michael Lipskey, *Street-Level Bureaucracy: Dilemmas of the Individual in Public Services* (New York: Russel Sage Foundation, 1980); Laurence E. Lynn Jr., *Managing Public Policy* (Boston: Little, Brown, 1987), chs. 2–4.

5. Vince Blasi, *The Checking Value in First Amendment Theory,* Samuel Pool Weaver Constitutional Series no. 3 (New York: American Bar Foundation, 1977). Also see Edward Weisband and Thomas M. Franck, *Resignation in Protest: Political and Ethical Choices between Loyalty to Team and Loyalty to Conscience in Ameri-*

can Political Life (New York: Viking Press, 1975); Deanna Weinstein, *Bureaucratic Opposition: Challenging Abuses in the Workplace* (New York: Pergamon Books, 1979).

6. Robert C. Solomon, *Ethics and Excellence: Cooperation and Integrity in Business* (New York: Oxford University Press, 1992). Also see Martha Nussbaum, *The Fragility of Goodness: Luck and Rational Self-sufficiency in Greek Ethical Thought: The Tragic Poets, Plato, and Aristotle* (Cambridge: Cambridge University Press, 1986).

7. Stephen L. Carter, *Integrity* (New York: Basic Books, 1996), 3–68, 229–42; Lynne McFall, "Integrity," *Ethics* 98 (1987): 4–20, provides a seminal account of integrity that is consistent with this conception.

8. Christine M. Korsgaard, "Personal Identity and the Unity of Agency: A Kantian Reply to Parfit," *Philosophy and Public Affairs* 15 (1989): 101–32; J. Patrick Dobel, *Compromise and Political Action: Political Morality in Liberal and Democratic Life* (Savage, Md.: Rowman and Littlefield, 1990), chs. 1–2, and "Personal Responsibility and Public Integrity," *Michigan Law Review* 86 (1988): 1450–65, esp. 1450–53.

9. Nancy Sherman, *The Fabric of Character: Aristotle's Theory of Virtue* (Oxford: Clarendon Press, 1989).

10. Dennis F. Thompson, "Ascribing Responsibility to Advisors in Government," *Ethics* 93 (1983): 546–60, and "Moral Responsibility and the New York Fiscal Crisis," in *Public Duties: The Moral Obligations of Government Officials*, ed. Joel L. Fleishman et al. (Cambridge: Harvard University Press, 1991), 266–88, and especially "Moral Responsibility in Government: The Problem of Many Hands," *American Political Science Review* 74 (1980): 905–16.

11. John Rawls, *A Theory of Justice* (Cambridge: Belknap Press, 1971), 17–22, 48–51.

12. Herbert Fingarette, *Self-deception: Studies in Philosophical Psychology* (London: Routledge and Kegan Paul, 1969).

13. Dobel, *Compromise and Political Action*, chs. 1–2; Thomas Nagel, "Ruthlessness in Public Life," in *Public and Private Morality*, ed. Stuart Hampshire (Cambridge: Cambridge University Press, 1978), 75–92.

14. John Rohr, *To Run a Constitution: The Legitimacy of the Administrative State* (Lawrence: University of Kansas Press, 1986); Kathleen Clark, "Do We Have Enough Ethics in Government Yet? An Answer from Fiduciary Theory," *University of Illinois Law Review* 1 (1996): 57–102.

15. Dobel, "Personal Responsibility," 1453; also see Thompson, *Public Office*, ch. 1.

16. William Richardson and Lloyd G. Nigro, "Administrative Ethics and Founding Thought: Constitutional Correctives, Honor, and Education," *Public Administration Review* 47 (1987): 167–376.

17. Max Weber, "Politics as a Vocation," in *A Centennial History of American Public Administration*, ed. Ralph C. Chandler (New York: Wiley, 1988).

18. For the most sophisticated and clear updating of this model see John P. Burke, *Bureaucratic Responsibility* (Baltimore: John Hopkins University Press, 1986).

19. Weber, "Politics as a Vocation," 95.

20. For an insightful but overstated account of the pathology of self-interest in public organizations, see William Niskanen, *Bureaucracy and Representative Government* (Chicago: Aldine, 1971).

21. Stanley Milgram, *Obedience to Authority* (New York: Harper Torchbooks, 1975).

22. Donald Warwick, "The Ethics of Administrative Discretion," in Fleishman, *Public Duties*, 93–127.

23. Eugene Bardach and Robert A. Kagan, *Going by the Book: The Problem of Regulatory Unreasonableness* (Philadelphia: Temple University Press, 1982).

24. Benjamin N. Cardozo, *The Nature of the Judicial Process* (New Haven: Yale University Press, 1949); Rohr, *To Run a Constitution*, chs. 11, 14.

25. Stephen Toulmin and Albert R. Jonsen, *The Abuse of Casuistry* (Berkeley: University of California Press, 1988), chs. 1–2, analyze the nature of presumptive moral commitments.

26. This summarizes my extension of John Rohr's theory of public discretion in *Ethics for Bureaucrats: An Essay on Law and Values* (New York: Marcel Dekker, 1978).

27. Scott Moore, "The Theory of Street Level Bureaucracy: A Positive Critique," *Administration and Society* 19 (1987): 74–94.

28. The most powerful accounts of this thesis exist in the work of Dennis Thompson, who gives a seminal account in the "Moral Responsibility in Government." His *Political Ethics and Public Office* expands on this account in a wide variety of contexts. See also Debra Stewart, "The Moral Responsibility of Individuals in Public Sector Organizations," in *Ethical Insight: Ethical Action Perspectives for the Local Government Manager*, ed. Elizabeth K. Kellar, Practical Management Series (Washington, D.C.: International City Management Association, 1988), 22–29.

29. Harmon, *Action Theory*, ch. 14; James G. March and Johan P. Olsen, *Ambiguity and Choice in Organizations* (Bergen: Universitetsforlaget, 1976). Lynn, *Managing Public Policy*, 1–52, emphasizes how public management involves negotiating the meaning of actions.

30. Bailey, "Ethics and the Public Service."

31. Norman Bowie, *Business Ethics* (Englewood Cliffs, N.J.: Prentice Hall, 1982); Solomon, *Ethics and Excellence*, chs. 1–4.

32. Joel L. Fleishman and Bruce L. Payne, *Ethical Dilemmas and the Education of Policymakers* (Hastings-on-Hudson, N.Y.: Hastings Institute, 1980), 15; Dwight Waldo, "Public Administration and Ethics: A Prologue to a Preface," in Stillman, *Public Administration*, 460–70.

33. Terry L. Cooper and N. Dale Wright, eds., *Exemplary Public Administrators* (San Francisco: Jossey-Bass, 1994).

34. In the most plausible cases these are tied to the need to rectify the deficiencies of a democratic system, which severely discounts the least well-off, children, or future generations. See John P. Burke, "Reconciling Public Administration and Democracy: The Role of the Public Administrator," *Public Administration Review* 49 (1989): 180–85, for a synthetic review of some of the "democratic" accounts. See also Kathryn G. Denhardt, "The Management of Ideals: A Political Perspective on Ethics," *Public Administration Review* 49 (1989): 192.

35. Denhardt, *Ethics of Public Service*, presents a far-ranging statement of this model that makes little discrimination between personal judgments and public judgments.

36. Cardozo, *Nature of Judicial Process*, 141.

37. Debra W. Stewart, "An Ethical Framework for Human Resource Decision Making," 72–74, in Kellar, *Ethical Insight*. I have modified the terms slightly.

38. Joel Fleishman, "Self-interest and Political Integrity," in Fleishman, *Public Duties*, 52–92. Thompson, *Ethics in Congress*, discusses the complexities of using the self-interest limitations on legislators.

39. Henry Louis Gates Jr., "The End of Loyalty," *New Yorker* (9 March 1998): 34–44, reflects on these conflicts and decline of loyalty in public life.

40. Frederick C. Mosher, *Democracy and the Public Service*, 2d ed. (New York: Oxford University Press, 1968); Thompson, *Ethics in Congress*.

41. Timothy J. O'Neill, "Liberal Constitutionalism and Bureaucratic Discretion," *Polity* 19 (1987): 371–93, quotation on 385. O'Neill argues that the Constitution presumes a much more aggressive and interpretive day-to-day politics in which bureaucratic discretion within an accountable order is quite compatible.

42. Thompson, *Public Office*, 3.

43. Ibid., chs. 1–3.

44. Lynn, *Managing Public Policy*, 24–36, discusses how a "good action" becomes one that can "stand up to partisan scrutiny and debate."

45. Niccolò Machiavelli, *The Prince*, trans. George Bull (New York: Penguin, 1963), chs. 10, 15.

46. Dobel, *Compromise and Political Action*, ch. 5.

47. J. Patrick Dobel, "Reflection and Good Reasons in Policy Analysis," in *The Handbook of Political Theory and Policy Science*, ed. Edward Bryan Portis and Michael B. Levy (New York: Greenwood Press, 1988), 29–44. For an application of it to an organizational setting see Solomon, *Ethics and Excellence*, 101–91.

48. Bardach, *Implementation Game*; Niskanen, *Bureaucracy and Representative Government*.

Chapter 2. The Temptations of Power

1. 2 Sam. 11–12 and Psalms 25 and 116, *The New English Bible* (New York: Oxford University Press, 1972).

2. Bruce L. Payne, "Devices and Desires: Corruption and Ethical Seriousness," in *Public Duties: The Moral Obligations of Government Officials*, ed. Joel L. Fleishman et al. (Cambridge: Harvard University Press, 1981), 175–203.

3. This debate goes to the heart of American public philosophy. For the classic formulation see Carl J. Friedrich, "Public Policy and the Nature of Administrative Responsibility," versus Herman Finer, "Administrative Responsibility," in *Bureaucratic Power in National Politics*, ed. Francis E. Rourke, 2d ed. (Boston: Little, Brown, 1972), 316–36.

4. E. J. Dionne, *Why Americans Hate Politics* (New York: Simon and Schuster, 1991); Hugh Heclo, *A Government of Strangers: Executive Politics in Washington* (Washington, D.C.: Brookings Institution, 1977); James Q. Wilson, *Bureaucracy: What Government Agencies Do and Why They Do It* (New York: Basic Books, 1989).

5. John Rohr, *To Run a Constitution: The Legitimacy of the Administrative State* (Lawrence: University of Kansas Press, 1986).

6. This approach builds upon the basic insights of social psychology and attri-

bution theory. See Lee Ross and Richard N. Nisbett, *The Person and the Situation: Perspectives of Social Psychology* (Philadelphia: Temple University Press, 1991). The approach is influenced by the work of Bruce Buchanen, *The Presidential Experience* (Englewood Cliffs, N.J.: Prentice Hall, 1978), and Ralph K. White, *Nobody Wanted War: Misperception in Vietnam and Other Wars* (Garden City, N.Y.: Doubleday, 1968). I have raised the level of generality of the concepts employed by them and detached them from any specific search for the ideal personality types that can weather the pressures of office. I have integrated the work of David Kipnis, *The Powerholders* (Chicago: University of Chicago Press, 1976), on the metamorphic effects of power and that of Phillip G. Zimbardo on the notion of deindividuation in "The Human Choice: Individuation, and Order versus Deindividuation, Impulse, and Chaos," in *Nebraska Symposium on Motivation*, ed. William J. Arnold and David Levine (Lincoln: University of Nebraska Press, 1969). The work of Irving Janis on the distortions of groups upon integrity and rationality and on commitment and decision stress also underlies the analysis. See Irving Janis, *Groupthink: Psychological Studies of Policy Decisions and Fiascoes*, 2d ed. (Boston: Houghton Mifflin, 1982), and Janis and Leon Mann, *Decision Making: A Psychological Analysis of Conflict, Choice, and Commitment* (New York: Free Press, 1977).

7. Buchanen, *Presidential Experience*, chs. 1–3; Ross and Nisbett, *Person and Situation*, chs. 1–4; Janis and Mann, *Decision Making*, chs. 3–7.

8. Janis and Mann, *Decision Making*, chs. 5–9.

9. Ross and Nisbett, *Person and Situation*, chs. 3–5; Janis, *Groupthink*, chs. 8–11.

10. Larry Berman, *Lyndon Johnson's War* (New York: Norton, 1989), 20 ff., 80–88; David Halberstam, *The Best and the Brightest* (New York: Random House, 1969), epilogue, especially 624–28.

11. Buchanen, *Presidential Experience*, chs. 1, 2, 6.

12. Leon Festinger, Henry W. Riecken, and Stanley Schachter, *The Theory of Cognitive Dissonance* (Evanston, Ill.: Row, 1957); Leon Festinger, *When Prophecy Fails: A Social and Psychological Study of a Modern Group That Predicted the End of the World* (New York: Harper and Row, 1964).

13. Herbert Fingarette, *Self-deception* (London: Routledge and Kegan Paul, 1969).

14. Doris Kearns Goodwin, *Lyndon Johnson and the American Dream* (New York: Harper and Row, 1976), 312–13, quotation on 394.

15. J. Patrick Dobel, *Compromise and Political Action Political Morality in Liberal and Democratic Life* (Savage, Md.: Rowman and Littlefield, 1990).

16. Buchanen, *Presidential Experience*, chs. 1–2; Kipnis, *Powerholders*, chs. 1–4.

17. Martin Linsky, *Impact: How the Press Affects Federal Policy Makers* (New York: Norton, 1986); Larry Sabato, *Feeding Frenzy: How Attack Journalism Has Transformed American Politics* (New York: Free Press, 1991). For instance, during the middle of the Vietnam War, Lyndon Johnson warned his staff, "Don't let newspapermen divide us" (Berman, *Lyndon Johnson's War*, 19).

18. Elizabeth Drew, *Showdown: The Struggle between the Gingrich Congress and the Clinton White House* (New York: Simon and Schuster, 1996), 19–20. For a sobering discussion of the lengths to which this anger and defensiveness can be carried and create its own reinforcing dynamic see Howard Kurtz, *Spin Cycle* (New York: Simon and Schuster, 1998).

19. Thomas Cronin, *The State of the Presidency* (Boston: Little, Brown, 1975), 153.

20. George E. Reedy, *Twilight of the Presidency* (New York: World Publishing, 1970), 10.

21. Kipnis, *Powerholders*, chs. 3–6.

22. Plato, *The Republic*, trans. H. D. P. Lee (New York: Penguin Books, 1974), 2.359D–360B, quotation 360A–B.

23. Philip Zimbardo, "The Human Choice."

24. Stanley Milgram, *Obedience to Authority* (New York: Harper Torchbooks, 1975), chs. 10–11.

25. Janis, *Groupthink*, chs. 1, 10, 11.

26. *The American Heritage Dictionary*, 2d ed. (Boston: Houghton Mifflin, 1985), 1252.

27. Halberstam, *Best and Brightest*, 433.

28. Pitrim A. Sorokin and Walter A. Lunden, *Power and Morality: Who Shall Guard the Guardians* (Boston: P. Sargent, 1959).

29. Janis, *Groupthink*, ch. 10.

30. White, *Nobody Wanted War*, chs. 1–3.

31. Newt Gingrich, *Lessons Learned the Hard Way: A Personal Report* (New York: Harper and Row, 1998), 54. Drew, *Showdown*.

32. Duff Cooper, Viscount Norwich, *Old Men Forget* (London: Hart-Davis, 1953), 279.

33. Drew, *Showdown*, 273–74, 227–44, 305–42.

34. John W. Dean III, *Blind Ambition: The White House Years* (New York: Simon and Schuster, 1976).

35. Robert Blake, *Disraeli* (London: Eyen and Spottiswoode, 1966), 343.

36. Niccolò Machiavelli, *The Chief Works and Others*, ed. and trans. Allan Gilbert (Durham: Duke University Press, 1965), vol. 2, 947, 969.

37. Dennis F. Thompson, *Ethics in Congress: From Individual to Institutional Corruption* (Washington, D.C.: Brookings Institution, 1995), 55–69, 80–84.

38. R. H. S Crossman, *The Diaries of a Cabinet Minister* (London: Hamilton Cape, 1975–77).

39. Kipnis, *Powerholders*, chs. 1, 6.

40. Robert Caro, *The Power Broker: Robert Moses and the Fall of New York* (New York: Alfred Knopf, 1974), esp. 399–401, 500–504, 608–12, 815–23, 848–50.

41. H. R. Haldeman, *The Ends of Power* (New York: New York Times Books, 1978).

42. Joseph Haroutunian, *The Lust for Power* (New York: Scribner's Sons, 1949), 9.

43. Christopher Hansen, "Clinton Wins Second Term," *Seattle Post Intelligencer* (6 November 1996): 1, A6.

44. White, *Nobody Wanted War*.

45. Ibid., ch. 3. For a study of how central this is to maintaining institutions of oppression see Orlando Patterson, *Slavery and Social Death: A Comparative Perspective* (Cambridge: Harvard University Press, 1982). Also see David Brion Davis, "At the Heart of Slavery," *New York Review of Books* (17 October 1996): 51–56.

46. Richard Gid Powers, *Secrecy and Power: The Life of J. Edgar Hoover* (New York: Free Press, 1987), 439–70.

47. Dean, *Blind Ambition*.

48. John M. Barry, *The Ambition and the Power* (New York: Viking, 1989), chs. 1, 5, 10–13.

49. Drew, *Showdown*, 215–17, 277–79, 300–303, 312–15, 331–76. Gingrich's own sobered account, replete with his rhetorical thrusts against "liberals" and the media, cites his problems of overconfidence, underestimating opponents, and not listening to good advice (Gingrich, *Lessons Learned the Hard Way*, chs. 1, 4, 5).

50. Herbert Goldhamer, *The Adviser* (New York: Elsevier, 1978), 8–12, 20–25, 109–16.

51. Robert S. McNamara, with Brian VanDeMark, *In Retrospect: The Tragedy and Lessons of Vietnam* (New York: Times Books, 1995).

52. Albert Speer, *Inside the Third Reich*, trans. Richard and Clara Winston (New York: Avon, 1971).

53. Caro, *The Power Broker*, 465–80, 484–90, 729–40, 814–20, 864–69.

54. Henry Kissinger, *Diplomacy* (New York: Simon and Schuster, 1994), provides an extended defense of this position.

55. Dean, *Blind Ambition*, 215–19. Also see Jeb Stuart Magruder, *An American Life: One Man's Road to Watergate* (New York: Atheneum, 1974); Janis and Mann, *Decision Making*, 226 ff.

56. Hannah Arendt, *Eichmann in Jerusalem: A Report on the Banality of Evil* (New York: Penguin, 1965), ch. 2.

57. Powers, *Secrecy and Power*, 179–228, 353–439.

58. Bob Woodward, *Veil* (New York: Simon and Schuster, 1987).

59. Caro, *The Power Broker*, 207–20, 299–307, 314–20, 405–10.

60. Powers, *Secrecy and Power*.

61. Robert Jackall, *Moral Mazes: The World of Corporate Managers* (Oxford: Oxford University Press, 1988), chs. 1–3.

62. Janis, *Groupthink*, chs. 6–8.

63. William Shawcross, *Sideshow: Kissinger, Nixon and the Destruction of Cambodia* (New York: Simon and Schuster, 1979).

64. Milgram, *Obedience to Authority*, chs. 10–12.

65. Robert Klitgaard, *Controlling Corruption* (Berkeley: University of California Press, 1988).

66. *The New American Bible*, Luke 4:5–7.

Chapter 3. The Moral Realities of Public Life

1. Kathryn G. Denhardt, *The Ethics of Public Service: Resolving Moral Dilemmas in Public Organizations* (New York: Greenwood Press, 1988); Joel L. Fleishman et al., eds., *Public Duties: The Moral Obligations of Government Officials* (Cambridge: Harvard University Press, 1981).

2. John A. Rohr, *Ethics for Bureaucrats: An Essay on Law and Values* (New York: Marcel Dekker, 1978); John P. Burke, *Bureaucratic Responsibility* (Baltimore: John Hopkins University Press, 1986); Max Weber, "Politics as a Vocation," in *From Max Weber*, trans. and ed. H. H. Gerth and C. W. Mills (New York: Oxford University Press, 1958), 77–128.

3. Terry Cooper, "Hierarchy, Virtue, and the Practice of Public Administration,

Public Administration Review 47, no. 4 (1987): 320–28; Terry Cooper and Dale N. Wright, eds., *Exemplary Public Administrators: Character and Leadership in Government* (San Francisco: Jossey-Bass, 1992).

4. Charles T. Goodsell and Nancy Murray, eds., *Public Administration Illuminated and Inspired by the Arts* (New York: Praeger, 1995).

5. William Shakespeare, *Henry IV (Parts I and II)*, The Yale Shakespeare (New Haven: Yale University Press, 1957); *Henry V*, The Yale Shakespeare (New Haven: Yale University Press, 1957).

6. William Shakespeare, *The Tragedy of Coriolanus*, The Yale Shakespeare (New Haven: Yale University Press, 1957).

7. John Le Carré, *Tinker, Tailor, Soldier, Spy* (New York: Knopf, 1974).

8. C. P. Snow, *The New Men* (New York: Charles Scribner's Sons, 1954, 1980); *Homecomings* (New York: Charles Scribner's Sons, 1956, 1980).

9. John Le Carré, *Smiley's People* (New York: Knopf, 1980).

10. John Le Carré, *The Honourable Schoolboy* (New York: Knopf, 1977).

11. Robert Penn Warren, *All the King's Men* (New York: Harcourt Brace, 1946).

12. Fyodor Dostoevsky, *The Grand Inquisitor*, trans. Constance Garnett (Indianapolis: Library of Liberal Arts, 1982).

13. Anthony Trollope, *Phineas Finn* (London: Oxford University Press, 1975); Anthony Trollope, *Phineas Redux* (London: Oxford University Press, 1975).

14. Louis Auchincloss, *Honorable Men* (Boston: Houghton Mifflin, 1985).

15. John Hersey, *A Bell for Adano* (New York: Alfred Knopf, 1944).

16. See Howard E. McCurdy, "How Novelists View Public Administration," in *A Centennial History of the American Administrative State*, ed. R. Chandler (New York: Free Press, 1987), 543–57, for a fine study of *A Bell for Adano*.

17. Robert Bolt, *A Man for All Seasons* (New York: Vintage Books, 1960), 60.

18. Snow, *Homecomings*, 207.

19. Edwin O. Connor, *The Last Hurrah* (Boston: Little, Brown, 1956).

20. William Shakespeare, *Richard II*, The Yale Shakespeare (New Haven: Yale University Press, 1957).

21. John Le Carré, *The Spy Who Came in from the Cold* (New York: Coward-McCann, 1963), 144.

22. Auchincloss, *Honorable Men*, 125–26.

23. Jean Anouilh, *Becket or the Honour of God*, trans. L. Hill (London: Methuen, 1961).

24. Ibid., 62, 70.

25. Herman Melville, *Billy Budd* (New York: Washington Square Books, 1972).

26. Thomas More, *Utopia*, trans. and ed. H. V. S. Ogden (Northbrook, Ill.: AHM Publishing, 1949), 22–23.

27. Snow, *Homecomings*, 250.

Chapter 4. Character and Moral Attrition

1. John Le Carré, *Smiley's People* (New York: Knopf, 1980), 202.

2. John Le Carré, *The Honourable Schoolboy* (New York: Knopf, 1977), 460.

3. Robert C. Solomon, *Ethics and Excellence: Cooperation and Integrity in Business* (New York: Oxford University Press, 1992).

4. John Le Carré, *The Secret Pilgrim* (New York, Alfred Knopf, 1991), 224. The need for individuals on the ground making judgment calls because of the limits of technology continuously arises. See, for instance, "Director Warned CIA Staff about Relying on Spy Satellites," *Seattle Times* (25 May 1998): A4.

5. Terry L. Cooper and N. Dale Wright, eds., *Exemplary Public Administrators: Character and Leadership in Government* (San Francisco: Jossey-Bass, 1992), illustrate how studies of individuals provide exemplary models of emulation. Also see Louis C. Gawthrop, "Democracy, Bureaucracy, and Hypocrisy Redux: A Search for Sympathy and Compassion," *Public Administration Review* 57, no. 3 (1997): 205–10, for reflection on the broader issues of the stress of hypocrisy in public office.

6. Charles T. Goodsell and Nancy Murray, eds., *Public Administration Illuminated and Inspired by the Arts* (New York: Praeger, 1995), make the case for such a role of fiction in teaching public virtue. See J. Patrick Dobel, "Review of Goodsell," *Administrative Theory and Praxis* 18, no. 1 (1996): 154–57, for a more explicit defense of this view.

7. John Le Carré, *The Spy Who Came in from the Cold* (New York: Coward-McCann, 1963), 144.

8. John Le Carré, *A Murder of Distinction* (New York: Bantam Books, 1963, 1981), 177. The character of George Smiley first occurs in two mysteries, *A Murder of Distinction* and *Call for the Dead* (New York: Bantam Books, 1962, 1981), before Smiley becomes the central character of the three books of the Karla trilogy.

9. The problems with utilitarianism are aptly summarized in Bernard Williams, "A Critique of Utilitarianism," in *Utilitarianism: For and Against*, ed. J. J. C. Smart and Bernard Williams (Cambridge: Cambridge University Press, 1973), 75–150. Michael Walzer addresses the same issues from a perspective consistent with this article in "Political Action: The Problem of Dirty Hands," *Philosophy and Public Affairs* 2 (1973): 160–79. Williams also addresses the notion of character in political life in "Politics and Moral Character," in *Public and Private Morality*, ed. Stuart Hampshire (Cambridge: Cambridge University Press, 1978), 23–53.

10. *The Spy Who Came in from the Cold*, 184.

11. Ibid., 24–25.

12. *The Secret Pilgrim*, 177.

13. *The Spy Who Came in from the Cold*, 252–53.

14. *The Honourable Schoolboy*, 317.

15. *The Secret Pilgrim*, 260.

16. *The Spy Who Came in from the Cold*, 149–50.

17. *Tinker, Tailor, Soldier, Spy*, 342–43.

18. *The Spy Who Came in from the Cold*, 24.

19. *The Honourable Schoolboy*, 164.

20. *The Secret Pilgrim*, 181–91.

21. Hannah Arendt, *Eichmann in Jerusalem: A Report on the Banality of Evil* (New York: Penguin, 1965).

22. *The Honourable Schoolboy*, 219.

23. *The Spy Who Came in from the Cold*, 24–25.

24. *Smiley's People*, 264–69.

25. Ibid., 66.

26. *The Spy Who Came in from the Cold*, 144.

27. *Call for the Dead*, 5.

28. *Tinker, Tailor, Soldier, Spy*, 196; *Smiley's People*, 335–46.

29. *Tinker, Tailor, Soldier, Spy*, 206.

30. *Smiley's People*, 203–4. In a tantalizing double take, Connie adds, "Others said she wasn't dead at all, the story was disinformation to end the trail." Karla, on the other hand, relates a vaguely true but fictitious cover story to Anton Greigoriev, his liaison with his daughter. In this story, Karla's daughter's mother was exiled to "a far province" and "died of a broken heart" (*Smiley's People*, 343, 344). Karla's daughter, Alexandra, tells Smiley only that her mother "was punished. . . . She was not obedient to history" (*Smiley's People*, 360–61).

31. *Tinker, Tailor, Soldier, Spy*, 90–91.

32. Ibid., 148.

33. *The Honourable Schoolboy*, 322.

34. *Smiley's People*, 70.

35. John Le Carré, *The Russia House* (New York: Alfred Knopf, 1989).

36. *Call for the Dead*, 6–7.

37. *Tinker, Tailor, Soldier, Spy*, 146–48.

38. *The Secret Pilgrim*, 117–51.

39. *Tinker, Tailor, Soldier, Spy*, 125–29.

40. Ibid., 70.

41. *The Honourable Schoolboy*, 67.

42. *Smiley's People*, 75.

43. Ibid., 56.

44. *The Honourable Schoolboy*, 187.

45. *Smiley's People*, 274–75, 266.

46. *The Honourable Schoolboy*, 532.

47. *Smiley's People*, 262.

48. *The Honourable Schoolboy*, 70.

49. *Tinker, Tailor, Soldier, Spy*, 12.

50. *The Honourable Schoolboy*, 450.

51. Ibid., 257–69, 436.

52. *The Secret Pilgrim*, 321.

53. *Tinker, Tailor, Soldier, Spy*, 24, 204.

54. Max Weber, "Politics as a Vocation," in *From Max Weber: Essays in Sociology*, ed. H. H. Gerth and C. W. Mills (New York: Oxford University Press, 1958), 77–128.

55. *Call for the Dead*, 130.

56. *The Honourable Schoolboy*, 104, 533, 319.

57. *Smiley's People*, 252–53.

58. *Tinker, Tailor, Soldier, Spy*, 332.

59. Ibid., 1–17, 211–13, 355.

60. Ibid., 327.

61. *Call for the Dead*, 114.

62. Ibid., 75.

63. *Tinker, Tailor, Soldier, Spy*, 30.

64. *Smiley's People*, 277; *The Secret Pilgrim*, 249.

65. *Smiley's People*, 275–77; quotation in *The Honourable Schoolboy*, 219. Karla also confronts bureaucrats and careerists who resent his commitment and success. Moscow Center teems with "jealous beavers" "longing for an excuse to knife him." Karla's very purity amid the climbers made him all the more vulnerable to exposure for breaking rules to give care to his daughter.

66. *The Honourable Schoolboy*, 533.

67. Ibid.; *Smiley's People*, 271, 355, 362.

68. *Tinker Tailor, Soldier, Spy*, 72–73, 140–41.

69. *Smiley's People*, 150–53.

70. Ibid., 370–71.

71. *A Murder of Distinction*, 73.

72. *Smiley's People*, 205–6.

73. *Tinker, Tailor, Soldier, Spy*, 207.

74. *Smiley's People*, 287, 150–53.

75. *The Secret Pilgrim*, 8–10.

76. *Smiley's People*, 371.

77. *The Secret Pilgrim*, 264.

Chapter 5. Staying In: The Ethics of Commitment in Office

1. Irving Janis, *Groupthink: Psychological Studies of Policy Decisions and Fiascoes*, 2d ed. (Boston: Houghton Mifflin, 1982), and Irving Janis and Leon Mann, *Decision Making: A Psychological Analysis of Conflict, Choice and Commitment* (New York: Free Press, 1977), chs. 1, 3, 4, 10, 11, 12, analyze the psychological pressures and explore numerous case studies of the distorting effects of groups and commitment. Also see Sidney Verba, *Small Groups and Political Behavior: A Study of Leadership* (Princeton: Princeton University Press, 1961), esp. 26–45 and 231–43.

2. Lawrence F. O'Brien, *No Final Victories: A Life in Politics from John F. Kennedy to Watergate* (Garden City: Doubleday, 1974), 217–18.

3. Albert Hirschman, *Exit, Voice, and Loyalty: Responses to Decline in Firms, Organizations, and States* (Cambridge: Harvard University Press, 1977), 30–44, 106–20, argues that the use of effective "voice" and dissent both renews institutions and makes them more accountable. James C. Thomson Jr., "How Could Vietnam Happen? An Autopsy," *The Atlantic* (April 1968): 47–53, and "Getting out and Speaking out," *Foreign Policy* 13 (1973–74): 49–67, as well as Anthony Lake, "Lying around Washington," *Foreign Policy* 2 (1971): 91–113, discuss the central importance of effectiveness for any policy maker and explore the complex moral loyalties that tie dissenting decision makers to an institution.

4. Thomas More, *Utopia*, ed. Edward Surtz, S.J. (New Haven: Yale University Press, 1973), 50.

5. J. Patrick Dobel, *Compromise and Political Order: Morality in Liberal and Democratic Life* (Savage, Md.: Rowman and Littlefield, 1990), chs. 1–3.

6. William Shakespeare, *The Tragedy of Hamlet Prince of Denmark*, *The Yale Shakespeare* (New Haven: Yale University Press, 1966), 3.1.68.

7. For an illustrative case see Henry Kissinger, *The White House Years* (Boston: Little, Brown, 1979), 18–20, 42–43. Also see Roger Morris, *Uncertain Greatness:*

Henry Kissinger and American Foreign Policy (New York: Harper and Row, 1977), 94 ff., 136 ff.

8. John P. Burke, *Bureaucratic Responsibility* (Baltimore: John Hopkins University Press, 1986); O. Glen Stahl, "Loyalty, Dissent and Organizational Health," *The Bureaucrat* July (1974): 162–71; Hirschman, *Exit, Voice, and Loyalty*, 76–106.

9. Bernard Crick, *In Defense of Politics*, 2d ed. (Chicago: University of Chicago Press, 1972); Dobel, *Compromise and Political Order*, chs. 3–7.

10. National security provides the most easily abused set of justifications for such actions. Jeb Stuart Magruder, *An American Life: One Man's Road to Watergate* (New York: Atheneum, 1974), 65–168, describes how "intelligence operations" were justified by the Committee to Re-elect the President in order to discover what domestic "enemies" were up to. John W. Dean III, *Blind Ambition: The White House Years* (New York: Simon and Schuster, 1976), 60–67, 183–89, 199–201, 262, explains how claims of "executive privilege" or "national security" were used to hide evidence of the ITT bribes or to keep incriminating evidence out of testimony.

11. The violated rules need not be just electoral rules. Rules designed to ensure accountability through formal procedures are also vital. The Strategic Air Command reporting procedures enable government civilians to keep control over the magnitude, location, and actual dropping of bombs. During the illegal and secret bombing of Cambodia, the military were ordered to falsify the reporting procedure by changing the information fed into the computers and falsely reporting flight plans and locations. The violation of these basic rules that control the integrity of the United States' nuclear arsenal led several ex-pilots to report the acts to Congress. William Shawcross, *Sideshow: Kissinger, Nixon and the Destruction of Cambodia* (New York: Simon and Schuster, 1979), ch. 1.

12. Patrick Anderson, *The President's Men: White House Assistants of Franklin Roosevelt, Harry S. Truman, Dwight D. Eisenhower, John F. Kennedy and Lyndon B. Johnson* (Garden City, N.Y.: Doubleday, 1968), 340–47.

13. David Halberstam, *The Best and the Brightest* (New York: Random House, 1969), 533–36, and Townsend Hoopes, *The Limits of Intervention: An Inside Account of How the Johnson Policy of Escalation in Vietnam Was Reversed* (New York: David McKay, 1969), 31–37, 163–65.

14. Herbert Fingarette, *Self-deception: Studies in Philosophical Psychology* (London: Routledge and Kegan Paul, 1969), 47; also see Leon Festinger, *A Theory of Cognitive Dissonance* (Stanford: Stanford University Press, 1962).

15. Janis and Mann, *Decision Making*, chs. 8–12.

16. Stanley Hauerwas, "Self-deception and Autobiography: Reflections on Speer's *Inside the Third Reich*," in *Truthfulness and Tragedy: Further Investigations into Christian Ethics*, ed. Stanley Hauerwas, Richard Bondi, and David Burrell (Notre Dame, Ind.: University of Notre Dame Press, 1977), 86.

17. Fingarette, *Self-deception*, 140.

18. Dean, *Blind Ambition*, 167–71, 182–86, quotations on 167 and 182.

19. Albert Speer, *Inside the Third Reich*, trans. Richard and Clara Winston (New York: Macmillan, 1970), 479–89.

20. Doris Kearns Goodwin, *Lyndon Johnson and the American Dream* (New York: Harper and Row, 1976), 268–73; Michael Walzer, "Political Action: The Problem of Dirty Hands," *Philosophy and Public Affairs* 2 (1973): 176–79.

21. Edward Weisband and Thomas M. Franck, *Resignation in Protest: Political and Ethical Choices between Loyalty to Team and Loyalty to Conscience in American Public Life* (New York: Grossman, 1975), discuss the public alternatives available to a dissenter who leaves government. They emphasize the pressures that lead individuals to stay. Robert Jackall, *Moral Mazes: The World of Corporate Managers* (Oxford: Oxford University Press, 1988), provides a rich analysis of the linguistic and psychological traps of organizational life.

22. George E. Reedy, *The Twilight of the Presidency* (New York: New American Library, 1970), 91.

23. Morris, *Uncertain Greatness*, 3, 46–94; Kissinger, *White House Years*, 3–73, especially 29–32.

24. Halberstam, *Best and Brightest*, 40 ff., 133 ff., 291 ff.; Goodwin, *Lyndon Johnson and the American Dream*, ch. 6.

25. Thomson, "How Could Vietnam Happen," 49.

26. Morris, *Uncertain Greatness*, 73.

27. Robert S. McNamara, with Brian VanDeMark, *In Retrospect: The Tragedy and Lessons of Vietnam* (New York: Times Books, 1995), 145–273, especially 95–99, 311–17. Also see Halberstam, *Best and Brightest*, 516–21, 622–46; Hoopes, *The Limits of Intervention*, 83–91, 161–66; Henry L. Trewhitt, *McNamara* (New York: Harper and Row, 1971), 236–47.

28. Magruder, *An American Life*, 122–29, 149–53, 168–75; Dean, *Blind Ambition*, describes similar experiences (27, 38, 168).

29. George M. Ball, *The Past Has Another Pattern: Memoirs* (New York: W. W. Norton, 1982), 360–434.

30. McNamara, *In Retrospect*, 277–85.

31. William Safire, *Before the Fall: An Inside View of the Pre-Watergate White House* (New York: Ballantine Books, 1977), 352.

32. Thomson, "How Vietnam Could Happen," 49; Anderson, *The President's Men*, 339–52.

33. Hirschman, *Exit, Voice, and Loyalty*, ch. 9.

34. Morris, *Uncertain Greatness*, 157–62, 196–99, 249 ff.

35. Felix Gilbert, *Machiavelli and Guicciardini: Politics and History in Sixteenth-Century Florence* (Princeton: Princeton University Press, 1973), 281–82.

36. Dean, *Blind Ambition*, 46–49. Eric F. Goldman, *The Tragedy of Lyndon Johnson* (New York: Alfred Knopf, 1969), recounts how Kennedy appointments such as Nicholas Katzenbach or Lawrence O'Brien had to earn their access with President Johnson with their hard-line stands on Vietnam.

37. Lyndon Baines Johnson, *The Vantage Point: Perspectives of the Presidency 1963–1969* (New York: Holt, Rinehart, and Winston, 1971), 2.

38. Halberstam, *Best and Brightest*, 213–50, 516–28, 581–90, 633. McNamara, *In Retrospect*, disagrees with this characterization but does make clear that because he could see no serious alternatives to graduated escalation, he rejected many other alternatives. He also admits he was mistaken to do so.

39. Goldman, *Tragedy of Lyndon Johnson*, 262–68.

40. Halberstam, *Best and Brightest*, 502–9, 579–85, 622–29.

41. Dean, *Blind Ambition*, 167–68, 182–83; Magruder, *An American Life*, 220, 229, 317.

42. Goodwin, *Lyndon Johnson and the American Dream*, 317, 394, quotation on 311.

43. More, *Utopia*, 48.

44. McNamara, *In Retrospect*, 51–88, 169–206, 319–36.

45. Trewhitt, *McNamara*, 227–60, especially 239–41. Also see *The Pentagon Papers: The Defense Department History of United States Decisionmaking on Vietnam*, vol. 4, Senator Gravel Edition (Boston: Beacon Press, 1971), 177–277.

46. Safire, *Before the Fall*, 65–80, 373–401, 445–50; Morris, *Uncertain Greatness*, 105–7; Madeleine Edmondson and Alden Duer Cohen, *The Women of Watergate* (New York: Stein and Day, 1975).

47. McNamara, *In Retrospect*, 216–17, 258.

48. Speer, *Inside the Third Reich*, 480.

Chapter 6. Getting Out: The Ethics of Resigning from Office

1. Resigning has a high threshold given the economic and reputational costs. Resigning a job without civil service protection or another sure job can be very economically costly. Family support obligations often deter resigning. Resigning can also affect the reputation and employability of people. Sometimes it marks them as a person of integrity, at other times it marks them as disloyal and not team players. At the same time internal social pressures press them to stay in an organization. See Irving Janis, *Groupthink: Psychological Studies of Policy Decisions and Fiascoes* (Boston: Houghton Mifflin, 1982), and Robert Jackall, *Moral Mazes: The World of Corporate Managers* (Oxford: Oxford University Press, 1988).

2. The discussions arose from the crisis of conscience many policy makers experienced during the Vietnam War of which Edward Weisband and Thomas M. Franck, *Resignation in Protest: Political and Ethical Choices between Loyalty to Team and Loyalty to Conscience in American Public Life* (New York: Grossman, 1975), is the best and only sustained study on the morality of resignation in the United States. James C. Thomson Jr., "Getting out and Speaking out," *Foreign Policy* 13 (1973–74): 49–67, provides a remarkable account of the process and issues. More recently Norton Long, "The Ethics and Efficacy of Resignation in Public Administration," *Administration and Society* 25, no. 1 (1993): 3–12, comments upon the importance of resignation to defend an agency trusteeship understanding of office.

3. Stephen L. Carter, *Integrity* (New York: Basic Books, 1996), 3–14.

4. The capacity to act despite costs to oneself is central to most definitions of integrity. For a seminal work see Lynne McFall, "Integrity," *Ethics* 98 (October 1987): 5–23; also see Carter, *Integrity*, 15–52.

5. Dennis Thompson, "Moral Responsibility in Government: The Problem of Many Hands," *American Political Science Review* 74 (1980): 905–16; J. Patrick Dobel, "Personal Responsibility and Public Integrity," *Michigan Law Review* 86, no. 6 (1988): 1450–65, expands this argument.

6. Public officials regularly make this point. For clear expositions see George Ball, *The Past Has Another Pattern: Memoirs* (New York: W. W. Norton, 1982), 424–34; Cyrus Vance, *Hard Choices: Critical Years in America's Foreign Policy* (New York: Simon and Schuster, 1983), 398–413; George P. Shultz, *Turmoil and Triumph:*

My Years as Secretary of State (New York: Charles Scribner's Sons, 1993), 783–840. Colin Powell, *My American Journey* (New York: Random House, 1995). For the classic statement of the position see Stephen Bailey, "Ethics and the Public Service," in *Administration and Democracy*, ed. R. C. Martin (Syracuse, N.Y.: Syracuse University Press, 1965), 283–98.

7. Weisband and Franck, *Resignation in Protest*, 112.

8. Albert Hirschman, *Exit, Voice, and Loyalty: Responses to Decline in Firms, Organizations, and States* (Cambridge: Harvard University Press, 1977).

9. Shultz, *Turmoil and Triumph*, 725–26.

10. Ibid., 792.

11. "The Saturday Night Massacre," part C, Kennedy School of Government Case C1477-543, 16 (1977).

12. See Chapter 5. Myron Peretz Glazer and Penina Migdal Glazer, *The Whistle-Blowers: Exposing Corruption in Government and Industry* (New York: Basic Books, 1989); John P. Burke, *Bureaucratic Responsibility* (Baltimore: John Hopkins University Press, 1986); Deena Weinstein, *Bureaucratic Opposition: Challenging Abuses in the Workplace* (New York: Pergamon Press, 1979), all discuss the ways in which individuals can come to terms with morally troubling policy as well as the legitimate methods of moral dissent within office.

13. John Rohr, *To Run a Constitution: The Legitimacy of the Administrative State* (Lawrence: University of Kansas Press, 1986); Thompson, "Moral Responsibility in Government," 905–16; J. Patrick Dobel, *Compromise and Political Action: Political Morality in Liberal and Democratic Life* (Savage, Md.: Rowman and Littlefield, 1990), chs. 1–3, extends the promissory conception to integrity.

14. James G. March and Johan P. Olsen, *Rediscovering Institutions: The Organizational Basis of Politics* (New York: Free Press, 1989).

15. Robert D. Behn, *Leadership Counts: Lessons for Public Managers from the Massachusetts Welfare, Training, and Employment Program* (Cambridge: Harvard University Press, 1991). The implementation literature of political science commonly addresses these issues. For a fine example see Eugene Bardach, *The Implementation Game: What Happens after a Bill Becomes a Law* (Cambridge: MIT University Press, 1977).

16. Nancy Sherman, *The Fabric of Character: Aristotle's Theory of Virtue* (Oxford: Clarendon Press, 1989).

17. Janet Hook, "Morris Udall May Soon Resign as Health Problems Continue," *Congressional Quarterly Weekly Report* (13 April 1991): 934.

18. Forrest C. Pogue, *George C. Marshall: Statesman 1945–1959* (New York: Viking, 1987), 477–514.

19. Helen Dewar, "The Democrats Lose Their Big Gun from the South," *Washington Post Weekly Edition* (16–22 October 1995): 14.

20. Burke, *Bureaucratic Responsibility*, chs. 3–5.

21. Jackall, *Moral Mazes*, 101–34.

22. For an illuminating account of this type of moral conflict and resolution see Shultz's explanation of why he did not resign in *Telling the Boss He's Wrong: George Shultz and Iran/Contra*, Kennedy School of Government Case C16-94-1254.0 (1994): 12–13.

23. Laurence E. Lynn Jr., *Managing Public Policy* (Boston: Little, Brown, 1987).

24. R. K. Alderman and J. A. Cross, *The Tactics of Resignation* (London: Routledge and Kegan Paul, 1967).

25. Kerry Murakami, "Soliz Exit Revives Talk of DSHS Split," *Seattle Times* (2 November 1995).

26. Brooks Jackson, "John Fedders of SEC Is Pummeled by Legal and Personal Problems," *Wall Street Journal* (25 February 1985): 1; Stuart Taylor Jr., "Life in the Spotlight: Agony of Getting Burned," *New York Times* (25 February 1985): 1.

27. Congressional Quarterly, *Congressional Ethics: History, Facts, and Controversy* (Washington, D.C.: Congressional Quarterly Press, 1992), 87–88.

28. Weisband and Franck, *Resignation in Protest*; Jackall, *Moral Mazes*.

29. Duff Cooper, Viscount Norwich, *Old Men Forget* (London: Hart-Davis, 1953), 224–51, quotations on 241, 248.

30. Robert S. McNamara, with Brian VanDeMark, *In Retrospect: The Tragedy and Lessons of Vietnam* (New York: Times Books, 1995), 282–83.

31. Andrew Rosenthal, "Sununu Resigns under Fire as Chief Aide of President: Cites Fear of Hurting Bush," *New York Times* (4 December 1991): 1.

32. "The Saturday Night Massacre," part A, Kennedy School of Government Case C14-77-151 (1977).

33. "The Saturday Night Massacre," parts A and B, Kennedy School of Government, Cases C14-77-151 and 152 (1977).

34. "The Saturday Night Massacre," part D, Kennedy School of Government, Case C14-77-544 (1977).

35. "A Change of Management," Public Service Curriculum Exchange, the Electronic Hallway Network (1987).

36. Vance, *Hard Choices*, 411; also see 398–413.

37. Ibid., 35–38, 44, 113–49, 248–50, 328–40, chronicles the battle. Zbigniew Brzezinski, *Power and Principles: Memoirs of the National Security Advisor 1977–81* (New York: Farrar Straus Giroux, 1983), presents his own account of the struggle (36–44, 470–513).

38. Michael A. Fletcher, "Mfume Takes NAACP Helm Today," *Washington Post Capitol on Line* (15 February 1996).

39. George Shipman, "The Silver Affair," in *Public and Budgetary Policy*, ed. Fremont Lyden (New York: Wiley, 1972), 234–49.

40. Dean Acheson, *Present at Creation: My Years in the State Department* (New York: Norton, 1969), 735–36.

41. *George Shultz and the Polygraph Test*, Kennedy School of Government, Case C16-86-681, (1986), 1; see also Shultz, *Turmoil and Triumph*, 800–803.

42. Robert Caro, *The Power Broker: Robert Moses and the Fall of New York* (New York: Alfred Knopf, 1974), 3–6, 313–16, 447–49, 801–6, 866–70, 1074–79; "The City-Shaper," *New Yorker* (5 January 1998): 38–55.

43. *Facts on File* (2 February 1995), 55, n. 2826 64.

44. See David Halberstam, *The Best and the Brightest* (New York: Random House, 1969). Weisband and Franck, *Resignation in Protest*, 163–65, argue that Ball was used in this role.

45. Ball, *The Past Has Another Pattern*, 425. His description and analysis of his resignation remain one of the clearest and best available in memoirs (424–35).

Chapter 7. The Political Morality of Sleaze and Honor

1. Dennis F. Thompson, *Ethics in Congress: From Individual to Institutional Corruption* (Washington, D.C.: Brookings Institution, 1995), 28–30, quotation on 28; J. Patrick Dobel, "The Corruption of a State," *American Political Science Review* 72 (1978): 958–73.

2. F. H. Bradley, "My Station and Its Duties," in *Ethical Studies* (Indianapolis: Bobbs Merrill, 1951), 98–147, provides a clear if overstated argument for this position. For a more comprehensive set of statements without Bradley's rigidity or metaphysics see Stephen Bailey, "Ethics and the Public Service," in *Public Administration and Democracy*, ed. R. C. Martin (Syracuse, N.Y.: Syracuse University Press, 1965), 283–98. See Robert C. Solomon, *Ethics and Excellence: Cooperation and Integrity in Business* (New York: Oxford University Press, 1992), 200–222, for an updated account of honor in an institutional setting.

3. William L. Riordon, *Plunkitt of Tammany Hall: A Series of Very Plain Talks on Very Practical Politics* (New York: Dutton Paperback, 1963), ch. 1, quotation on 3.

4. Ibid., ch. 2, quotation on 9.

5. Ibid., ch. 4.

6. Edward Walsh, "Big Jo Rusty's Son Learned the Game of Politics in a Bygone Era," *Washington Post* (1 June 1994): A-12.

7. Jeffrey H. Birnbaum and Alan S. Murray, *Showdown at Gucci Gulch: Lawmakers, Lobbyists, and the Unlikely Triumph of Tax Reform* (New York: Vintage, 1988), 151.

8. Ibid., 127–51, quotation on 134; Peter Carlson, "Stamped by Scandal: Dan Rostenkowski Worries That He May Be about to Lose His Battle or Respect," *Washington Post National Weekly Edition* (1–7 November 1993): 6–10.

9. Milton L. Rakove, *Don't Make No Waves, Don't Back No Losers: An Insider's Analysis of the Daley Machine* (Bloomington: Indiana University Press, 1975).

10. Birnbaum and Murray, *Showdown*, 96–106.

11. "A Betrayal of the Public Trust," statement by U.S. Attorney Eric H. Holder Jr., *Washington Post Capitol Edition on Line* (1 June 1994); "The Rostenkowski Indictment," *Washington Post Capitol Edition on Line* (1 June 1994); Myra MacPherson, "Tip O'Neill, One with His Roots," *Washington Post Capitol Edition on Line* (7 January 1994); "Big Joe Rostenkowski's Son Learned the Game of Politics in a Bygone Era," *Washington Post Capitol Edition on Line* (1 June 1994).

12. Birnbaum and Murray, *Showdown*, 126–52, 204–34.

13. Toni Locy, "Rostenkowski Fraud Plea Brings 17 Month Sentence," *Washington Post Capitol Edition on Line* (10 April 1996); Daniel Klaidman and Evan Thomas, "Rosty's Difficult Winter," *Newsweek* (12 January 1998).

14. Jonathan Agronsky, *Marion Barry: The Politics of Race* (Latham: N.Y.: British American Publishers, 1991).

15. "Defiant FBI Chief Removed from Job by President," *New York Times* (20 July 1993); Michael Isikoff, "Sessions Said Likely to Quit as FBI Chief within Days," *Washington Post* (17 July 1993); Lloyd Grove, "Unresigned to His Fate: For William Sessions, a Slow Walk to the Door, *Washington Post* (20 July 1993).

16. "The Reign of King John," *Newsweek* (13 May 1991); "The 'Air Sununu' Flap," *Newsweek* (6 May 1991); "More Turbulence for Air Sununu," *Washington Post Weekly Edition* (13–19 April 1992).

17. Maureen Dowd, "Indispensability of Sununu Is Creating Hard Questions," *New York Times* (26 June 1991); Meg Greenfield, "Washington's Revenge," *Newsweek* (13 May 1991).

18. Richard Gid Powers, *Secrecy and Power: The Life of J. Edgar Hoover* (New York: Free Press, 1987), provides the most balanced biography, which verifies all the abuses and how early they started. Anthony Summers, *Official and Confidential: The Secret Life of J. Edgar Hoover* (New York: Putnam, 1993), provides a more polemical account, focusing upon Hoover's personal life and how it entangled the FBI in abusive policy.

19. For a partial listing of the 225 indictments and people who left government under ethics charges during the administration see Shelley Ross, *Fall from Grace: Sex, Scandal, and Corruption in American Politics from 1702 to Present* (New York: Ballantine Books, 1988), 269–85.

20. Memorandum, United States Office of Government Ethics, "Guidance on Ethics Program Issues Raised in the Report of the Independent Counsel Dated July 5, 1988" (12 September 1988).

21. Bob Woodward, *Veil: The Secret Wars of the CIA 1981–1987* (New York: Pocket Books, 1987); U.S. House of Representatives Select Committee to Investigate Covert Arms Transactions with Iran, U. S. Senate Select Committee on Secret Military Assistance to Iran and the Nicaraguan Opposition, *Report of the Congressional Committees Investigating the Iran-Contra Affair with Supplemental, Minority, and Additional Views, November 1987* (Washington, D.C.: U.S. Government Printing Office, 1987), 321–75.

22. Ben Bradlee Jr., *Guts and Glory: The Rise and Fall of Oliver North* (New York: Donald I. Fine, 1988), 35–120, quotation on 559.

23. Ibid., 266–89, 457–96.

24. Oliver L. North with William Novak, *Under Fire: An American Story* (New York: HarperCollins, 1991), 405–12; *Report of the Iran-Contra Committees*, 255–375.

25. Bradlee, *Guts and Glory*, 148, 156–59, 200, 219–21, 425, 496–560.

26. William S. Cohen and George Mitchell, *Men of Zeal* (New York: Viking, 1988); Bradlee, *Guts and Glory*, 533.

27. J. Anthony Lukas, *Nightmare: The Underside of the Nixon Years* (New York: Viking, 1976), provides the best and most coherent accounts of the whole web of actions enmeshed in Watergate.

28. *Report on Iran-Contra Affair*, 327–75; Bradlee, *Guts and Glory*, 281–402.

29. Bradlee, *Guts and Glory*, 1–18, 536–60.

30. Ibid., 431–36. For North's own version see North, *Under Fire*, 263–77, 350–76.

31. Bradlee, *Guts and Glory*, 534–35.

32. This argument focuses upon the internal moral assessments of private gain in public office and how these can be both explicit or corrupted. It presumes a fairly clear dividing line between office and self-interested gain. For an analysis of the difficulty of maintaining the clarity of this distinction in practice, see Andrew Stark, "Beyond Quid Pro Quo: What's Wrong with Private Gain from Public Office," *American Political Science Review* 91, no. 1 (1997): 108–20.

33. Solomon, *Ethics and Excellence*, 210–20, provides a plausible and interesting account of how honor can be linked to the ethics of roles in institutions.

Thompson, *Ethics in Congress*, 17–27, discusses the obligations of public representatives to protect and build the honor and integrity of public institutions and to avoid bringing an institution into "dishonor and disrepute." Yet honor has its own limits, especially if aggravated by the pathologies of groupthink. See Michael Walzer, "Political Solidarity and Personal Honor, in *Obligations: Essays on Disobedience, War, and Citizenship* (Cambridge: Harvard University Press, 1970), 190–202.

34. Terry L. Cooper, *An Ethics of Citizenship for Public Administration* (Englewood Cliffs, N.J.: Prentice Hall, 1991).

35. J. Patrick Dobel, *Compromise and Political Action: Political Morality in Liberal and Democratic Life* (Savage, Md.: Rowman and Littlefield, 1991), 35–79, discusses the nature of these moral tensions.

Chapter 8. Building the Common amid Differences

1. Stephen Holmes, *Passions and Constraints: On the Theory of Liberal Democracy* (Chicago: University of Chicago Press, 1995).

2. Charles Taylor, "The Politics of Recognition," in *Multiculturalism*, ed. Amy Gutman (Princeton: Princeton University Press, 1994), 25–75, provides a compatible analysis.

3. C. B. MacPherson, *The Real World of Democracy* (Oxford: Clarendon Press, 1966).

4. Daniel Patrick Moynihan, *Pandemonium: Ethnicity in International Politics* (Oxford: Oxford University Press, 1993).

5. Stephen K. White, *Political Theory and Postmodernism* (Cambridge: Cambridge University Press, 1991). See also William E. Connolly, *Identity/Difference: Democratic Negotiations of Political Paradox* (Ithaca: Cornell University Press, 1991).

6. Michael J. Sandel, *Liberalism and the Limits of Justice* (Cambridge: Cambridge University Press, 1982).

7. Carole Pateman, "Equality, Difference and Subordination: The Politics of Motherhood and Women's Citizenship," in *Beyond Equality and Difference: Citizenship, Feminist Politics and Female Subjectivity*, ed. Gisela Brock and Susan James (London: Routledge, 1992); Anne Philips, "Democracy and Difference: Some Problems for Feminist Theory," *Political Quarterly* 93 (1991): 79–90.

8. William A. Galston, *Liberal Purposes: Goods, Virtues, and Diversity in the Liberal State* (Cambridge: Cambridge University Press, 1991), 140–43. For the most rigorous statement of the political position see Iris Marion Young, *Justice and the Politics of Difference* (Princeton: Princeton University Press, 1991). Will Kymlicka and Wayne Norman, "The Return of the Citizen: A Survey of Recent Work on Citizenship Theory," *Ethics* 104 (January 1994): 352–81, provide an admirably balanced assessment of many of the recent arguments.

9. K. Anthony Appiah, "Identity, Authenticity, Survival: Multicultural Societies and Social Reproduction," in Gutman, *Multiculturalism*, 149–64; also see Amy Gutman, "The Challenge of Multiculturalism to Political Ethics," *Philosophy and Public Affairs* 22–23 (1993): 171–206.

10. Lyle Downing and Robert Thigpen, "After Telos: The Implications of MacIntyre's Attempt to Restore the Concept," *Social Theory and Practice* 10, no. 1 (1984):

39–54. For a thoughtful review of the literature on politics identity see Kenneth Hoover, *The Power of Identity: Politics in a New Key* (Chatham, N.J.: Chatham Publishers, 1997), especially chs. 1–4.

11. Harold Isaacs, *Idols of the Tribe: Group Identity and Political Change* (New York: Harper and Row, 1975), 32–33; Moynihan, *Pandemonium*, 64–66.

12. A. Oldenquist, "Community and De-Alienation," in *Alienation, Community, and Work*, ed. A. Oldenquist and M. Rosner (New York: Greenwood, 1991).

13. John Stuart Mill, *On Liberty*, ed. Alburey Castell (Northbrook, Ill.: Northbrook Publishing, 1974); Robert Nozick, *Anarchy, State and Utopia* (New York: Basic Books, 1974), 297–334. See also Kenneth E. F. Watt et al., *The Unsteady State: Environmental Problems, Growth, and Culture* (Honolulu: University of Hawaii Press, 1977).

14. Reinhold Niebuhr, "Law, Conscience, and Grace," in *Justice and Mercy* (San Francisco: Harper and Row, 1974), 41–45.

15. Fyodor Dostoevsky, *The Grand Inquisitor*, trans. Constance Garnett (Indianapolis: Hackett, 1993); also see George Kateb, "Notes on Pluralism," *Social Research* 61, no. 3 (1994): 511–37.

16. Anthony Oberschall and Hyojoung Kim, "Ethnic Conflicts and Collective Identity," Global Forum Series Occasional Papers (Durham: Duke University Center for International Studies, 1994); Hoover, *Power of Identity*, chs. 5–6.

17. Ronald J. Schmidt, "Politics and Cultural Identity: What's at Stake," paper presented at the 1994 annual meeting of the American Political Science Association, September 1994; J. Donald Moon, *Constructing Community: Moral Pluralism and Tragic Conflicts* (Princeton: Princeton University Press, 1993), 129–45.

18. Aeschylus, *The Orestes Plays*, trans. Paul Roche (New York: Mentor Books, 1962). Foustel de Coulanges, *The Ancient City* (Garden City, N.Y.: Doubleday Books, 1972), examines the home nature of the polis.

19. Steven Kelman, "What Is Wrong with the Revolving Door," in *Public Management: The State of the Art*, ed. Barry Boseman (San Francisco: Jossey-Bass, 1993), 224–51.

20. Thomas Hobbes, *Hobbes Leviathan: Reprinted from the Edition of 1651* (Oxford: Clarendon Press, 1967), part 1, ch. 11. See Carl Schmitt, *The Concept of the Political*, trans. George Schwab (Chicago: University of Chicago Press, 1996), for a modern apotheosis of group conflict and domination informed as the center of all politics.

21. Galston, *Liberal Purposes*, 165–91.

22. Judith N. Shklar, *Faces of Injustice* (New Haven: Yale University Press, 1990), and *Ordinary Vices* (Cambridge: Harvard University Press, 1988), discusses the absolute importance of toleration and of stopping cruelty and how difficult this minimal virtue is to live and how much effort it takes to sustain.

23. R. Kent Weaver and Bert A. Rockman, "When and How Do Institutions Matter?" in *Do Institutions Matter? Government Capabilities in the United States and Abroad*, ed. R. Kent Weaver and Bert A. Rockman (Washington, D.C.: Brookings Institution, 1993), 445–81.

24. Susan Wolff, "Comment upon Politics of Recognition," in Gutman, *Multiculturalism*, 76–79; David A. Hollinger, "National Solidarity at the End of the

Twentieth Century: Reflections on the United States and Liberal Nationalism," *Journal of American History* 84 (1997): 559-69.

25. Camilla Stivers, "The Listening Bureaucrat: Responsiveness in Public Administration," *Public Administration Review* 54, no. 4 (1994): 364-69; also see Galston, *Liberal Purposes*, 217-28.

26. Anthony Oberschall, *Social Conflicts and Social Movements* (Englewood Cliffs, N.J.: Prentice Hall, 1973); Juan Linz, "Toward Consolidated Democracies," *Journal of Democracy* 7, no. 2 (1996): 14-20.

27. Kymlicka and Norman, "The Return of the Citizen"; Stephen L. Carter, *The Dissent of the Governed: A Meditation on Law, Religion, and Loyalty* (Cambridge: Harvard University Press, 1998), discusses the strains between group allegiance and the efforts to achieve a national affiliation.

28. Paula D. McClain and Joseph Steward Jr., *"Can We All Get Along?" Racial and Ethnic Minorities in American Politics* (Boulder: Westview Press, 1996), chs. 3-5.

29. Erwin C. Hargrove, "'The Better Angels of Our Nature': The Moral and Cultural Dimensions of Political Leadership," *Miller Center Journal* 2 (1995): 3-17.

30. Laurence Thomas, "Morality and Human Diversity," *Ethics* 103, no. 1 (1992): 117-34.

31. Robert A. Dahl, "Is Civic Virtue Relevant in a Pluralistic Democracy," in *Diversity and Citizenship: Rediscovering American Nationhood*, ed. Gary Jeffrey Jacobson and Susan Dunn (Lanham, Md.: Rowman and Littlefield, 1996), 1-16.

32. Kymlicka and Norman, "The Return of the Citizen," 376-77.

33. R. W. Cobb and C. P. Elder, *Participation in American Politics: The Dynamics of Agenda-Building* (Baltimore: Johns Hopkins University Press, 1983), 31; Fred M. Frohock, "The Boundaries of Public Reason," *American Political Science Review* 91-94 (1998): 833-44.

34. Robert N. Bellah et al., *Habits of the Heart: Individuals and Commitment in American Life* (Berkeley: University of California Press, 1985). See David H. Hollinger, "National Culture and Communities of Descent," *Reviews in American History* 26 (1998): 312-28, for a thoughtful assessment of how the narratives of national culture could accommodate these ideas.

35. Richard Lamm and Gary Imhoff, *The Immigration Time Bomb: The Fragmenting of America* (New York: Dutton, 1985). See Will Kymlicka, *Liberalism, Community, and Culture* (New York: Oxford University Press, 1989), for a subtle analysis of the moral legitimacy of requirements of language acquisition from immigrants in order to further basic political and justice aims. Also see Michael Walzer, "Comment on Politics of Recognition," in Gutman, *Multiculturalism*, 99-104.

36. Martha Craven Nussbaum and Amartya Kumar Sen, eds., *The Quality of Life* (New York: Oxford University Press, 1993), 288-89.

37. Moon, *Constructing Community*, 116-18; Steven C. Rockefeller, "Comment on The Politics of Recognition," in Gutman, *Multiculturalism*, 87-98; Elizabeth V. Spelman, "On Treating Persons as Persons," *Ethics* 88, no. 2 (1978): 150-61.

38. David A. Hollinger, "Postethnic America," *Contention* 2, no. 1 (1992): 79-96.

39. Arthur Kuflik, "The Inalienability of Autonomy," *Philosophy and Public Affairs* 13 (1984): 271-98; Thomas Hurka, "Why Value Autonomy," *Social Theory and Practice* 13, no. 3 (1987): 361-83.

40. Moon, *Constructing Community*, 85–115.

41. Albert Hirschman, *Exit, Voice, and Loyalty: Responses to Decline in Firms, Organizations, and States* (Cambridge: Harvard University Press, 1977), discusses the options of exit and voice and how one can use them in various ways depending upon commitment.

42. Hannah Fenichel Pitkin, "Justice: On Relating Public and Private," *Political Theory* 9, no. 3 (1981): 327–52.

43. John Rawls, *A Theory of Justice* (Cambridge: Harvard University Press, 1971), provides the clearest exposition of this basic moral point.

44. Mari J. Matsudo, *Words That Wound: Critical Race Theory, Assault Speech and the First Amendment* (Boulder: Westview Press, 1993).

45. Nancy Fraser, "Toward a Discourse Ethic of Solidarity," *Praxis International* 5 (1986): 425–29; Young, *Politics of Difference*.

46. Jean Bethke Elshtain, "The Politics of Displacement," in *Democracy on Trial* (New York: Basic Books, 1995), 37–64.

47. This term is employed by Moon, *Constructing Community*, 163–89. His subtle and probing critique of differentiated rights informs much of this discussion.

48. Gutman, "The Challenge of Multiculturalism."

49. Amelie Oksenberg Rorty, "The Hidden Politics of Cultural Identification," *Political Theory* 22, no. 1 (1994): 152–66.

50. Alaka Wali, "Multiculturalism: An Anthropological Perspective," *Report from the Institute for Philosophy and Public Policy* 12, no. 1 (1992): 6–9.

51. Jon Elster, "Self-realization in Work and Politics," *Social Philosophy and Policy* 3, no. 2 (spring 1986): 97–126, examines the dynamics of such control. On the attempts to claim and control cultural authenticity see Claudia Mills, "Multiculturalism and Cultural Authenticity," *Report from the Institute for Philosophy and Public Policy* 14, nos. 1–2 (1994): 1–6, and Robert Fullwinder, "Ethnocentrism and Education in Judgment," *Report from the Institute for Philosophy and Public Policy* 14, nos. 1–2 (1994): 6–112. Also see Robert Hughes, "The Fraying of America," *Time* (3 February 1992): 44–49.

52. Thomas W. Pogge, "Cosmopolitanism and Sovereignty," *Ethics* 103 (1992): 48–75; Daniel Philpott, "In Defense of Self-determination," *Ethics* 105 (1995): 352–85.

53. "On Borders and Belonging: A Conversation with Richard Rodriguez," *Utne Reader* (March-April 1995): 76–79; Henry Louis Gates Jr., "The Charmer," *New Yorker* (29 April and 6 May 1996), provides an insightful analysis into the tensions and politics of authenticity in the American black community.

54. Lisa Funderburke, *Black, White, Other* (New York: Basic Books, 1995), provides a telling portrait of the pressures, both black and white, on mixed-race children to become "black" and the efforts of many to carve out a new identity. See Hollinger, "Postethnic America," for a fine discussion of the permutations of multiculturalism as well as a sustained defense of this vision.

55. Tom Morganthau, "What Color Is Black?" *Newsweek* (13 February 1995): 63–72.

56. Henry Shue, *Basic Rights: Subsistence, Affluence, and U.S. Foreign Policy* (Princeton: Princeton University Press, 1980), provides an extended defense of the capacity to make informed moral judgments across states and cultures.

57. Václav Havel, *Summer Meditations*, trans. Paul Wilson (New York: Vintage, 1993), 31.

Chapter 9. Saints, Sinners, and Politicians: How Private Lives Matter

1. R. W. Apple Jr., "Note Left by White House Aide: Accusation, Despair and Anger," *New York Times* (11 August 1993): 1. For a thoughtful reflection on the erosion of private lives, see Henry Louis Gates Jr., "The Naked Republic," *New Yorker* (25 August 1997): 114–15.

2. Larry J. Sabato, *The Rise of Political Consultants: New Ways of Winning Elections* (New York: Basic Books, 1981); *Feeding Frenzy: How Attack Journalism Has Transformed American Politics* (New York: Free Press, 1991).

3. Judith Lichtenberg, "The Politics of Character and the Character of Journalism," Joan Shorenstein Barone Center, J.F.K. School of Government Discussion Paper D-2 (1990), provides a classic statement of it. Sabato, *Feeding Frenzy*, provides the most sophisticated analyses of the breakdown of press reserve and a defense of the relevance requirement.

4. The private lives of officials is mentioned in many studies of public ethics but usually in a cursory fashion. For example, see Carol Lewis, *The Ethics Challenge in Public Service: A Problem Solving Guide* (San Francisco: Jossey-Bass, 1991), 53–59; Peter French, *Ethics in Government* (Englewood Cliffs, N.J.: Prentice Hall, 1983); Harold F. Gortner, *Ethics for Public Managers* (New York: Praeger, 1991), 42–50. The most systematic and thoughtful assessments have been written by Dennis F. Thompson, "The Private Lives of Public Officials," in *Political Ethics and Public Office* (Cambridge: Harvard University Press, 1987), 123–47. An earlier version, "The Private Lives of Public Officials," appeared in *Public Duties: The Moral Obligations of Government Officials*, ed. Joel H. Fleishman et al. (Cambridge: Harvard University Press, 1981), 221–47. My argument builds upon his discussions.

5. Jeffrey H. Reiman, "Privacy, Intimacy, and Personhood," *Philosophy and Public Affairs* 6 (1976): 26–44.

6. Stephen L. Carter, *Integrity* (New York: Basic Books, 1996), 3–69.

7. Robert S. Gerstein, "Intimacy and Privacy," *Ethics* 89 (1978): 76–81.

8. James Rachels, "Why Privacy Is Important," *Philosophy and Public Affairs* 4 (1975): 95–133. Ferdinand Schoeman, *Privacy and Social Freedom* (Cambridge: Cambridge University Press, 1992); Dean Cocking and Jeanette Kennett, "Friendship and the Self," *Ethics* 108, no. 3 (1998): 502–27.

9. Stanley I. Benn, "Privacy, Freedom, and Respect for Persons," in *Today's Moral Problems*, ed. Richard Wasserstrom (New York: Harper, 1975), 7–11.

10. George Orwell, *1984* (New York: Penguin, 1947).

11. Orlando Patterson, *Slavery and Social Death: A Comparative Study* (Cambridge: Harvard University Press, 1982).

12. For a thoughtful commentary upon the importance of a private boundaries in maintaining civil relations see Thomas Nagel, "Concealment and Exposure," *Philosophy and Public Affairs* 27, no. 1 (1998): 3–30.

13. Patricia Boling, *Privacy and the Politics of Intimate Life* (Ithaca: Cornell Uni-

versity Press, 1996), provides an excellent survey of the discussions within feminist scholarship over the role and limits of privacy claims.

14. Jean B. Elshtain, *Public Man, Private Woman* (Princeton: Princeton University Press, 1981); Wendy Brown, *Manhood and Politics: A Feminist Reading in Political Theory* (Totowa, N.J.: Rowman and Littlefield, 1988); Glenna Matthews, *The Rise of Public Women: Woman's Power and Woman's Place in the United States, 1630–1970* (Oxford: Oxford University Press, 1992).

15. Benjamin Ginsberg and Martin Shefter, *Politics by Other Means: The Declining Importance of Elections in America* (New York: Basic Books, 1990).

16. John M. Barry, *The Power and the Ambition: A True Story of Washington* (New York: Penguin, 1996), chs. 8, 13, 14, 23–25; Peter Madsen and Jay Shafritz, eds., *Essentials of Government Ethics* (New York: Meridian Books, 1992), 122–23.

17. James Davison Hunter, *Culture Wars: The Struggle to Define America* (New York: Basic Books, 1991).

18. *Covering the Presidential Primaries* (New York: Freedom Forum Media Studies Center, 1992), 11–15, 30–33, 79–82.

19. Richard Schickel, *Intimate Strangers: The Culture of Celebrity* (Garden City, N.Y.: Doubleday, 1985); Lloyd Grove, "Looking for President Perfect," *Washington Post National Weekly Edition* (6–12 April 1992); Neil Postman, *Amusing Ourselves to Death: Public Discourse in the Age of Show Business* (New York: Penguin, 1986).

20. Anthony Barker, "The Upturned Stone: Political Scandals and Their Investigation Processes in Twenty Democracies," *Crime, Law and Social Change* 21 (1994): 337–73; Sabato, *Feeding Frenzy*.

21. Howard Kurtz, CNBC Interview, 22 June 1993.

22. Doris Kearns Goodwin, *Franklin and Eleanor Roosevelt on the Home Front* (New York: Simon and Schuster, 1994).

23. Richard Reeves, *President Kennedy: Profile of Power* (New York: Simon and Schuster, 1993).

24. Freedom Forum, *Covering the Presidential Primaries*; Jonathan Alter, "How Phil Donahue Came to Manage the '92 Campaign," *Washington Monthly* (11–13 June 1992).

25. Barker, "The Upturned Stone"; Suzanne Garment, *Scandal: The Crisis of Mistrust in American Politics* (New York: Times Books, 1991).

26. *Political Scandals and Causes Celebres since 1945: An International Reference Compendium* (Harlow, U.K.: Longman Group, 1990), 414–15, 420–21, 431–32, provides a chronicle of a number of careers destroyed by unproved accusation.

27. Cass R. Sunstein, "Unchecked and Unbalanced: Why the Independent Counsel Act Must Go," *American Prospect* 38 (1998): 20–27; Jeffrey Rosen, "Is Nothing Private?" *New Yorker* (1 June 1998): 36–41; Jeffrey Tobin, "Starr Can't Help It," *New Yorker* (18 May 1998): 32–38.

28. Mary P. Ryan, *Women in Public: Between Banners and Ballots, 1825–1880* (Baltimore: John Hopkins University Press, 1990).

29. Michael Walzer, *Spheres of Justice: A Defense of Pluralism and Equality* (New York: Basic Books, 1983).

30. Lichtenberg, "The Politics of Character."

31. James G. March and Johan P. Olsen, *Rediscovering Institutions: The Organizational Basis of Politics* (New York: Free Press, 1988).

32. Henry Adams, *The Education of Henry Adams*, ed. Ernest Samuels (Boston: Houghton Mifflin, 1918), 128–67; Clinton Rossiter, *Alexander Hamilton and the Constitution* (New York: Harcourt, Brace and World, 1964), 28–31; Shelley Ross, *Fall from Grace: Sex, Scandal, and Corruption in American Politics from 1702 to the Present* (New York: Ballantine Books, 1988), 20–29.

33. John P. Burke, *Bureaucratic Responsibility* (Baltimore: John Hopkins University Press, 1986).

34. David Kipnis, *The Powerholders* (Chicago: University of Chicago Press, 1976).

35. French, *Ethics in Government*, 243–48; Stuart Hampshire, "Public and Private Morality," in *Public and Private Morality*, ed. Stuart Hampshire (Cambridge: Cambridge University Press, 1978), 23–54.

36. Bernard Williams, "Politics and Moral Character," in Hampshire, *Public and Private Morality*, 55–74; Michael Walzer, "Political Action: The Problem of Dirty Hands," *Philosophy and Public Affairs* 2 (1973): 160–80.

37. Peter J. Steinberger, *The Concept of Political Judgment* (Chicago: University of Chicago Press, 1993).

38. Congressional Quarterly, *Congressional Ethics: History, Facts, and Controversy* (Washington, D.C.: Congressional Quarterly Press, 1992), 86–89, 94–96.

39. Thompson, "Private Lives of Public Officials," 141.

40. Sabato, *Feeding Frenzy*, 216–19, provides an excellent set of standards that members of the media could use to judge the merits of information they obtain about private lives of public officials and decide whether to reveal the information or not. However, he is very pessimistic about the capacity of the modern media to implement them except on a sporadic basis.

41. Howard Kurtz, "The Dole Affair," *Washington Post Weekly* (25 November–1 December 1996): 10–12, describes the debate over how to cover a past extramarital affair by presidential candidate Bob Dole. The affair was discovered and documented but went largely unreported in the media. The unusual and rare debate for today's media agreed that the affair occurred too long ago and was irrelevant and not germane to Dole's presentation of himself. However, many editors believed that if Dole had attacked President Clinton for his own "character" flaws around this area, the report would have become legitimate. The whole debate relied extensively upon the type of standards presented here.

42. Ross, *Fall from Grace*, 141–43.

43. Renee Sanchez, "Barry's Presence Turned the Campaign into a Test of His Personal Redemption," *Washington Post Capitol Edition on Line* (15 September 1994); DeNeen Brown and James Ragland, "Barry Win Transcends City's Barriers: His Supporters Come from Many Classes, Sections of District," *Washington Post Capitol Edition on Line* (15 September 1994).

44. Dennis F. Thompson, *Ethics in Congress: From Individual to Institutional Corruption* (Washington, D.C.: Brookings Institution, 1995), 49–97, develops the case that individuals in public office do have rights to develop private sources of income.

45. Frank Z. Nebeker, "Memorandum: Guidance on Ethics Program Issues Raised in the Report of the Independent Counsel dated July 5, 1988," United States Office of Government Ethics, 12 September 1988, Congressional Quarterly, *Congressional Ethics* 7–9 (1988): 63–68.

46. Thompson, *Ethics in Congress*, 43–48.

47. Paul Douglas, "Daniel Webster's Retainer," in Madsen and Shafritz, *Essentials of Government Ethics*, 78–83.

48. *The Packwood Report: The Senate Ethics Counsel on Senator Robert Packwood* (New York: Times Books, 1995); "Hatfield Career Is Sullied over Conflict of Interest," *Seattle Times* (31 May 1991); "Couples, Careers, and Conflicts: Washington's Debate over Power Partnerships," *Business Week* (21 February 1994): 32–34.

49. Congressional Quarterly, *Congressional Ethics*, 39–41, 48–48, 88–89.

50. J. Patrick Dobel, "The Corruption of a State," *American Political Science Review* 72 (1978): 958–73.

51. Richard A. Serrano, "Some in White House Had Used Crack," *Seattle Times* (18 July 1996): A-3.

52. For instance, Joe Klein, "The Politics of Promiscuity," *Newsweek* (9 May 1994): 16–20, argues that President Clinton's promiscuity in his private life flows into a political promiscuity and pattern of deal making in public life.

53. Ross, *Fall from Grace*, 131–34, 266–68; Congressional Quarterly, *Congressional Ethics*, 90; E. J. Dionne, "Bill & Dan & Murphy Brown," *Washington Post Capitol Edition on Line* (13 September 1994).

54. "Helms to Fight HUD Appointment of Avowed Lesbian," *Seattle Times* (16 May 1993); "Senate Confirms Achtenberg," *Seattle Times* (25 May 1993); Howard Fineman and Mark Miller, "Hillary's Role," *Newsweek* (15 February 1993); Robert Pear, "Court Rules That First Lady Is a 'Defacto' Federal Official," *New York Times* (23 June 1993).

55. Deborah L. Rhode, "Moral Character: The Personal and the Political," *Loyola University Law Journal* 20 (1988): 1–19.

56. *New York Times*, "Ginsberg Withdraws as Court Nominee Citing Clamor on Drugs" (8 November 1987): 1.

57. *Packwood Report*; Ross, *Fall from Grace*, 120–30, 287–88; Gary Wills, *Under God: Religion and American Politics* (New York: Simon and Schuster, 1990), ch. 2.

Chapter 10. Political Prudence

1. Niccolò Machiavelli, *The Prince*, trans. George Bull (New York: Penguin, 1963), ch. 15, quotation on 91.

2. Thucydides, *The Complete Writings of Thucydides: Peloponnesian War*, trans. R. Crawley (New York: Modern Library, 1934), 331.

3. Hans J. Morgenthau, *Politics among Nations*, 2d ed. (New York: Alfred Knopf, 1959); Kenneth Waltz, *Man, State, and War* (New York: Columbia University Press, 1957). For an overview of the school see Marshall Cohen, "Moral Skepticism and International Relations," in *Political Realism and International Morality: Ethics in the Nuclear Age*, ed. Kenneth Kipnis and Diana T. Meyers (Boulder: Westview Press, 1987), 15–34.

4. Otto Gierke, *Natural Law and the Theory of Society, 1500–1800*, trans. Ernest Barker, 2 vols. (Cambridge: Cambridge University Press, 1934); Immanuel Kant, *Perpetual Peace*, trans. L. W. Beck (New York: Bobbs Merrill, 1957). For an interesting update on the claims see Michael Doyle, "Kant, Liberal Legacies, and Foreign Affairs," parts 1 and 2, *Philosophy and Public Affairs* 12, nos. 3–4 (1983).

5. Richard E. Neustadt, *Presidential Power: The Politics of Leadership with Reflections on Johnson and Nixon* (New York: Wiley, 1976); Robert C. Tucker, *Politics as Leadership*, rev. ed. (Columbia: University of Missouri Press, 1995). For exemplars of classic approaches of leadership see Baltasar Gracián, *The Art of Worldly Wisdom*, trans. Christopher Maurer (New York: Doubleday, 1992), or Francis Bacon, *Essays* (Oxford: Oxford University Press, 1975).

6. James MacGregor Burns, *Leadership* (New York: Harper and Row, 1978); John W. Gardner, *On Leadership* (New York: Free Press, 1990); Ronald A. Heifetz, *Leadership without Easy Answers* (Cambridge: Harvard University Press, 1994).

7. David Norton, *Democracy and Moral Development: A Politics of Virtue* (Berkeley: University of California Press, 1991); Ronald Beiner, *Political Judgment* (Chicago: University of Chicago Press, 1983); William Galston, *Liberal Virtues* (Cambridge University Press, 1988).

8. John Dunn, in *Rethinking Modern Political Theory* (Cambridge: Cambridge University Press, 1985) and *Interpreting Political Responsibility* (Cambridge: Cambridge University Press, 1990), especially 199-215, has been the most sophisticated exponent of this position.

9. Max Weber, "Politics as a Vocation," in *From Max Weber: Essays in Sociology*, ed. and trans. H. H. Gerth and C. W. Mills (New York: Oxford University Press, 1958), 77-128. While this chapter focuses upon political leadership, John Dunn has correctly emphasized the need to "democratize prudence" and its obligations beyond those who have assumed office; see Dunn, "Reconceiving the Content and Character of Modern Political Theory," in *Interpreting Political Responsibility*, 199-215.

10. Adam Smith, *The Theory of the Moral Sentiments* (Indianapolis: Liberty Press, 1976), 3.3.22-30.

11. Ibid., 6.3.1-19; Bacon, *Essays*, nos. 5, 18, 58; Gracián, *Worldly Wisdom*, par. 8, 52, 69 155, 162, 287.

12. Terry Cooper, "Hierarchy, Virtues, and the Practice of Public Administration," *Public Administration Review* 47, no. 4 (1987): 320-28.

13. Nancy Sherman, *The Fabric of Character: Aristotle's Theory of Virtue* (Oxford: Clarendon Press, 1989).

14. Jay Budziszewski, *The Nearest Shore of Darkness: A Vindication of the Politics of Virtues* (Ithaca: Cornell University Press, 1988).

15. Václav Havel, *Living in Truth*, trans. Jan Valdislav (London: Faber and Faber, 1986), 136-58, quotation on 144.

16. Charles W. Anderson, *Statecraft: An Introduction to Political Choice and Judgment* (New York: John Wiley and Sons, 1977); Peter J. Steinberger, *The Concept of Political Judgment* (Chicago: University of Chicago Press, 1993), chs. 1, 2, 5.

17. Sherman, *Fabric of Character*.

18. Aristotle, *The Nichomachean Ethics*, trans. Sir David Ross (Oxford: Oxford University Press, 1969), book 2.

19. Smith, *Moral Sentiments*, 6.3.12.

20. Thomas Aquinas, *Summa Theologiciae. Vol. 36: Prudence*, part 2 of the 2nd part (2a2ae), ed. and trans. Thomas Gilby, O.P. (London: Blackfriars, 1967), Qu. 47, Art. 2, 5, 7; Josef Pieper, *The Four Cardinal Virtues* (Notre Dame, Ind.: Notre Dame University Press, 1966).

21. Thomas Hobbes, *The Leviathan* (Oxford: Clarendon Press, 1967), chs. 22–25. Nathan Grundstein, *The Futures of Prudence: Pure Strategy and Aristotelian and Hobbesian Strategists* (Hudson, Ohio: Enterprise Achievement Associates, 1986); Smith, *Moral Sentiments*, 6.3.3.

22. The classic modern account of prudence is Derek Parfit, "Prudence, Morality and the Prisoner's Dilemma," in *Rational Choice*, ed. Jon Elster (New York: New York University Press, 1986), 34–59. Also see Phillip Bricker, "Prudence," *Journal of Philosophy* 77 (1986): 381–401, and David Gauthier, *Morals by Agreement* (Oxford: Clarendon Press, 1986).

23. Smith, *Moral Sentiments*, 6.1.14.

24. Morgenthau, *Politics among Nations*, 10–11.

25. Michael Walzer, "Political Action: The Problem of Dirty Hands," *Philosophy and Public Affairs* 3 (1973): 160–79. Sebastian de Grazia, *Machiavelli in Hell* (Princeton: Princeton University Press, 1989), provides a brilliant account of the moral risk and cost to the "prince" or leaders who risk their souls to provide for the welfare of the state. See especially chs. 4, 14, 15.

26. Alberto R. Coll, 1991, "Normative Prudence as a Tradition of Statecraft," *Ethics and International Affairs* 5 (1991): 33–51.

27. Aquinas, *Prudence*, Qu. 47, Art. 2, 5, 7.

28. Alasdair C. MacIntyre, *After Virtue: A Study in Moral Theory*, 2d ed. (Notre Dame, Ind.: University of Notre Dame Press, 1984). Cooper in "Hierarchy, Virtues, and Practices" successfully applies this approach to administrative politics.

29. As a preliminary account of these see J. Patrick Dobel, "Reflection and Good Reasons in Policy Analysis," in *The Handbook of Political Theory and Policy Science*, ed. Edward Bryan Portis and Michael B. Levy (New York: Greenwood, 1988), 29–44.

30. Both Aquinas and Aristotle develop more elaborate lists of characteristics necessary to judge with prudence; see Coll, "Normative Prudence." Their characteristics deeply inform the approach I have developed, which attempts to provide more operational terms for them.

31. Duff Cooper, *Talleyrand* (New York: Fromm International, 1932, 1988), 43, passim.

32. Richelieu, *The Political Testament of Cardinal Richelieu*, trans. Henry Bertram Hill (Madison: University of Wisconsin Press, 1961).

33. Herbert Goldhamer, *The Adviser* (New York: Elsevier, 1978); Gracián, *Worldly Wisdom*, par. 15, 181–82, 235.

34. Richard E. Neustadt and Ernest R. May, *Thinking in Time: The Uses of History for Decision Makers* (New York: Free Press, 1986), provides an interesting and illuminating update of the importance of the historical dimension for leaders.

35. Machiavelli, *The Prince*, ch. 34.

36. This remains one of Machiavelli's most important concerns: see ibid., chs. 15–25; Gracián, *Worldly Wisdom*, par. 151.

37. Duff Cooper, *Talleyrand*, 149.

38. Antony Lentin, "Several Types of Ambiguity: Lloyd George at the Paris Peace Conference," presented to the International Conference on Ethics and Statecraft, University of British Columbia, 6–10 October 1993.

39. Dorothy V. Jones, "Dag Hammarskjöld and the Ethics of the Long Term,"

paper presented to the International Conference on Ethics and Statecraft, University of British Columbia, 6–10 October 1993.

40. Carl Cavanagh Hodge, "Konrad Adenauer and the Diplomacy of German Rearmament," paper presented to the International Conference on Ethics and Statecraft, University of British Columbia, 6–10 October 1993.

41. Margaret Jane Wyszomirski, "The Politics of Art: Nancy Hanks and the National Endowment of the Arts," in *Leadership and Innovation: A Biographical Perspective on Entrepreneurs in Government*, ed. Jameson W. Doig and Erwin C. Hargrove (Baltimore: John Hopkins University Press, 1987), 207–45.

42. Mark V. Tushnet, *Making Civil Rights Law: Thurgood Marshall and the Supreme Court, 1936–1961* (New York: Oxford University Press, 1994).

43. Forrest C. Pogue, *George C. Marshall: Statesman 1945–59* (New York: Viking, 1987), chs. 12–15.

44. Machiavelli, *The Prince*, ch. 18; also see Gracián, *Worldly Wisdom*, par. 55.

45. Aquinas, *Summa Theologiciae*, Qu. 47.

46. Richard E. Cohen, *Washington at Work: Back Rooms and Clean Air* (New York: Macmillan, 1992).

47. George P. Shultz, *Turmoil and Triumph; My Years as Secretary of State* (New York: Charles Scribner's Sons, 1993), 712, 800–804.

48. Cohen, *Washington at Work*.

49. Erwin C. Hargrove, "David Lilienthal and the Tennessee Valley Authority," in Doig and Hargrove, *Leadership and Innovation*, 2–62.

50. David W. Ellwood, *Rebuilding Europe: Western Europe, American and Postwar Reconstruction* (London: Longman, 1992).

51. James Thomas Flexner, *Washington: The Indispensable Man* (Boston: Little, Brown, 1974), chs. 14, 22, 23.

52. Garry Wills, *Cincinnatus: George Washington and the Enlightenment* (New York: Doubleday, 1984).

53. Michael W. Doyle, "Liberal Institutions and International Ethics," in Kipnis and Meyers, *Political Realism*, 185–210, demonstrates that even Kantian understandings of ethics are consistent with the insistence upon the importance of interests being accommodated and flourishing under a moral regime.

54. James A. Baker III, *The Politics of Diplomacy: Revolution, War & Peace 1989–1992* (New York: G. P. Putnam, 1995), especially chs. 15–20, provides a clear exposition of the ways in which building policy and coalitions must attend to meeting the needs of the various actors. Also see William H. Riker, *The Art of Political Manipulation* (New Haven: Yale University Press, 1986).

55. Sheldon Wolin, "Machiavelli: The Politics and Economy of Violence," in *Politics and Vision: Continuity and Innovation in Western Political Thought* (Boston: Little, Brown, 1960).

56. Paul Kennedy, *The Rise and Fall of the Great Powers* (New York: Vintage, 1987), provides an insightful account of the costs of the projection of power and coercion for dominant powers.

57. Václav Havel, *Summer Meditations*, trans. Paul Wilson (New York: Vintage Books, 1993), 4.

58. Nelson Mandela, *Long Road to Freedom: The Autobiography of Nelson Mandela* (Boston: Little, Brown, 1994).

59. John Dunn, "Trust and Political Agency" and "Reconceiving the Content and Character of Modern Political Community," in *Interpreting Political Responsibility*.

60. G. M. Trevelyan, *Lord Grey of the Reform Bill* (London: Longman, 1920), 268, 372. Walter Williams, *Washington, Westminster and Whitehall* (Cambridge: Cambridge University Press, 1988), 18–20, 187–93, discusses the conservative, in the broad sense of the term, meaning of prudence.

61. Shultz, *Turmoil and Triumph*, chs. 8, 10, 12, 17, 18, 25–30, 34–36, 40–41, 46, 49–51.

62. Both Machiavelli and Gracián emphasize that prudence holds an aspect of insight and boldness: Machiavelli, *The Prince*, ch. 25; Gracián, *Worldly Wisdom*, par. 54.

Epilogue

1. *The New English Bible with the Apocrypha* (Oxford: Oxford University Press, 1972), Matt. 27:11–26; Luke 22, 23:1–25.

Index

Printed in the United States
1236200004B/190-216